Winnicott and 'Good Enough' Couple Therapy

Claire Rabin innovatively applies the Winnicottian theory of the 'good enough mother' to couple therapy, redirecting attention to the therapeutic relationship and the therapist's self-awareness regardless of the methods used. Using this lens, even the therapist's mistakes become an opportunity for repairing both the therapeutic relationship and the partners' own personal maturity.

The intensity and pressure of couple therapy can make each case a test of the therapist's competence. The need for neutrality constitutes ongoing pressure on the therapist and the proliferation of therapeutic methods can cause confusion about which might be most useful in each situation. Applying theory effectively is easier said than done within the context of the powerful emotions unleashed in sessions, which can result in a catastrophic atmosphere. These factors can make it hard for therapists to utilize their own skills and knowledge within sessions of couple therapy.

This book explores how therapists and couples can unintentionally further 'false selves' without realising how the very tools of change may counter authenticity. Featuring interviews with an international range of couple therapists and case studies from the author's own experiences, the key aspects of the 'good enough' concept are elaborated. Rabin shows how these ideas can strengthen therapists' sense of security and safety in using their lived experience and intuition.

Winnicott and 'Good Enough' Couple Therapy is the ideal book for clinicians seeking an overarching framework for working with couples or families, as well as those concerned with the importance of the client–helper relationship.

Claire Rabin is director of the family and couple training programme at Tel Aviv University, Israel, and the founder and director of the Claire Rabin Clinic for Couples Therapy. Her previous publications include *Equal Partners – Good Friends: Empowering couples through therapy.*

Winnicott and 'Good Enough' Couple Therapy

Reflections of a couple therapist

Claire Rabin

Routledge
Taylor & Francis Group
LONDON AND NEW YORK

First published 2014
by Routledge
27 Church Road, Hove, East Sussex, BN3 2FA

and by Routledge
711 Third Avenue, New York, NY 10017

Routledge is an imprint of the Taylor & Francis Group, an informa business

British Library Cataloguing in Publication Data
A catalogue record for this book is available from the British Library.

Library of Congress Cataloging in Publication Data
Rabin, Claire Low.
Winnicott and "good enough" couple therapy : reflections of a couple therapist / Claire Rabin. -- First Edition.
pages cm
Includes bibliographical references.
ISBN 978-0-415-53016-3 (hardback) -- ISBN 978-0-415-53017-0 (pbk.) -- ISBN 978-1-315-81796-5 (ebook) 1. Marriage counseling. 2. Psychotherapist and patient. 3. Countertransference (Psychology) 4. Winnicott, D. W. (Donald Woods), 1896-1971. I. Title.
BF636.7.G76R33 2014
616.89'1562--dc23
2013038352

ISBN: 978-0-415-53016-3 (hbk)
ISBN: 978-0-415-53017-0 (pbk)
ISBN: 978-1-315-81796-5 (ebk)

Typeset in Times
by Saxon Graphics Ltd, Derby

MIX
Paper from responsible sources
FSC www.fsc.org FSC® C013056

Printed and bound in Great Britain by
TJ International Ltd, Padstow, Cornwall

Contents

Foreword

Judith Siegel

Therapists who work with couples have a myriad of clinical models to choose from. Theories that espouse systemic dynamics, structure, communication patterns, behavior and cognition have generated multiple ways of conceptualizing and intervening in the kinds of problems couples encounter (Gurman & Fraenkel, 2002; Johnson & Lebow, 2007). And yet, approaches to couple therapy that incorporate object relations principles continue to flourish. These principles have provided a rich base upon which to build a comprehensive understanding of intimacy. From this perspective, the desire to build an authentic connection, completed by mutual acceptance and nurturance, is the force that draws partners toward each other, but that all too often fails to be realized.

Object relations theories emerged in different parts of the world as a response to the limitations of psychoanalytic theory to explain the complexity of infant and child development in a relational context. Through observation and analysis of childhood memories, different analysts offered conceptualizations of the ways that the mother–child (or object–child) relationship affected the psychic development of the child. Early relational experiences were viewed as influencing the capacity to trust, creating defenses that were formed to protect the self, and forming core aspects of identity. Object relations couple therapists understand that these core experiences of self in relation to caregivers resurface in intimate relationships. Therapists who can help the couple unravel and identify these critical themes can facilitate repair (Siegel, 1992).

Over the years, couple therapists have incorporated the contributions of several different object relations scholars. While the Scharffs (Scharff & Scharff, 1991) have been guided by the writings of Fairbairn and Klein, other therapists have been influenced by the theories of Kohut (Livingston, 2009; Solomon, 2009), Jacobson, and Kernberg (Siegel, 2010). Clare Rabin offers an important addition to this cadre by translating and applying the rich theoretical contributions of Winnicott.

Among the principles that Rabin has eloquently described is the importance of the holding environment. The mother's ability to recognize, mirror and respond to the affective state of her child requires a sensitivity to the child's being 'in the moment' as well as the correct use of the space between them. Rabin applies this principle not only to the functions marital partners must provide for each other, but also to the role that the therapist must assume. This requires an ability to make use of unconscious communication and the skill to enter into another's emotional experience. It is through 'knowing' the partners and the relationship they have constructed that the therapist is able to earn the level of trust that allows couples to access vulnerable longings and needs that have often been sealed from awareness.

Therapists who seek to work from this relational perspective need more than theory. In order to receive and comprehend the emotional communications of their clients, they need to access and develop their own authentic selves. Winnicott's notion of the true self is as important in today's world as it was 60 years ago. What combination of self-awareness and self-acceptance will allow us to spontaneously operate in the here-and-now? What kind of understanding allows us to respond to subtle emotional cues with the confidence that we are reacting to the couple's world rather than our own? When and why does our need to prove our competence take over the therapy and create obstacles to the couple's growth?

Winnicott's concepts create opportunities for personal reflection and growth. Rabin has taken full advantage of this to demonstrate how her personal journey toward authenticity has enriched her ability to comprehend and work with couples. Here, there is no pursuit of the superficial or 'false'. Instead, we are offered the contradictions and paradoxes that more thoughtfully address the complexity of human emotions and needs. Rabin shares her own relationship struggles as a daughter, wife and therapist in pursuit of the kind of honesty and accountability needed to do the work. Her process of self-scrutiny and ultimate self-acceptance demonstrates qualities that lead to healing and maturity – the acceptance of a self and loved ones that are far from perfect, but perfectly good enough.

Rabin has integrated her insights with other theoretical approaches, particularly the Internal Family systems model developed by Schwartz (1997). However, her application of Winnicott's concepts stands on its own, and can stimulate clinical development in therapists who have been trained in other practice models. Object relations therapists have consistently valued the therapist's use of self in the therapy process (Siegel, 1997). The level of understanding that can be gained through emotional awareness often leads to the most important discoveries. The personal qualities that are called upon to provide a responsive holding environment require a level of sensitivity and tolerance that are the cornerstones of all successful relationships. Winnicott's understanding of relational experiences exemplifies the best that object relations theory can offer. Thanks to Rabin, these important contributions are now accessible to all who pursue the relational path.

References

Gurman, A. S. & Fraenkel, P. (2002) The history of couple therapy: A millennial review. *Family Process* 41(2), 199–260.

Johnson, S. & Lebow, J. (2007) The coming of age of couple therapy: A decade review. *Journal of Marital & Family Therapy* 26(1), 23–38.

Livingston, M. (2009) Sustained empathic focus and its application in the treatment of couples. *Clinical Social Work Journal* 37(3), 183–189.

Scharff, D. E. & Scharff, J. S. (1991) *Object relations couple therapy.* Northdale, NJ: Jason Aronson.

Schwartz, R. C. (1997) *Internal family systems therapy.* New York: Guilford.

Siegel, J. P. (1992) *Repairing intimacy: An object relations approach to couples therapy.* Northvale, NJ: Aronson.

Siegel, J. P. (1997) Applying countertransference theory to couples treatment. In M. F. Solomon & J. P. Siegel (Eds.), *Countertransference in couples therapy*, pp. 3–22. New York: Norton.

Siegel, J. P. (2010) A good enough therapy: An object relations approach. In A. Gurman (Ed.), *Clinical casebook of couple therapy*, pp. 134–152. New York: Guilford.

Solomon, M. F. (2009) Attachment repair in couples therapy: A prototype for treatment of intimate relationships. *Clinical Social Work Journal* 37(3), 214–223.

Preface

Alan MacKenzie

Claire Rabin's profoundly stimulating and insightful book will inspire anyone reading it to take their very own personal pilgrimage – revisiting life both as parents and therapists (all the while reacquainting the reader with Winnicott's central tenets). Her book encouraged me to write a very personal preface … a 'dialogue' of sorts about the notion of 'good enough' parental relations (in my case, especially with my father). This preface intends to focus on fatherhood as an elaboration born of my own (and her) self-reflections.

Her book confirms the understandings most recent research supports (as I've always believed) – what is most important to therapeutic outcomes is not the *type* of therapy, but the quality of the therapeutic *relationship*. Three further things bubbled up for me, personally: (a) my earliest memories of couple therapy (where I truly experienced the ire of the male partner in narcissistic/borderline couples); (b) the importance of my own self-understanding in aiding this paramount therapeutic alliance; and finally, (c) my own partnership 'journey' with my current spouse – and how that helped facilitate my own personal growth as a therapist and as a father, husband and human being.

'Good enough' fathering/mothering

My earliest therapeutic work focused primarily on middle-aged males (facing mid-life crises) and couples in strife. In both cases, more often than not, I became for many of my clients a 'father figure' they never had. Like me, they too were searching to 'fill the inexplicable void' that persisted in their lives and intimate relations. I never felt I really knew my own father. Serious and stoic, he seemed to me to be a 'ghost dad' – *present*, but not really there. He was a superb provider, but not much else. As a therapist and father to my own family, I've always been fascinated by the value of the father's role for both the mother and infant during the most impressionable years of early childhood development. Even recognizing that the father cares deeply for the infant can seem to me to provide the mother some relief and maybe even allow her to risk parting with her child to have a well-deserved hiatus (Marks, 2002). According to Winnicott (1964), the father's role with the new-born is protecting the mother/child relationship. This provides a *secure enough* environment for the mother which, in turn, enables her to provide a beneficial, nurturing environment for the baby. One might even surmise that a *good enough* father could possibly contribute richly to secure attachment in the infant and toddler.

As a father to three rambunctious boys, I've always seen my role as offering both physical and emotional support. Physically, I'm viewed as helping with practical matters (provisional, pragmatic support). Emotionally, my role as father allows my wife Raewyn to cope better with the frustrations of motherhood (a là Winnicott, 1964). In some instances, I can even imagine fathers might provide parenting for the mother, who might be struggling with the intensive demands of motherhood (Tuttman, 1986). In some respects, these actions parallel those revivified again and again in the therapy room.

The father object

Rabin's book endorses the supreme tenet of the internal mental and emotional world of psychotherapy. Within this inner world are created mental representations of other people, and experiences, that are referred to as 'objects' (as understood by object relations theorists). These objects, created early in life, profoundly influence later emotional and mental health. As such, understanding how these internal objects are formed seemed of central importance to Winnicott and his successors. Rabin also supports the notion that the mother/infant pair is experienced by the infant as a single entity. As such, the mother object comes into being by being separated out from the merged mother–infant dyad. In other words, the infant experiences the mother as emerging from within.

Strangely enough, how the father object develops is still a matter of considerable debate. Many argue that there is a significant difference in how the mother object and the father object develop. Some researchers even hold the father as the *first* object to come from the external world, entering the infant's consciousness from the outside. In this sense, I've often pondered whether the father object can offer an initial representative 'opening up' of the *potential space* a là Ogden, and if introduction of this male representation may appropriately set the stage for the term Rabin uses, 'the analytic third ... [referring to] a third subject, unconsciously co-created by analyst and analysand, which seems to take on a life of its own in the interpersonal field between analysts and patients' (Ogden, p. 17). As therapists, do we in some respects represent the 'father figure' to either or both partners in a dyad – thereby affording them the same 'liminal space' for (re)parenting to commence?

Following on from this, Davids (2002) maintains that the two parental objects occupy two mental domains of the infant – the mother's domain being that of nurturer, comforter and attending to the infant's needs, whereas the father's domain consists of boundary setting and reality testing. Similarly Wisdom (1976) explains that the father encourages the infant to tolerate frustrations, and to bear difficulties. If this is so, Rabin's book leaves me wondering whether adequately trained, 'good enough' therapists ensconce the esteemed role of the 'container contained', and thereby become a backdrop for all hostile projections (i.e. in projective identification – where the therapist 'holds' the bad that the couple cannot bear to hold). Are we then asked to stand 'in dialectical tension with the separate, individual subjectivities of analyst and analysand in such a way that the individual subjectivities and the third create, negate, and preserve one another' (Ogden, p. 17)?

Many writers have observed that fathers are often more exhilarating, interactional, playful, and stimulating than mothers in the way they relate to infants. This includes encouraging 'rough-and-tumble play', a sense of body self and exploration of space. This provides the infant/toddler a 'rock to which he can cling and against which he can kick' (Winnicott, 1964, p. 115). This ultimately is what much of my own 'fathering' lacked.

Further evidence suggests that if a parental couple is missing in the mother's (or father's) mind (i.e. if there is little 'Us' acknowledged), it can lead to impairment of the infant's ability to think creatively (Feldman, 1989). Indeed Marks (2002) cites evidence that links poor parental relationship and impaired cognitive and social development in the child. Are these our client's experiences, also? And could the therapist offer an anchoring experience for their own lifetime exploration of 'internal paradoxes'? I suspect so.

Is 'good enough therapy' likened to the 'good enough fatherhood'?

Under optimal conditions, the father plays many roles for both the infant and the mother. From conception, the father supports the mother by providing a secure environment, protecting the mother–infant child relationship (Winnicott, 1960). Fathers assist in the formation of the child's identity as a source of early identification and offer support against re-engulfment by the mother (Greenspan, 1982) and provide a real relationship for the infant (Winnicott, 1964). Under optimal conditions, the actual (real) father both offers a real relationship and contributes towards the development of the father object. It is not only his role that influences the infant, but by his very essence, the father is different to the mother (Forrest, 1966) and the infant can learn to distinguish subtleties in his presence.

Like the 'good enough mother', the 'good enough father' is not required to be perfect. Rather, he is required to fail from time to time, enabling the infant to develop. The father assists the infant in separation from the mother (Mahler *et al.*, 1975). The father is a model of work and the world (Winnicott, 1964), boundary-setting and reality-testing (Davids, 2002). As a therapist I've had a growing appreciation of the father's role for emotional health. The father is one half of the 'parental couple' and the presence of this relationship in the parent's mind is also important to the infant (Marks, 2002). Interestingly, I've often wondered if the ambiguities experienced by the therapist reflect similar ambiguities and paradoxes in early life. Mindful of the complexities of the role of therapeutic 'fathering' in couple therapy, and differing theoretical perspectives in the literature and in this exquisite book, I concur with Rabin – just as the 'good enough' mother (father) plays a pivotal role in the infant's emotional development, so can a 'good enough' therapist serve this same function in successful and efficacious couples work. In this notion rests our boundless hope – 'It is in this space where intuition finds a voice'.

References

Davids, M. (2002) Fathers in the internal world. In J. Trowell & A. Etchegoyen (Eds.), *The importance of fathers*, pp. 67–92. New York: Brunner-Routledge.

Feldman, M. (1989). In R. Britton, M. Feldman, & E. O'Shaughnessy (Eds.), *The Oedipus complex today*, pp. 102–128. London: Karnac Books.

Forrest, T. (1966) Paternal roots of female character development. *Contemporary Psychoanalysis* 3, 21–37.

Greenspan, S. (1982) The third other. In S. H. Cath, A. Gurwitt, & J. M. Ross (Eds.), *Father and child: Developmental and clinical perspectives*, pp. 123–139. Boston, MA: Little Brown.

Lamb, M. E. (1981) The development of father–infant relations. In M. E. Lamb (Ed.), *The role of the father in child development*, pp. 459–488. New York: John Wiley & Sons.

Marks, M. (2002) Letting fathers in. In J. Trowell & A. Etchegoyen (Eds.), *The importance of fathers*, pp. 93–106. New York: Brunner-Routledge.

Ogden, T. (1994) The analytic third: working with intersubjective clinical facts. *International Journal of Psychoanalysis*, 75, 3–20.

Trowell, J. & Etchegoyen, A. (Eds.) (2002) *The importance of fathers*. New York: Brunner-Routledge.

Tuttman, S. (1986) The father's role in the child's development in the capacity to deal with separation and loss. *Journal of American Academy of Psychoanalysis* 14, 309–322.

Winnicott, D. W. (1960) The theory of the parent–infant relationship. In D. W. Winnicott (Ed.), *The maturational processes of the facilitating environment: Studies in the theory of emotional development*, pp. 37–55. New York: International Universities Press.

Winnicott, D. W. (Ed.) (1964) *The child, the family and the outside world*. London: Penguin Books.

Wisdom, J. (1976) The role of the father in the mind of parents, in psychoanalytic theory and in the life of the infant. *International Review of Psycho-analysis Journal of Psychoanalysis* 3, 231–239.

Acknowledgments

It takes a village to write a book.

My village extends back to all my teachers. My awareness of their contribution to me is explored in this book. However, there are specific people I wish to give special thanks to. These people not only influenced me years ago but have remained good friends since then.

Professor Eileen Gambrill stands out in her professionalism and depth. Eileen began mentoring me as advisor on my doctoral research over 30 years ago. As we moved through time, we remained firm and fast friends. It is hard to find words to describe the importance to me of this relationship. As I look forward to our next meeting, I already know it will be filled with interesting talk, fun times and emotional nourishment.

I want to thank the staff at Routledge, who have been amazing in their guidance, patience and professionalism. Joanne Forshaw has been especially important in guiding this book from its first idea to its completion. She has shown me what real professionalism looks like and has created a hard act to follow. It is my hope to continue to work with her on projects as interesting as this one.

My art therapist Roni believed in me from the start and let me move on in crucial ways. I see my own painting as an offshoot of our work together. My painting teacher Ronit Binder has guided me in my journey towards becoming an artist. She has always supported me and continues to be a steadfast mentor and friend.

I need to thank all my clients throughout my career as a therapist. They remain firmly entrenched in my mind as my teachers as well.

Similarly I want to thank all the therapists from Israel, Canada, the United Kingdom, Turkey and Malta who were interviewed for this book. Special thanks to Angela Abata, who has become a devoted friend and professional support group all on her own. She does the work of several people and is committed to truth and understanding on many levels.

Special thanks to Yona Bressler, who is both a friend and colleague. I have worked with Yona in many different capacities, with our friendship remaining firm throughout the many changes in our relationship. What would I be without you?

To Nurit Binstock, who encouraged me to start the Claire Rabin Clinic for couples and who has been a positive part of my life for many years in many changing roles. Client, student, colleague and friend, our relationship keeps on evolving beyond what I could have imagined. I am so grateful for the gifts you give me.

To all the angels who have come into my life as support for the many changes I experience in my journey. Special thanks to Etti Rushti, who while only coming into my life recently knows how much she is giving to me out of the depths of her heart. Similar, but unique, are Merav Harmose and Yankele Raz, and others who appear just when I need them.

My close friends have contributed so much to my ability to take the time to write. They offered time off, support, and ideas. These include Eleanor Parness, Tsippi Minsk, Eric Moss, and many others who have supported me during difficult times and continued into good times as well.

My family is my first line of support. These include my eldest daughter Noa, who came into my life to make me a 'good enough mother' for the first time and who has taught me as much as I taught her. My middle son Omri has been a constant source of joy and celebration since his arrival in my life. I so often see myself in him, but watch him taking even greater risks and challenges than I took. My youngest daughter Shani has been my challenge and teacher since her late arrival on the family scene. She is a trailblazer to me in her steadfast honesty to her values. She has been and continues to be, like my other children, my mentor about life as it really is.

Last, but certainly not least, is my husband, lover, and friend Yossi. There can be no words that adequately sum up our 40 years together. Together we travelled the 20s, 30s, 40s, and 50s of our lives. Now we are into our sixth decade. I could write another book about these years, but here I can only say that I have truly been blessed since I first met you. You are the world authority on me, remembering far more than I can remember. You saw many things coming before they did. You have steadfastly believed in me and in our relationship, despite the storms and turbulence of so many years. I am grateful for having you to get old with. But I also rely on you to help me stay young.

The letter from D. W. Winnicott to Clare Winnicott dated 2 April 1943 on p. 57 and the poem 'The Tree' by D. W. Winnicott are reproduced here by permission of The Marsh Agency Ltd on behalf of The Winnicott Trust.

1 Winnicott and I

Why look to Winnicott for help in treating couples?

Before examining this basic question, I want to share the ambivalence that arose in me while writing this book. I believe Winnicott would have been delighted with this self-disclosure: Winnicott was the champion of the 'real self' and knew about the anxiety that any creative expression entails. He firmly believed in self-reflection and awareness by the therapist, more than techniques or tools for changing other people.

Why am I ambivalent about applying Winnicott to couple therapy?

First of all, I am not a psychoanalyst, although I did an analysis of my own. Initially, I studied a course on Winnicott and family therapy at the Seattle Family Therapy Institute under Rusty Palmer, but over the past three years I have continued to study him on my own. Thus a lot of this book arises from my own self-reflection. Also, I am primarily a couple therapist, but Winnicott did not write about couple therapy. My inner critic warns me about criticism from both sides. Those who use primarily psychoanalytic methods might see me as a naïve interloper. Therapists doing couple therapy might rightly ask why we need another method when couple therapy is inundated with new methods each year.

I believe that couple therapy has lost out by not recognizing the value of Winnicott's ideas. Some of his ideas were incorporated into modern couples object relations. But there are few books or articles that apply Winnicott's ideas to couples. Winnicott presented a series of ideas gleaned from watching mothers and babies. People told me that they have a hard time with his idiosyncratic language, paradoxes and rather strange oblique statements. Often those who know of Winnicott have not read his papers but utilize the many secondary explanations that try to explain what Winnicott really meant.

For me stepping out into a new direction in couple therapy invites anxiety of all kinds and certainly ambivalence about my knowing enough to do this. There is a strong pull in me to understand Winnicott as applied to couples. But there is also a fear of not being 'good enough' to be able to pull this off.

Winnicott believed deeply in ambivalence. When he wrote about mothers, he was vivid in his description of how ambivalent a mother is. He connected this to the ambivalence of the therapist. He wrote that however much the therapist loves his patients, he cannot avoid hating them and fearing them. His writing is full of paradoxical and contradictory thinking. From everything I have read, it seems he rebelled against the psychoanalysis of his times but also invested much energy and creativity to reach into the psychoanalytic world and change it. He was a child and adult psychoanalyst who also had (through his second wife Clare) a strong affinity for social work. His writings are replete with his own unique ways of using language, a way that allowed paradoxes and contradictions to enliven the reading. He believed that the state of ambivalence marks maturity. If that is true, than I have certainly reached my own maturity!

Looking back on my personal and professional experiences, I have come to appreciate factors that helped and hindered my development. One of the discoveries I made is that Winnicott's ideas provide a mirror through which I have been able to make sense of these experiences. Talking to other therapists about their work, I have found that they have wrestled with similar concerns, notably what it means to be good enough as a therapist. The pressure to be 'good enough' is in the work: the problem of feeling bad about oneself in the work (especially when feeling hateful towards couples), the uncertainties resulting from becoming involved in the couple's affective field, the value of therapy in creating a special kind of space for the partners and so on. Gathering together the seminal ideas that Winnicott introduced about the role of mothers in infant development, and his application of these to therapeutic practice, related directly to concerns that I have had, and those of the therapists I interviewed. So I shall summarize these ideas, illustrate them appropriately, and then apply them to couple therapy, again providing illustrative vignettes of the therapeutic process that relate to his ideas.

As such this book marks a significant development in my professional and personal movement towards maturity as I reach the age of 65. As Winnicott criticized his colleagues out of intense concern and caring, I will allow myself here to criticize the tendency in couple therapy to overemphasize positive thinking and the teaching of so-called constructive communication skills. Using Winnicott's ideas I want to bring back the therapist and the therapeutic relationship to the center of the process of work with couples.

This is certainly not to say that the methods of creating change in couples available today have no use. Rather this is an appeal to return to the roots of the therapeutic environment as the basic medium for change. Infancy is about as basic as we get, although as I show later there are now psychologists dealing with 'gestational' psychology of the fetus. Like an educated parent, the most sophisticated intervention will fail if the holding environment is not firmly in place. For example, I remember watching a mother teach her one-year-old toddler words by flash cards. I was instinctively turned off by this seemingly advanced training. Twenty years later I heard that the son had a nervous breakdown when he tried to leave home.

We can use Winnicott's ideas to bring back the interaction between the therapist and the couple as central to the therapy process. From this good enough holding relationship we can then move to utilizing different methods available today. There are enough tools and methods. We need an umbrella concept to hold all of these. Good enough couple therapy is offered here as a generic set of related concepts that can hold the therapist who is trying to make sense of both the complexity of the couple and the complexity of the field of couple therapy. I need something more concrete to find my way through the over 300 methods available today to couple therapists.

Winnicott versus goal-centered treatment

Winnicott eschewed techniques, tools and 'how to' prescriptions in his work. He did not like his trainees to ask him what to do. He mostly asked questions. He was a social constructivist before there was a name for this. He had ideas about health and maturity but was also firm in his support for patience and allowing our clients to proceed at their own rate. He positioned himself alongside the greatest psychoanalysts, such as Melanie Klein, Anna Freud, Marion Milner and others carrying on the traditions of Freud. As opposed to the current bent toward clear goals and even protocols for treatment of couples, Winnicott brings us back to the basics.

The good enough mother is a metaphor that can be used to understand the process going on between the couple therapist and the couple, and between the couple. We can use his ideas to view therapy like an infant at play. Winnicott's ideas can be woven throughout therapy, with a couple using different methods just as a mother would offer the infant different foods and toys.

In the family and couple therapy literature he is more like Murray Bowen, who advocated patient reconstruction of family of origin issues (Brown and Wright, 2010). While his ideas centered on the mother–infant attachment, reflected today in Emotion Focused Therapy, he was clearly not interested in mapping out stages of treatment, as promoted by Susan Johnson's work (Johnson and Whiffen, 2003). On the contrary, he viewed each infant as unique, and so therapy based on this model cannot have a protocol for every couple.

Winnicott dazzles with the richness of his ideas. He was often paradoxical, which very much fits couple interactions as well as interactions of babies and mothers. For example, in writing about Winnicott's thinking on play and fantasy, Tuber (2008) gives an example of Winnicott's unique style of thinking: Winnicott explains how the baby solves his own potential loneliness by creating mental symbols of his mother, allowing the infant to hold his own mother in his mind and solving his predicament of knowing too early how alone he is.

This idea could also be said about couples, who struggle with awareness and imagination, fantasies of togetherness and being alone. Winnicott's writings are filled with such paradoxical thinking. Thus his papers can be read and re-read over and over, and the paradoxical manner of thinking lights up different associations on each reading. His writings are so rich that books have been written to help people navigate his special use of language (Abrams, 1996).

I don't think I am alone. Sometimes when I mentioned to people I was writing about Winnicott we would share a smile, as if we both knew a secret and wonderful genius who was so much himself, so real and yet so hard to reach. He was one of a kind, unique, obscure and deep.

A 'relational' professional identity

This book will show that being good enough for our couples helps them be good enough for each other. It will make the case that aiming for 'good enough' is better than aiming for a perfect record, trying to help everyone all the time with every problem. By having less perfectionist goals we are freed from performance anxiety, which can get in the way of sincere connection and clear thinking. Hamady wrote:

> Performance anxiety is an elephant-in-the-room sized issue for everyone who spends time on any kind of a stage. Its management is the subject of a thousand books, workshops and programs that teach how to deal with and mitigate its effects ... how to ride its wave rather than have it come crashing down upon you. Yet only a fundamental shift in how performance anxiety is perceived will allow you to overcome and indeed, transcend it. This shift begins by considering how the majority of us view stage fright: as a barrier between a performer and an audience. That performance anxiety is a barrier is not news to most of you. But what may come as a surprise is that its status as such only exists when another much larger barrier is already in place: the perception of the performance as a performance, rather than as a communion, a conversation and a connection.
>
> (2010, p.10)

Therapy as connection not performance

What are the steps toward reducing viewing the therapy role as a performance and staying with the connection, communication and conversation, which is the essence of therapy? These are the resources that lead to becoming a 'good enough' couple therapist.

In the time I set aside to write this book, I have gone through a period of deep reflection. I have come to view theoretical tools as fundamentally intertwined with the people who taught them to me. I have come to see these people as mentors rather than teachers. I was a therapist searching for a theory. The people I met on the way helped me self-define and become reflexive. Theories contradict each other and focus on different aspects of life (emotional, behavioral, cognitive, body, brain, etc.), and in choosing a theory we make choices about what we believe and who we are.

In preparing this book I interviewed therapists in five different cultures. When I began to write, I realized this project was becoming a journey back through time and the book was going to be about being and becoming a couple therapist using Winnicott's ideas as an umbrella for other theories. As I reflected on my own development, an intense curiosity about other couple therapists and their experiences ignited in me. As I started to develop the idea of 'good enough couple therapy', I wondered how others would react to this idea. I wondered if it made sense to them and in what way it might help them. I was well rewarded, because the therapists were mostly focused on their own inner worlds and the connections they made with couples. Few really focused on what has been the center of couple therapy – different theories and methods. Rather, therapists need help in dealing with the volatile turbulence of couples and couple therapy.

The role of theory

A theory is far more than a theoretical construction of reality. It goes beyond abstraction of concepts from the details of life. It means more than whose professional company feels right and whose does not.

It is the choice of theory that is a basic and fundamental professional action and activity. It is the ongoing choice of how to view the world and what sense to make of clients' and one's own reality. If we see theory in terms of our choices, like all our choices we would expect our professional choice of theories to change over time. We would expect to see the development of the 'self' of the therapist grow and become increasingly articulated over the years through these theoretical models and the different colleagues and teachers who taught these theories. When do we ever really feel like an expert inside? Often couples expect us to present ourselves like a medical doctor treating a disease. Deep down we know that the medical metaphor doesn't fit therapy. But what metaphor does? I am offering the idea of the good enough therapist as an alternative to the expert therapist.

Choice of theory

We become what we choose. Our choice of methods reflects where we are at the time, and thus would be expected to change as we change. It would not be an exaggeration to say that there has been an explosion of material to guide couple therapists. Some of this intensive effort to help couples comes from rising divorce rates, and some from the research showing the importance of good couple relationships for partners' mental health and for the mental health of children. Thirty years ago couple therapists did not have much choice in methods they used for guiding couples. There were a few different approaches, but nothing like the options that became available from the beginning of the new millennium. The types of therapies continue to increase.[1]

Making the choice of methods is easier when the goals are reasonable and attainable. Thus the idea of the 'good enough' therapist doing 'good enough therapy'. Having supervised many trainees and advanced family/couple therapists, I know that deep down many 'experts' feel some confusion when faced with the diverse choice of methods. Some therapists chose according to what they think they would like to have if they were in couple therapy. Some have seen good results for certain methods and thus tend to return over and over to the same tools. Others have been exposed to certain theories in their training programs.

An interesting study of choice of methods shows that beginners who don't have a clear notion of what theory to use are more effective and liked better by their clients than advanced therapists who choose one method and stick to it. Lambert and Barley's (2001) research shows surprising results. As therapists became better at techniques and theory with increasing experience, they became worse at interpersonal joining abilities! Clients might be impressed by the technique, but the relationship between the client and the therapy suffers the more the therapist knows – or thinks he/she should know.

The good enough therapist is self-confident but willing to change direction.

Mira, aged 35, came to therapy for help. Married for one year and now three months pregnant she was desperately unhappy with her husband. She came alone and talked confidently about wanting a divorce. She felt she had made a bad choice and was sure she wanted to change that. Yet over time in therapy it seemed that she was not really that sure. She then asked me to invite her husband into the sessions to see what really was needed; a new therapy or a divorce. When her husband Don came to a session, Mira and I had already contracted that she and not the marriage was my client. She did not want to automatically move into couple sessions; they had had couple therapy and it had not helped. She did not feel safe in the therapy because she found out that Don was secretly taping the session. Yet she still hesitated about the divorce and wanted Don to attend one session, for me to get a feel for what was going on. I had believed we had agreed that she would observe most of the session and I would interact with Don.

As I interviewed Don about how he saw things, I learned much that could help me help Mira come to a decision. But as I interviewed him on how he viewed the situation, I saw Mira getting more and more upset. I felt I was doing what she had asked for, to get to know Don and to talk with her after meeting him. I even thought I was doing a good job!

After half an hour, Mira exploded with anger at me and him. She went into a rather long diatribe about Don using the session to make his agenda clear, but in her words her agenda was to find out if they needed a divorce, to decide where she should live (she had moved out a month before and gone home to her parents) and most importantly she needed to know what he would pay for now. I asked her if she believed that we could solve all that in one session and she said 'yes' emphatically, and that this was all she was interested in. She repeated many times 'I am paying for this session and I want to get out of it something real'.

I was momentarily confused. Don was using her explosion to emphasize how difficult it was to live with her, how immature she was and that he had no real interest in staying in such a relationship. When I asked him if he wanted a divorce, surprisingly he said 'I am not ready for that yet'. When I asked what he did want, he did not know.

I had to rethink my strategy. I realized that although I had contracted with Mira that she was the client, she sensed in the session that Don was using me as a platform for his positions, feelings and actions. While very important information, I could not carry on interviewing Don. So I shifted to writing down the exact issues that she wanted to deal with and worked with him around those issues. At first I felt manipulated by her, but then something in her aggressive attack seemed to me to be very alive, very vital and I felt a sort of admiration for her ability to stand up for herself. She would have failed if we were in an assertiveness course, but, as will be shown, Winnicott was an admirer of people's aggression.

By the end I also realized that she had been right and that in being more practical (not gathering information for Don), I was helping her to deal with her panic about where she would live if separated and who would pay for her apartment. Although the focus had shifted, the therapy seemed to move along much better because Don had revealed his lack of engagement in the practical side of the relationship. Thus in the end I not only better met her needs as my client, but I did actually see what she was up against in the relationship.

As I worked with this couple I felt the contribution of Winnicott's ideas. I had contracted that Mira was the client yet I had gone on to give half of the session to Don. This felt wrong for Mira and I picked up the signs, just as a good enough mother would notice a change in infant affect. But I did nothing to change this. She had to explode angrily at me for me to realise that although what we had contracted did match the session, the outcome was not what she had anticipated or intended.

As a good enough couple therapist, I don't feel I have to get it right immediately. I would have hoped to have noticed her anger earlier, but I believe that rupture and repair are more important than getting it right straight away. I saw her smiles and happiness as she left the session, and understood that I had both withstood her aggression and fostered an experience of repair.

I believe people who come to therapy do not really expect a therapist to catch everything right away. While perhaps this fantasy has a certain appeal, it also would mean that the couple had been stupid. Even if we could catch everything, the people in therapy could feel inferior to an overly-smart therapist.

The therapist as a good enough mother

The book will take the position that the therapist is like a mother to the infant 'relationship'. Even if a relationship is 40 years old, when a couple begin therapy, with regard to the therapy they are in the stage of relationship infancy. If couples would just see this, they would already be on the way to change. That is, they would be willing to allow themselves to be in the infant state with the new 'good enough' mother/therapist. How the therapist 'holds' this infant will determine the outcome of therapy. It is through this medium that fears are confronted, new behaviors tried out, emotional soothing becomes a habit and finally new ideas and beliefs about oneself and the other are created.

'Know thyself'

Knowing yourself is a central concern for me when teaching couple therapists. 'Know thyself' is actually what my mother wrote on my first ever diary at age 8. As we shall see, she knew a lot about not being oneself. To help my students begin to think inwardly about their own definitions of therapy, I usually start with an exercise I learned from Jill Freeman and Gene Combs. First students are asked to go around and introduce each other. Most classes seem to go the same way with this. The first people who talk pretty much establish what will be revealed. People will talk about their professional degrees, places of employment and changes in careers or type of problems or populations they work with. The second stage of the exercise asks the group for another round of introductions. This time they are asked to think about their professional life as a journey. I ask for introductions to be based on their answers to this question: if you were to write a book today about your life as a therapist, what name would you give to that book? After a shocked silence, the group usually dives with relish into the narrative meanings they can give to their professional lives. Their 'book titles' range from 'The victory of hope over despair' to 'How my family has influenced my work' and everything in between. It is rare that there are two similar answers.

I see my own experience with different types of therapy as a journey through different ways of viewing problems. Along this personal and professional journey, I met others on the road who influenced my development. I privilege Winnicott not because I gave up other theories and methods to use his ideas. Rather it seems to me that his ideas can form the basis of good enough therapy and from there we can let the process determine what methods we choose.

Outline of this book

Chapter 2 begins my own professional journey by describing the effects of significant teachers and supervisors in my life and how they all helped me move to the position of 'good enough couple therapist'. Through them I was exposed to behavior therapy, family and couple therapy, narrative therapy and others. Professionally, during my personal analysis focusing on the self and throughout many experiences with different theories, I once more came back to the self.

But my training as a therapist really began in my family of origin and this chapter will link my professional and my personal self. While it is hard to use the right words for this, our personal and professional selves are a seamless coat of many colors. Sometimes we focus on our history, sometimes on a workshop we just went to. Theory, personal experience going back to infancy and the methods we work with are all made of one garment. I revisit my own personal journey because it reflects what I can give to couples, and where I needed help for my own lack of good enough parenting.

Chapter 3 describes a series of interviews with couple therapists in Canada, the UK, Malta, Turkey and Israel. I wondered how they would all view the concept of good enough couple therapist and what that might contribute to their work. I look at differences and similarities between these therapists and come to some conclusions about the good enough concept, as well as the difficulties many have in doing couple therapy.

In encounters with therapists from different cultures, I was struck by some outstanding similarities. Over and over, I found there was pressure on these therapists to be perfect, not just 'good enough'. I discovered the ubiquitous difficulty in dealing with couples' hateful feelings and the emotions stirred up in the therapist. There were many anxieties stirred up by doing couple therapy. Therapists were unsure how much to lead and how much to follow the couples.

Chapter 4 introduces the reader to the work of Winnicott and focuses especially on the 'good enough mother' as a central organizing principle. This chapter introduces the reader to the building blocks of Winnicott's theories. He never pulled all his ideas together into a cohesive theory for practice, and this limited his usefulness to therapists outside of individual psychoanalysis. I show here some ways that the process of being good enough can help couple therapists use Winnicott's ideas to help couples.

Chapter 5 looks at the importance Winnicott gave to feelings of hate and aggression in his view of good enough relationships. As opposed to theories that promote 'positive' communication skills, central to his thinking was that theories on negative types of experience are especially appropriate for couples in therapy. Couples' problems are not related to being nice to each other but to how aggressive and hateful they can feel. The interviews discussed in Chapter 3 also show how these feelings and their concomitant behaviors are especially hard for couple therapists to handle. Winnicott's ease with the negative side of human emotional worlds helps us to use these emotions to help couples and couple therapists cope in a more vitalized way.

Chapter 6 looks at transitional objects and space as well as potential space. These are ideas unique to Winnicott and very relevant to the interaction between partners in intimate relationships. Also these ideas have a lot to say about how people change and what the process of change includes. One idea especially associated with Winnicott is the idea of play as a positive use of potential space.

The chapter stays close to the original ideas proposed by Winnicott for helping the process of good enough mothering.

Chapter 7 explores countertransference in couple therapy. Countertransference needs to be seen in context. The chapter includes specific situations that are hard for couple therapists, such as having to cope with intense negative feelings and feeling part of a triangle. In some contexts these are difficult moments for therapists. However, we can view the potential use of these feelings for helping couples. Countertransference is described in case studies where the therapist attempts to use countertransference for the benefit of the couple.

Chapter 8 discusses transitional and potential space in relation to true and false self in the therapist and partners. The chapter also looks at what might go wrong in the potential space as well as how to move towards play and creativity. The idea of potential space is one of Winnicott's outstanding contributions to understanding how infants and mothers creatively construct a mutual and individual identity. The same process of potential space has much to give us about how the couple moves out of its relationship infancy (needing an active therapist) to maturity (having the therapist there internally and if needed for future work). The chapter also looks at my own marriage and the ways that it has affected my work with couples, as well as being affected by my work.

In Chapter 9, Winnicott's thinking about false and true selves in all of us leads to a discussion of how viewing the self as made up of parts can be helpful to couples. This chapter raises the idea of parts of the self as discussed in internal family systems (IFS) therapy, a method that links internal and external interaction. Developed by Dr. Richard Schwartz, this approach fits many of the concepts offered by Winnicott. A case example shows how this work is done and how we are led through this work back to the idea of the good enough mother.

Chapter 10 is a summary of the book. It sums up Winnicott's central focus of the self of the therapist and the importance of self-introspection for helping couples. Winnicott showed how self-awareness on the part of the therapist is at the crux of being able to repair ruptures in the therapeutic relationship. In this final chapter I sum up how writing the book has affected me and how it has influenced my view of helping couples. It ends with my hopes for the future development of Winnicott's ideas applied to couple therapy.

All case studies and examples in this book are a synthesis of real material. All identifying characteristics and names of those featured have been changed.

Note

1. For excellent lists of types of therapy available today, as well as criteria for what are good or questionable practices in therapy, visit http://www.GoodTherapy.org, an association founded by Noah Rubinstein.

2 My personal and professional journey and the connection between the two

How did I get to Winnicott? Our choices of theories are determined by where we have been and where we are personally and professionally. This chapter charts my professional and personal development and interweaves them. Winnicott was a champion of therapist introspection. He was open about his childhood, including his mother's depression and its effects on him. It was obvious to Winnicott that we are professionally determined by our personal history.

Where to start?

When I was just 18, I left home for college. I now see that as a very young age to go so far from home and as a difficult endeavor. In the USA, where I grew up, parents are extremely involved in their child's upbringing until their 18th birthday. At that point, I felt literally kicked out of the nest and told to fly. I now regard Israeli childrearing expectations as far healthier. In Israel, my daughter did indeed graduate from high school, as I did, by the age of 18. As I did, my daughter cried the night before leaving home (in her case to the army, in mine to university). However, my daughter then arrived home again two weeks later! I came home three months later and was expected to stay away except for holidays. The message then for me was you are 18, be independent!

Thus my introduction to therapy. During my first year away from home I missed my family terribly and was very unhappy. Since being independent was the ideal at that time, I could not share my sadness with my friends. It was the 1960s and a time of tremendous social upheaval. Most of the students were experimenting with drugs, sex and rock and roll. They seemed to be delighted not to be under the scrutiny of their parents. I did not take to the drug scene, felt very alone and thus turned to therapy.

Psychoanalysis

In Boston where I was studying, the most common and acceptable therapy was psychoanalysis, as Freud and his followers advocated. Psychoanalysis is suitable for families that can pay for it. My father willingly paid for four sessions a week for four years in the hope of helping me. I lay on a couch and shared my anxieties, hopes and dreams in free association of thoughts and feelings. The therapist offered little guidance but did come up with insights that I guess were supposed to magically cure me of my depression. When my anxiety only increased as I dropped deeper and deeper into my self-consciousness, the analyst, being a psychiatrist, prescribed tranquilizers. I doubt that the research on tranquilizers causing depression had come out. But looking back on all this now, 40 years later and after treating hundreds of clients, I see the methods used back then as primitive and outrageous for a lonely late teen missing her family. The last thing I needed was to drown myself in dreams and fantasies.

I needed real practical advice and help in making the transition from home to university. Had I been the therapist, I would have invited my family to take part in the therapy to help me let go gradually. Instead I transferred my dependency onto my therapist. When after four years I said I wanted to stop, he told me I was not finished. Somehow I had developed the strength to disagree; I felt ready to stop and I did.

This experience influenced me. I decided I wanted to be a therapist. I am not sure why my psychoanalytic experience did not turn me off therapy completely. Perhaps I identified with the power the therapist had over me and wanted some of that myself? Or perhaps, despite the fact that psychoanalysis had a regressive pull when actually I needed support to strike out on my own, there was enough 'good enough' experience with my analyst to make me want to be part of this enterprise. During the period I was in analysis, I spent a year abroad in Israel. I would call and talk with my analyst about my experiences and he listened. He was my good enough mother.

I remember his saying to me once 'Do you suppose that some of what you are experiencing has to do with you being a woman?' For him I suppose it was a mild suggestion, and we gave it little place in the therapy. But that one comment changed my life. It was 1967 and the feminist movement was beginning to bloom, especially in Boston. He sent me to read up on 'Bread and Roses' (an early feminist cooperative who published a well known newsletter), which I did, and I became very involved with women's groups in the Boston area.

I believe today that my analyst's timely suggestion influenced me more than the entire course of my psychoanalysis. I became a feminist and was part of that movement in the late 1960s, thanks to him. I also was very connected to him (transference?) and on my year abroad we often talked by phone. I think he missed me too and in him I found the available parent I never had. He probably thought his interpretations were what worked. I think otherwise.

Behavior therapy

Instead of getting as far from therapy as possible, I rejected the psychoanalytic way of thinking as an adolescent might reject their own parents' values on the way to self-definition. It is obvious that between that first rejection and taking on Winnicott, a lot has happened. I now realize that by taking on behaviorism I was trying to differentiate from my analyst and also from my own family of origin.

While in psychoanalysis I had spent many hours going back to my childhood; behaviorism was saying to me 'move forward, not back'.

But all our choices reflect our history. There are many different types of behavior therapy, such as relaxation and desensitization, assertiveness and social skills training. Yet I was attracted to behavioral therapy with families. If I thought I was rejecting psychoanalysis by choosing behavior therapy, now I see it differently. Family behaviorists advocate empowering clients by giving them the tools needed to solve their own problems. In analysis I spent most of my time talking about my family of origin. In my choice of behavior therapy, I returned again to the field of families. Only when linking all these trends together do I see a story of continual interest in families, no matter what method I was using. I also see myself reaching out through the theories I chose to work and rework my family-of-origin issues.

I first found out about behavior therapy when I was still in psychoanalysis. I had graduated from university and found my first job as a research assistant in a large private welfare organization in Boston. On the first day of my job, I was asked to sit in the basement and copy a list of numbers from one page to another. This was considered to be a research job, but I felt ridiculous and was severely bored. Within the first week, I 'accidentally' poured boiling water over my hand and had to go home. I came back refusing to continue the menial and punishing work. My boss, a social worker himself, was a smart man. Instead of firing me, he gave me a new job. I was to find and write-up interesting ideas for research that the agency would then look to fund.

It was while happily browsing through the public libraries that I came upon behavior therapy. The ideas that I read about thrilled me. The method, which was anti-psychoanalysis, seemed to want to hand power over to the clients. Instead of using the term therapy, behavior change was seen as training. For example, Patterson *et al.* (1982) experimented with a therapeutic model called 'Parent Training', which handed the therapeutic role over to parents who could create a 24-hour 7-day-a-week 'therapeutic environment' based on reinforcement rather than punishment. Having myself felt powerless and labeled as sick during my years in psychoanalysis, I was excited by a method that threw out the diagnosis system and gave clients tools for change.

My first contact in graduate school was with Professor Eileen Gambrill, a world-renowned expert in behavior therapy. I decided to do my doctorate with her. She insisted on my learning all that could be found on behavior therapy in those days – behavior analysis using rats, pigeons and dogs. I became an expert on reinforcement schedules. In some ways it felt like learning algebra in high school. I knew people wiser than me thought it important, but it was hard to see the application to real life. Professor Gambrill was open to my creativity in using behavior therapy in the ways that made sense to me. My doctoral research was on behavior training in parents of aggressive boys who were in behavior therapy. These parents learned to use the methods of changing behavior themselves. They worked with me as their co-therapists to teach them the principles of changing behavior. I then helped them reward and reinforce good behavior in their sons, for example, giving their children prizes and stickers for cooperative behavior.

I did notice that starting with my first training in behavior therapy, there was very little teaching about therapist self-awareness. Behavior therapy, which was in many ways a challenge to psychoanalytic thought, might have 'thrown out the baby with the bath water'.

Supervision

Marion Bar-Din was my first supervisor. I trained with her in a family service agency. Marion was consistently enthusiastic about my talents and abilities. She taught a kind of therapy with no brand name other than good social work practice with individuals, couples and families. When I left the agency, she said 'You are going to be a hard act to follow'. I felt this came from her heart and she really trusted me to do well despite the short time we had together and despite the limited number of clients I had managed to see in my practicum.

Marion's basic common sense was evident in her supervision of my first client, an adolescent I will call Jane.

> Jane had stayed home from school for a year. Our mutually agreed goal was to get her back to school by overcoming her phobia. In the later stage of therapy, when Jane was ready to return, Marion had the good sense to direct me in questioning Jane about what she would most miss when she was back at school. Jane, who usually looked anxious when thinking about going back, was suddenly delighted with my question. Her face lit up as Marion initiated a line of inquiry I never would have thought about. She apparently had filled her days at home watching the soaps on television. She now talked about each actor and their character as if they were real people for her. She shared with me all the drama of abortions, divorces, falling in love, family conflicts and all the other stuff of life. She talked about where they were at the present time and how she would miss them. We created a ritual in which she would say goodbye to those characters who were the most meaningful by writing letters of appreciation. Marion continued to support this direction in supervision, with me spending two more sessions with Jane saying goodbye to these people who had become dear to her and whose lives she had entered. 'Just listening' to her stories of their stories was enough to help her grieve their loss and become ready to exchange them with real-life friends.

I think of this incident as one of the bricks in the building of my secure therapist base. I learned to trust myself because Marion trusted me. My client Jane trusted herself to return to school because I knew she could do it. Thus from the start I was developing a professional relational self.

Family and couple therapy systems theory

During my doctoral studies I read about the new field of family and couple therapy. One of my teachers was the family therapist Professor Margaret Singer. She had worked with Professor Lyman Wynne in seeing entire families of schizophrenics together in treatment (Wynne & Singer, 1963). Psychotic people are generally assumed not suitable for psychoanalytic therapy and family therapy jumped into the gap in the world of severe mental illness. They were able to prove that family counseling can help a schizophrenic person, especially when combined with medication.

I found the ideas of family systems theory extremely exciting and knowing Margaret felt like being part of a new wave of thinking. Having been wrenched away from my family and taught that being independent was a major life goal, the idea of interdependency throughout the life cycle was very appealing to me. More than that, I began to realize that my anxiety disorder treated for four years with so many individual sessions and so much medication was a direct result of my family beginning to disintegrate. My parents divorced one year after I left home. I remember coming home for my first visit at Thanksgiving and not being able to sleep because of the tension in the house. Had my family been in treatment together, rather than me being the identified patient, this would have come out in the open. Instead, I carried alone the symptoms of distress and depression.

Family systems theory, especially the work of Murray Bowen (1978), got me back on track in the journey to know myself. Doing one's own genogram was a fundamental part of training in these methods and I re-engaged with my family of origin from the perspective of differentiation of self and all the other amazing ideas Bowen and other systems thinkers offered.

Narrative therapy

When I first met Michael White at a conference in Israel and saw his demonstrations of narrative therapy, I was open to adopting this new way of thinking while still using behavior therapy and systems therapy. By that time I was clear that no one method could ever cover all the types of problems brought to therapists, nor could one method meet the needs of all the different kinds of people who sought our help. Being open to all approaches is not easy. I remember envying therapists (like Michael White) who were 'True Believers' in a certain method. As I describe my first encounter with Michael and narrative therapy, it was especially hard that no one paid attention to how difficult the learning process was. While the teachings of narrative therapy were fascinating, there is an emotional level to being 'fed' a new theory. Not one of the people I worked with in Australia questioned us, the trainees, about how we were faring in taking on a whole new system of thought.

Today, when I teach methods like narrative therapy, I do a lot of sharing with the students about how the material is affecting their lives. Early on in the courses I take on the anxieties and fear that students have when faced with a radically different method. Questions arise like 'How does this relate to everything else I learned?' or 'What can I take from my previous learning into my learning narrative?'

So while on one hand narrative therapy appears to support self-disclosure of the therapist, it tends to create strict guidelines for the reflection. The reflecting team does not talk at all about the therapist's negative feelings. It is based on how the team is affected positively by the clients' stories. As shown later, the field of therapy and especially couple therapy is strongly concerned with positive feelings across methods. The relegation of negative feelings and behaviors to invisibility has had a profound influence both on how therapists treat couples and how they process the negativity that couples bring to therapy. The overemphasis on positivity leads to perfectionism, rather than aiming for 'good enough' outcomes.

I imagine that Winnicott would have been very ambivalent about narrative therapy. He was himself interested in people's stories and was a fine-tuned listener. But Winnicott was championing the true self, and I think he might have been horrified by the structure inherent in narrative therapy. For Winnicott each therapy was towards an unknown direction. His belief was that with good enough mothering from the therapist, the client reaches their own true self.

Journey back to the self: my introduction to Winnicott

During a sabbatical year in Seattle, Washington, I took a course at the Seattle Family Therapy Institute taught by Rusty Palmer. I really did not know what I was getting into. I had assumed we would continue to study family systems therapy. But his belief was that Winnicott had much to teach us as family therapists. As a small group we spent hours each week both reading the original Winnicott texts as well as watching behind a one-way mirror while Rusty interviewed people according to Winnicott's work. I really enjoyed it and was especially impressed by one idea that stuck with me. This idea is another seed leading to this book, but needing the time to grow and take root.

Of the many concepts taught, it was the good enough mother that most caught my attention. I finally had a concept that explained some of my rage and detachment from my own mother. My mother had believed in perfection and tried to practice perfection in everything she did, including childcare. If Dr. Spock told her that children need consistency and therefore I should be fed on schedule, my mother followed these guidelines to perfection. I remember real hunger as an infant and not having anyone come to me. The notion that good enough is better than perfect explained my own confusion. My mother made sure I learned how to type, had shoes that felt comfortable, and meals that were perfectly balanced. It was always so hard for me to explain to myself why I felt so alienated from this person who was sacrificing her life for her children. For example, she started doing art at one point and loved it. So she stopped it. She later told me that she was afraid that her interest in art would get in the way of caring for her children. How was it that I literally hated someone so giving?

Winnicott's idea of the good enough mother had a profound impact on me and still does. To understand why a child like myself might feel alienated from a perfectionist mother is to understand why the good enough path is so important. The part that is missing in the attempt to be perfect is not having the opportunity to go from rupture to repair. Winnicott believed that the site of both good attachment and the development of the self are in the process of rupture in the relationship and then repair as often as possible, which would not be 100% of the time. The repair attempts in a rupture show the baby, and later the client or partner, that the other really cares. That is combined with the times when there is no repair and the baby, client or partner has to move themselves to recreate the connection. The good enough mother does this gradually, first being almost perfect so that the child does not experience any rupture. But soon enough the good enough mother starts to allow ruptures (she goes into another room and leaves the child alone for moments) and then repair by coming back and holding the crying child.

Where was my mother?

Until learning about Winnicott's idea, I hardly saw my mother as affecting my life. As strange as this may sound, I always remembered myself as disconnected from her, connected only to my father instead. I knew something was wrong, but I had coped well by crossing her out of my life. Why did I do this?

During my psychoanalysis I remember my therapist trying to get me to talk about my mother. I had nothing much to say. I now think of all the pain I must have been defending against to withstand his attempts to analyze me with regard to my mother. Instead he became a substitute mother, perhaps as distant as she was and yet so familiar. My analysis was really about me and my father.

My family of origin: my father and mother

I was learning about behavior and family therapy while my own family was reeling from the traumatic and difficult divorce of my parents. Certainly this event affected my personal and professional life as much as, if not more than, the influence of my teachers, supervisors and analyst. But aside from my analyst, I was not encouraged to connect my own personal life with my professional one. This is my first attempt to integrate in writing how the personal and the professional are intertwined in me and how this led to writing a book on Winnicott.

My father

My father had spent 30 years of his life as a successful diamond importer. After building his business, inviting his younger brother and father into the venture, he began to question his whole life. It was the 1960s and everything was held up for questioning. Whereas when I went to college there was a 12 midnight curfew, one year later these old fashioned ideas were dumped. Within two years of my going to university, dormitories had a mix of men and women. My father had married the woman chosen by his family and hers, and he had been unhappy for most of his married life. This was known, but I just never thought about divorce because it was extremely uncommon during the 1950s when I was growing up.

When my father left home and divorced my mother, he also left the family diamond business. My father was very influenced by the 1960s, which was holding up most of the accepted social values for inspection. While he had done his duty as a son, father and husband, he started to think about what he really wanted. When he left he even refused to take most of the money he had acquired. He told me that money corrupts and that he wanted nothing to do with it.

He was accepted into a family therapy training program in New York. Margaret Rioch[1] had started a program to retrain people with 'life experience' and no degrees as family therapists. All the participants were housewives who had life experience and the one man was my father, who having fled the Holocaust certainly had life experience. A window of openness and change challenged usual accreditation. The fundamental power structures were being questioned: male oppression of women, white people's oppression of black people, and the hegemony of all the powerful groups in society were challenged. Life experience and academic learning were seen as potentially equal. My father had not graduated from high school as a child because of World War II. His life experience as an immigrant to the USA was equated with an academic degree. I remember going to his graduation from the family therapy program, where he was given a certificate from Einstein Medical School as an accredited family therapist. There were about 20 former housewives and him. He spent the next ten years of his life doing therapy with couples. He even published a paper on co-leadership of couples groups, which he ran with his new wife.

The 1960s were a window of opportunity for people like my father. His authentic self was ignored when he had to marry my mother. He moved into business because that is what a man did in the years after World War II. Suddenly the restrictions of a hierarchal society were challenged, affecting his decisions to leave the family and the business. The window closed soon afterwards: in the 1970s there were reaction movements to the 1960s. Traditional accreditation was back in place. The potential for radical change had ended.

My mother

My mother was also unhappy in her marriage, at least as unhappy as my father. I don't know when I first learned this, but it was known to me for as long as I can remember. From adolescence onwards, I avoided her, because closeness never felt good. I remember that she tried a lot to talk with me, but always about her own childhood, which had been very traumatic. She had suddenly lost an older sister to diphtheria when her sister was 12 and my mother only 10. None of the family coped well with the tragedy and instead of any kind of processing, they moved to another city in Europe. This event remained traumatic for her, unprocessed and unforgiving. Her need was to talk constantly about the losses she experienced, with no interest in how handling all her pain and depression might be for me. As I describe here, later I developed a highly functional false self that did listen to her until adolescence and that then became mired in perfectionist performance goals.

World War II started for my parents when Hitler marched into Vienna, leaving them aware that they had to run away. They both were responsible for getting their parents out and they were obviously both 'parental' children. As children, both were beaten by their father, who was in each case unhappily married and in each case taking that out on the child. My paternal grandmother (named Clara) was apparently also a battered wife, but she was warm and loving. My father was able to take that and give it to me. My mother's mother was described as 'awful' and was selfish and narcissistic. My mother did not have any parenting from either parent and was seriously deprived and neglected. She told me about experiences before the war in which she was left at school without someone picking her up. She was not loved or cared for. In her case it was not a matter of not good enough mothering, but no mothering at all.

My mother's deep unhappiness with her life was evident to me. I attempted to find a balance between listening to her heartbreaking stories of lost people and places and cutting off inside and not listening at all. I felt cut off from it because I intuitively knew that she was using me as a kind of substitute parent or therapist. Despite that, she showed little interest in my life and made it clear that she felt my attempts to have my own life were rebellious and selfish. My false self was active in being her therapist until I was an adolescent.

On the one hand she and my father demanded performances in school, piano, dancing and popularity. But when these were achieved, they never responded. They left my graduation ceremony because it was 'boring'. The contradictions come from conflicting parts in their own personalities. My parents themselves were too compliant and both were functioning almost totally in what Winnicott would call the 'false self' mode. Miller (1981) gives an emotionally engaging narrative of the damage done to the real self by narcissistic parents. I remember reading this book not long after it came out in English, and immediately recognizing myself. But none of the theories I had learned led me to understanding the paradox of the parents who pressure their child to perform and then (out of jealousy and competition) ignore their child's accomplishments. My mother once said to me when I was very young, 'You know, when you were born I felt jealous of the love I gave you since I never got it'. She had not read Miller or Winnicott, but had a streak of honesty that burst out sometimes. Of course, there isn't much a child can do with these self-disclosures except to feel rather guilty and confused.

My parents were desperately unhappy together, but were sticking with their parents' commands, so they had no way to release these feelings. Like children they gave me double messages, coming from splits in their own personalities. Their false selves were encouraging me to achieve. But their real selves were hungry children who wanted all the attention and admiration. Their own neediness was undermining what they thought that they wanted from me. When I left home, my father could not carry on with the charade of his false self any more.

Rejecting the listening role

As an adolescent I began to reject the listening role with my mother, resisting her invitations to go shopping or cook with her. I felt used and angry. I did not verbalize all this to myself and used my anger to try to individuate from her. I was seriously depressed, although I didn't know it. For example, I found it impossible to enjoy the summer camps she organized for me and my sister. I was too homesick to let go and have fun. She warned me that only when I finally had an adolescent girl would I know the pain I caused her. I felt nothing but anxiety and transferred this into an obsession to succeed. This would become my best defense, until it no longer worked.

Her solution was to distance herself from me as well. Over the years there were attempts for a 'rapprochement' from both our sides, but they never worked. Her idea of a good conversation about our relationship was her complaining about me. I wanted recognition for my feelings of deprivation, neglect and abandonment that she was unable to give. I thus cut off from her, saying there was no point in connection at all. She was very upset about this, but I felt my emotional survival demanded that I care for myself by distancing from her. To me, she always felt like a hungry, needy infant who would smother me with her pain. And indeed when I did agree to listen to her, it was all about her. It was about the losses of the war and her dysfunctional family she was still angry with.

Problems in the nursery

Winnicott's theories have helped me understand what might have happened between me and my mother at the earliest stages of infancy. He stresses the importance of the good enough mother to titrated doses of not holding so that the child has a chance to make gestures that are then continued by the mother. When the mother is trying hard to be perfect, she does not allow the child to create their own gestures, but the mother is there meeting the child's needs before the child has a chance to experience them. I suspect that the history of my mother, her family and my parents' relationship made being a perfect mother imperative to her.

My mother was living a false-self life. She was not in love with my father and once told me she should never have married but that she had wanted to study medicine instead. Rather than follow her own 'spontaneous gestures', which might have led to being single and a doctor, she became the perfect mother of four perfect children. She fulfilled her parents' wishes without having a chance to develop some that were her own. She turned their wishes into her wishes and her compliancy led to a need to become the perfect mother, perhaps hoping to finally get some recognition from them.

Having a false-self perfect mother is more dangerous according to Winnicott than castration of the infant. It is a kind of castration of the personality before it has had a chance to develop. Winnicott mentions that there are two alternatives for the infant with the perfect mother. One is to become as compliant as possible, being just what the mother seems to want. The other is to reject the mother entirely. I somehow chose the latter at such an early age that I wiped out all memories of mothering by her.

My intense alienation from and anger towards my mother would be explained by Winnicott as a result of interacting with a false-self mother. He follows a tradition also proposed by R.D. Laing, who wrote *The Divided Self* (1960), which argues that unlike the ego, the self, as such, is never divided but can be starved of a sense of 'core relatedness' with others. The distinction between the ego with its various modes of object-relatedness on the one hand, and the self with its capacity for core relatedness on the other, is used to clarify the concept of authentic relating and refine Laing's and Winnicott's distinction between the 'false self' and the 'true' or 'inner' self. Winnicott wrote 'such communication with the world as occurs from the false self does not feel real; it is not a true communication because it does not involve the core of the self, that which could be called a true self'.

Core relatedness from the true self of the mother is essential to a baby. If the child is to survive psychologically it must be born into a

> mother's responsive attunement to the infant as a real being – a self; less to do with the infant's developing capacity for ego-relatedness and much more to do with the mother's own capacity for core relating. Maternal absence is not the absence of the breast but the absence of the mother who isn't really 'there' for the infant with her whole being, who is absent as a self. According to Winnicott this leaves the infant vulnerable to 'impingements' on its sense of 'going on being'. The absent sense of core-relatedness to the mother in other words creates a basic *ontological* insecurity in the infant (Greek *ontos* – 'being'), an insecurity which Laing correctly analyzed as the basis of adult psychosis. Its essence is not the experience of being a mere object for the mother. It is this that leads the developing ego to fear all relationships with others.
>
> (Wilberg, no date)

The infant needs an empathic-responsive human milieu just as it needs an atmosphere that contains an optimal amount of oxygen. Hence the paradox that

> the loss of self … is a despair which does not clamor or scream. People go on living as if they were still in contact with this alive centre … Patients coming in for a consultation complain about headaches, sexual disturbances, inhibitions in work, or other symptoms; as a rule they do not complain about having lost touch with the core of their psychic existence.
>
> (Wilberg, no date, quoting Horney, 1950)

I have come to the conclusion that my mother was not able to relate from her core self. Having no access to her core self, she was more a role (happy housewife) than a person. I grew up with a sense that I did not have a mother. This was strangely easy to maintain in the face of my mother's continual attempts to be the perfect mother. She devoted herself to her children, in the mode of the perfect housewife of the 1950s. She took me to ballet, art, piano and other lessons. The meals were perfect and even back then she was aware of the right combinations of carbohydrates, proteins and vegetables. Everything looked to the world as wonderful, and I never quite grasped how I lived in this strange duality. I knew my mother was trying hard to be a good mother and at the same time I had no mother. I had everything but was continually sad, and very angry. Any expression of these feelings was strictly forbidden and could result in unfair changing of plans or removal of a cherished item. For example, I came home one day to find all my clothes gone. My mother had thrown them out. She said they no longer looked good on me; she then spent a large sum of money compulsively shopping with me for my new clothes. I remember sitting next to her on these outings, angry, confused and mostly very sad.

The normatic personality

Following and developing Winnicott's idea of the false self was a type of false self proposed by the psychiatrist Christopher Bollas (1987). Calling this type of self the 'normatic personality', Bollas formulated the idea that some people have sacrificed all their personality to be seen as normal. This is the development of a self that fits into society, the family and the mother–child dyad to the exclusion of any personal feelings, characteristics, or even personal thoughts and emotions.

Winnicott believed that we begin our lives in absolute dependence on our caregiver. In this state the child cannot adapt because there is no self to do the adapting. The move from absolute dependence to relative independence is the place where adaptation starts and the potential for over-adaptation (the normatic personality) is begun. Winnicott believed that mothers who demand adaptation very early on are interfering with the infant's development of the true self. The notion of the normatic personality takes Winnicott one step further in describing the emptiness of the infant who has to adapt too soon.

This personality does not allow the development of richly articulated false selves as well as lacking definition of the true self. The infant in this precarious situation is all adaption and no self (false or true). This is precarious because emotional survival depends on maintaining this normality at all costs. The infant continues throughout life to trample any idiosyncratic aspects and is totally focused on fitting in.

June and Harold are a couple in their sixties. They raised three children. All three had difficult childhoods and all kinds of symptoms. However, June rejected the idea of therapy for her children because it might reveal something about her. As soon as possible, each child left home, angry and rageful. No one, including June, understood what they were so angry about. However, their extreme adolescence gave June a focus. She thought she was the best mother possible and was arrogant and removed when her children tried to express their pain. They each tried in their own way to get a response from her. June was locked into her own view, which is that her children had the best life possible. She was not open to any discussion about that.

After the third child left there was an emptiness in June that Harold did not feel. He found it relatively easy to adapt to the empty nest because he had his own hobbies and was looking forward to retirement to start new hobbies as well. June had been a 'stay-at-home' mother even when the children no longer needed her presence at home. June had grown up herself in a traumatic atmosphere. Both her parents were killed in a road accident when she was four months old. She was moved to her maternal aunt's home but the arrangement did not work out. June never knew why and the family never talked about it. She was moved first to foster care and then to adoption when she was two. Her infant self had never had continuity of being from caretakers, nor did she have the good enough mother to allow the maturation from total dependence to relative dependence or towards independence. She married Harold when she was 18 because he lived next door and was a good catch for her. Mainly she wanted her own home and did not marry for love. Harold also was not passionate about her, but saw her as a potentially good mother for his children. Also she allowed him a lot of space so that he felt free to do his thing, whether it involved more work, travelling or his hobbies.

June never developed her own personality. Her trauma was very early and massive. There was no good enough mothering and to survive emotionally June killed off any feelings she had. She adapted totally to being the caretaker of the moment. This ability allowed her to survive but just barely. Depression and even suicidal thoughts were central in her life, but she never thought about treatment. The notion of another person probing her personality was terrifying to her. Her life was her children and as long as they stayed near her, she was functional.

June started to have a breakdown when her last child decided to travel and perhaps relocate to another country. With no child at home and Harold busy with his own activities, she was left helpless in a sea of emotions that she had never felt or coped with. She literally had nothing to do. She was terrified of new people, so could not take on all the advice Harold suggested such as volunteering, working or starting a hobby. The only kind of treatment that she allowed was couple therapy, since she felt that Harold needed to take better care of her.

Couple therapy was unsuccessful because June had absolutely nothing to contribute except to say that she was not appreciated enough by any of the family members. Giving them all she had was her way of hiding that she had nothing much to give. She was focused on giving the family what she thought the normal family needed: healthy food, lessons for the kids, a clean house and appropriate clothing. Since she had been so busy arranging all these, she had no sense why everyone was angry. In couple therapy she also refused to consider the possibility that Harold might be angry too. She had no access to her own feelings. Questions like 'What did that make you feel?' were met with bewildered silence. The therapist found it hard to get through the hour, as time seemed to drag on and on. There simply was no material to work on. Eventually the couple dropped out. They said that the therapy wasn't helping and the therapist agreed. The therapist tried to stay in touch, being worried about June's mental health. The couple were polite on the phone, but never asked for help again. Much later on the therapist heard that June had tried to commit suicide and was hospitalized briefly. Apparently Harold had tried to leave her and could not do it as long as she was defined as mentally ill.

One of the central problems for people like this is that they make others around them very angry. They see themselves and others as objects without subjective feelings. They can not empathize with even their closest family members. What is important to them is to look normal and that goal defines their lives. They are thus unable to look below the surface in their own personalities or the people surrounding them. This lack of empathy can cause rage in others that is not mirrored back by the normatic personality. That causes even more rage and eventually a need to back off and move away. These people live tragic lives since they were victims of poor mothering from the start. Their attempts to make everything right by being super-normal never work and just make others angry. The normatic personality then feels that others are ungrateful for all they give. Totally without insight, they do not respond to help from others and are doomed to a lonely and empty aging process.

Changing my story

I lived with rage and anger at my mother until Winnicott's ideas began to make a mark in my narrative. I started to question what 'good enough' might mean in my life as well. I started another therapy that was based on art and discovered a new language to express the deep hidden pain that my cut-off from my mother had instilled in me. It took years of work to move past the cut-off to having an internal relationship with her. Only after that could I also actually be with her in a different way. But I never was able to have a real maternal bond with the real mother. I was able to construct a good enough mother from memories that were real and that showed another side to the story.

Winnicott was very insistent on the creative impulse being behind many defensive behaviors such as splitting false and true selves. Indeed, I first began to remember my own attempts at artwork and my mother's competition with me. Apparently we both were talented in art, but she was highly ambivalent about my doing it as well as her. She bought me a wonderful set of oils and also set up art lessons, but she also ended them abruptly when I showed talent, and she painted over my paintings.

My therapist commented that my mother brought the Holocaust into our relationship and was doing to me what history had done to her. This resonated with me. Because I was searching for a good enough mother, I found her in distant memories that I had relegated to the bin of unimportant and forgotten. I come from a family of four children, of whom I was the eldest. My sister was two years younger than me. Then, when I was six, my mother had my first brother and when I was seven my second brother. In searching for the missing mother in my life, I began to remember that until the birth of my first brother she had lots of time for me and my sister. She liked to play creatively with us on the floor, using art materials and felt to create animals and stories. She loved to take us to the park and I remembered her teaching me to swing.

Little by little, I uncovered a child who did have a mother who once was 'good enough'. I had 'forgotten' the mother I once had, probably because the loss was so traumatic. Apparently, when she had her third and fourth child, something major and perhaps terrible happened. I knew that we moved away from New York, where I was born, to the suburbs because life there was supposed to be better. I did not realize, but I remembered this in therapy, that my mother had disappeared for me in that move. Perhaps she had been overwhelmed by quite suddenly having four children, being in a new place, and with my father moving up in his business perhaps leaving her more and more alone.

When I was about 8 years old, I bought my first diary. It was common in those days to ask people to write something for the diary. My mother wrote 'know thyself'. For an 8-year-old, this was an inaccessible philosophical idea. When I was hating my mother, I focused on the negative sides of my life with her. Her writing to me about knowing myself at age 8 was typical in that she was thinking of herself and was out of touch with the stage I was at and what I could absorb. Yet now I think she was reaching out to me in her own way. Without thinking what I could absorb, I think she was warning me about a life lived within a false and empty normatic self.

For me the uncovering of memories of good times with her was crucial to my building a sense of self out of connection with her. Not a real-life connection at first, but a reaching back into the past to reconstruct my memories that had split my reality. I had been convinced she was the bad object and I wanted no contact with her. Having her again through memories did not erase the pain of lost years and not having a warm mothering experience when I deeply needed it.

When I thought more about good enough ideas, I realized that I had rejected everything my mother tried to give me out of anger and disappointment. Of course, as a child I was unaware of my idealistic notions of mothering. I just knew something major was missing. But it was true that once she did love me and play with me, and remembering these times was strengthening for me and my efforts to uncover my real self. In rituals with my art therapist, I took images of the bad mother and cut them up, burying them in a pretty box that I chose as the coffin. This ritual of letting go of the false self, and mourning the real loss of a real mother, was helpful in being able to accept internally what she had given me. Accepting my mother as good enough meant to gradually let go of the rage and anger that defined my boundaries with her; only from a distance and with some help was I able to imagine taking something from her. It still is hard because opening at all to her floods me with the pain of her unlived life.

I could later come back to memories like the diary and see them differently. While she could not adjust to my cognitive level, she was giving me her life experience. She had not been able to be true to herself. She had never wanted to marry my father and once said she wanted to study medicine. Throughout my childhood she urged me to have a career and not make family life my focus. In beginning to look for what was good enough, I began to access more memories, even earlier memories of me in my crib. I remember enjoying the cracks on the wall. But I also remember crying out for someone and no one coming. I have worked and reworked those memories from many different angles. I think I did experience the disintegration and mental breakdown Winnicott talks about. The unspeakable agonies are real and I was able to reconnect to them and talk about them. Obviously in infancy there were no words for this. Perhaps my mother had a breakdown herself when I was born. She did tell me that I was *the family's* child, being the first grandchild on both sides of the family in the new world. Only when her second child was born did she feel that this child was hers.

So there were two levels of memories. First that she indeed had been a good enough mother at some point, perhaps when my sister was born. She loved playing with both of us, dressing us up in matching outfits and taking us places in New York where we lived. She took us to museums and instilled in me a love of art from the age of two onward, till we moved away from the city.

Winnicott says that the fear of mental breakdown reflects a breakdown that has already happened. In any case there was a deep hole in my earliest memories of infancy, which are hard to recover because they are preverbal. My psychoanalysis was aimed at these memories, but they were much too scary and powerful for me to handle at the age of 18.

Signs of impending burnout

I was recruited by my mother to listen to her. Not surprisingly, I chose being a therapist, like many neglected children. Interestingly my sister (two years younger and enmeshed with my mother throughout her life) did a doctorate in therapy, but then refused to see any clients. My sense is she was busy being my mother's therapist until my mother's death in her arms.

I, who had gone the opposite way and had cut off from my mother, stayed connected through my choice of profession – without any conscious link between my choice of profession and my mother. I suspect that I had hopes of curing her by my listening to her stories. I learned to become a good listener, although I rebelled against listening too much to her stories. Yet the act of listening was instilled in me and I acted out that need to cure her so she could be a mother to me. Unfortunately this maneuver with my clients did not work. The work with them started to deplete me, as I became aware that I needed something they could not give (as I had not been able to give to my mother).

I now remember a few couples coming to therapy for the first time saying 'We are coming to you because we heard you are a magician.' I remember being flattered by this, but now I view this compliment as a double-edged sword. It feels very good to be seen this way, and certainly is a quick fix for the underlying feeling that perhaps I don't know anything at all.

The danger for me was in relying too much on myself and not getting enough support from others. I did not adequately use supervision and peer support. As I became a teacher, writer and well-known therapist in Israel, I basked in the warm light of a good reputation. But this reputation had to be kept up, like Winnicott's false self. Mistakes can be tragic in this mind-set. Trying to keep up the façade of being a magician is not much fun. It reinforces perfectionist goals that are the antithesis of the good enough model. The interesting thing is that I was trained in Winnicott but did not generalize his writings enough to my own life. I did not want to go to supervision. I seemed to get caught up in maintaining my image and found asking for help very difficult. What was this about?

My training as a therapist started with my role as my mother's own mother. I learned early on how to listen to her pain. The need to be omnipotent was inculcated early on. I now think that she probably did give me some basic mothering at the start and that I had high (unconscious) hopes to cure her and get back what was lost. I probably enjoyed being the listener because I felt important. Did the need to become a magician start back then? Does becoming a therapist seem like a second chance to cure somebody, even though I could not cure my own mother?

The flattered 'magician's' own underlying needs for love are not met. There might be admiration and respect, but not love. The therapeutic situation is one in which listening and giving is the core of the therapeutic transitional space. The most we can expect to 'get' from the clients is the satisfaction of having helped another person. But, like the exhausted mother of a newborn, we therapists are often faced with needy couples in a great deal of psychic pain. Where do we get our needs met?

Magicians generally work alone. They may have an assistant, but they don't have a peer group of colleagues with whom they can discuss the stress of being a magician. Actually being a magician means keeping the secrets of the trade to oneself. Magic generally isn't what is going on, but illusion is what is happening.

Keeping up the illusion (of omnipotence, for example) is an integral part of the magician's role. I did not realize the importance of support in questioning my omnipotent fantasies. Eventually I did burn out and had to cut back drastically on my work with couples. I am saddened that I did not realize what was happening along the way. Rejecting help from others allowed me to keep my fantasy life going, which only led to having to make drastic changes in my professional life.

A better metaphor would have been the good enough mother who is not expected to be a magician but who gradually moves together with her infant through failures to learn what the infant needs over time. Good enough parenting/therapy is firstly an ongoing process and not a goal. The good enough mother doesn't overwork to impress anyone. Built into Winnicott's idea of the good enough mother is the need for her to fail her infant in order to keep his growth going. She will fail to meet needs in a graduated dosage and will make mistakes in that as well. The good enough mother model is one of both sides growing and changing over time. This fits therapy a lot better than the magician metaphor and I wish I had used it earlier.

I remember that when I had overworked with a large number of couples, afterwards I was completely depleted. Like the mother of an infant, all I wanted was sleep. I refused to relate to requests from my family for attention, feeling that I needed rest for myself, and was not interested in human interaction. Also in my family I am not seen as a magician. I am a human being with faults and problems, neither overly admired nor crucial to their existence every moment. In therapy I am crucial and know it. There were times I felt much better about myself in a therapy session than I did afterwards with my own partner.

I only stopped overworking when I no longer could do it physically. I think back over all those diseases coming one after the other as if the universe was shouting at me and saying 'When are you finally going to stop it? What new problem do we have to send you to make you realize?' It was only after two cancers and numerous autoimmune diseases that I did finally, finally, cut back the number of hours and started using peer supervision. I established a clinic in which, instead of direct hours, I supervised a group of wonderful couple therapists.

It took years for me to return to painting, which had been offered then taken away from me. When I was overworking as a therapist, I was enacting being the good enough mother for the hundreds of clients I saw over so many decades. But no matter how much I gave out, I did not feel nurtured within. Being a magician is a poor substitute for feeling loved. It simply doesn't work and that is good, because we eventually have to abandon that which no longer nurtures us.

Winnicott and my burnout

I wish I could say that Winnicott's ideas saved me or rescued me from my own burnout. I cannot make this claim. I have come to see my own burnout as far more entrenched than I would have hoped. It had probably started in elementary school, when I was continually anxious about achievement and unable to get any real help from my parents. That is, I was busy developing my false self as long ago as I can remember. My burnout started somewhere around third grade, and that was over 60 years ago. That is a long-term problem and not surprisingly my burnout is quite deep-rooted.

I can now claim that finding and creating my own true self has led me to new horizons. I no longer see many clients, nor do I supervise a great deal. I paint, make pottery and exercise. I await the next stage of my life with anticipation, excitement and happiness. So I would claim that Winnicott's emphasis on the inner self of the therapist has helped me disengage from a lifestyle of overwork, overdependence on adulation and competition to succeed. At times I am sad about the direction my personal and professional work has taken. Had I had a good enough mothering experience, I would have made other choices. But I didn't and right now it has to be enough to understand what happened and to do the best I can given what happened.

Note

1. In the 1960s, while working at the National Institute of Mental Health, she developed a training program for middle-aged women seeking to pursue careers in psychotherapy. She believed that this would create opportunities for women in search of careers or for those who sought to return to the workplace. It later became the model for programs around the country.

3 How therapists view good enough therapy

The interviews

As I delved into the material on Winnicott, I could not locate literature on the application of his ideas to couple therapy. For me, loving the work on Winnicott as I do, the silence on this topic was deafening. This is more apparent in light of the large recent literature continuing to develop the application of Winnicott's ideas to psychoanalysis and child therapy (Caldwell and Joyce, 2011). Also, this lack of application of Winnicott to couples is odd, given the current trend of applying other psychodynamic ideas to couples. Today, theorists and therapists using attachment, intersubjectivity, psychoanalytic and object relations theories are major contributors to couple therapy (Gurman, 2008).

Are Winnicott's ideas relevant for use by couple therapists? What would therapists say about good enough couple therapy and what might it mean for them to create a space to think about it? I embarked upon a path of interviewing couple therapists around the world. I see myself as co-creating knowledge with my informants – knowledge that might not have been written about previously. I turned to qualitative interviews to help me clarify my thoughts about the good enough couple therapist.

I decided to talk with experienced couple therapists from five different cultures: Israel, Canada, the UK, Malta, and Turkey. In all these places I went to the major cities where most couple therapists work. Most of the therapists in Israel, the UK and Canada were trained in their own countries, while those in Malta and Istanbul traveled abroad for training. The couple therapists came from Tel Aviv, Vancouver, London, Malta, and Istanbul. I chose these places because I had a couple therapist who was interested in these ideas and who took responsibility for organizing my interviews (except for Israel, where I did this myself). It was heartwarming how many couple therapists freely gave of their time to help understand Winnicott's ideas as applied to couples work. Most of the interviews took place in the therapist's own office on account of their hours with clients. For this I am very grateful.

In this chapter I will discuss the themes I found while interviewing a total of 42 couple therapists (10 from Israel; 10 from Canada; 7 from the UK; 7 from Malta and 8 from Turkey). I enjoyed this work immensely and would have gone on to interview more couple therapists. But I had achieved 'satiation', which is the point at which no really new information was forthcoming. It was obvious that there were universal themes in these interviews and more similarities than differences.

I expected to hear a lot about the theories they were trained in. As we will see in this chapter, therapists did not use the interviews to talk about theories they use; the common themes do not really reflect the training models that they all made sure to know by travel, conferences and reading. I did try hard to get each person's specific take on their work by asking for examples of cases and personal stories. The interviews of personal experiences did not generate a reflection of differing theories and methods. I will discuss the similarity in themes after presenting the interviews.

The interview took 1–2 hours, and was not structured, except for one question that was asked at the start. That opening question was 'What does being a good enough couple therapist mean to you?' I made sure that the therapist knew that I did not expect them to know what good enough couple therapy was. Rather I hoped they would think about this perhaps for the first time.

I have outlined the common themes found. For the sake of brevity I have chosen a few of them for each theme, although there are far more examples. However, I am not offering these interviews as a good example of qualitative research – this project falls short of more rigorous demands. They are the result of my own searching for an echo to my excitement about Winnicott's potential contribution to couple therapy. Would couple therapists see this? I planned to start with that question, 'What does good enough couple therapy mean to you?', and to go with whatever came up associatively.

The results of the interviews

There were eight common themes that emerged from this process. I have chosen one quote from each culture group as examples. They will be presented first and then I will discuss possible interconnections and implications.

1. Good enough applied to couple therapy

A common answer to the question 'What does good enough couple therapy mean to you?' revolved around the rejection of perfectionism.

A (UK): People are very demanding, can only feel they are good enough if they are perfect. I need to allow couples to accept disappointment and recover from it.

V (ISRAEL): The opposite of perfect. Allowing room for mistakes in therapy. Accepting that not all goals will be obtained. Sometimes good enough is different for the therapist and the couple. The therapist wants to give something that the clients don't want. Good enough is letting people off this hook.

C (MALTA): I am too perfectionist. I feel too responsible for them. For me being good enough helps me focus on the relationship between me and them. I always feel a lot of pressure to intervene, not just to listen but to take action. Good enough is in the relationship, being loving, generous, warm and helping in the engagement in the relationship.

Quite a few respondents immediately talked of feeling empowered just by playing with the concept of 'good enough':

B (CANADA): It is a relief thinking that therapy can be just good enough. People expect perfection, so they come to therapy after 2 years. They need to accept that most relationships are good enough.

E (UK): I like the idea that you don't have to be the best, perfect, it's empowering. Takes the pressure off, what you really need is good intentions. This influenced me in therapy when I have difficult clients. I allow myself to challenge them, so I say that I am going to challenge them because I am on their side. So it doesn't seem like a direct attack. You just need to clarify your trying to help them and then you can do anything. It means we are a team and I am being respectful of their team.

E (TURKEY): You don't have to be perfect. To be good enough you have to have emotional regulation. Understanding the couple, what they give importance to, how they calm themselves.

J (MALTA): Good enough involves helping the family feel good enough and bridging the differences in perspectives between the members. Good enough is being humble and open to change.

One therapist talked about lack of perfectionism and accepting good enough relationships with regard to the problems of gay and lesbian couple clients.

B (CANADA): Good enough is crucial in homosexual relationships because they don't have other things to keep them together. The quality of the relationship is what matters. Working with a gay couple living in a straight world, they feel they are not ok so they have trust issues and problems with receiving love. Shame and guilt shaped them.

Therapists often talked about working on themselves in order to be good enough:

S (TURKEY): As an ambitious student, one day I realized it keeps me from having a good life. Being perfect doesn't give room for learning and growth. For example, when I started being a couple therapist, I thought everyone has to wind up staying together, otherwise I have failed. But you need to let the couples lead you, don't come with an agenda. I try not to work harder than the couple.

R (ISRAEL): I feel better as a therapist that is good enough if I feel safe enough to deal with new things in the treatment. My self-esteem is solid enough that I can take small steps, regression, using my own feeling to understand what is going on.

M (CANADA): Keeping a balance between what people are telling me and what I feel is right. The concept of good enough humbles us, makes us easy with our mistakes. This humility creates compassion and self-esteem, even when faced with criticism.

D (UK): A good enough therapist is a reflexive therapist who is able to focus on the relationship of the couple and not on the individuals.

C (MALTA): Good enough is containing the couple. You are like the mother bird digesting the worms (emotions) for the young. You cannot be a therapist if you don't include yourself. People don't come for your techniques, they come for the genuine interactions.

There were only two therapists out of the whole group that did not like the good enough idea.

C (CANADA): Good enough sounds to me like judgment, like it's mediocre. I want great – really help the couple understand what each needs and what to give to the other … otherwise I feel like I am losing my skills.

T (ISRAEL): I suggest giving up the idea of good enough. Good enough creates pressure to be good. Giving up the idea of good enough frees one.

With the exception of these two therapists, most were enthusiastic about the concept of good enough therapist. Once introduced into the conversation, they seemed to easily take on the idea and use and develop it throughout the interview. Many linked good enough to being less perfectionist, more accepting of themselves and their clients, working on themselves to become more self-aware and reflexive.

2. Difficulties in doing couple therapy

The majority of the couple therapists talked about couple therapy as being quite difficult. Many of them had come to couple therapy after first doing individual work or were currently doing both. They mentioned that couples work is harder. I did not initiate this line of questioning, but when it came up I pursued it.

Here are some of the common difficulties mentioned by these couple therapists.

K (ISRAEL): We don't hear about our successes … failures come back to tell us, but success happens out there in their lives.

A (UK): Sometimes the couple has a hidden agenda. They avoid things that might help their relationship. They may know they would benefit from deeper work, but they still stick to their original goals.

A (MALTA): Couple therapy is especially difficult when there is a childhood trauma. It is hard for people to say what their trauma was in front of their partners. I try to find a way for them to share it. Trust is important.

B (CANADA): Couples work is the hardest kind. They hold back more, don't want to say stuff in each other's presence. I want to seem impartial, but that stuff isn't always easy. Couples say that the only time they really talk is with me, but I don't feel comfortable with that level of dependence. People come to me six years too late. Many times I don't enjoy it. But I still continue. I have a fear of couple therapy. I am used to only talking to one person. If there are affairs or drugs, then I see them alone. We don't know what couples should do; we don't know what works for other people. We have these theories; maybe they are making it worse.

C (TURKEY): They generally talk about each other's faults. But when it comes to reality, it is a communication problem. Certain kinds of personality types bother me a lot. They try hard to get me on their side. But I believe that there are two types of people. Some people come to find solutions. Others come to show you it is impossible to find solutions.

The most common difficulty is making the therapist party to destructive couple behavior. This came up in almost every interview in some way or another. Being a witness to one partner's humiliation by the other, attacking behavior, severe criticism, addiction to affairs, all place the therapist at risk for moving from the good enough position. They lose their neutrality and ability to maneuver.

D (CANADA): It is hard for me when the couple has attacking behavior. I think that in such cases I need a psychiatric assessment and believe that there are personality disorders involved. For example, there is this couple where the wife always attacks me or her husband. He is defensive. I cannot listen to this unhealthy commutation. If there is no safe environment, it is not good enough. I stop them within 20 minutes … if I can. Sometimes I cannot and that is very hard for me.

A (UK): What makes couples work very difficult for me is when they call my basic identity into question. The trust that is needed to do good enough work doesn't develop. You need to have been fed emotion to know how to receive it as an adult. It is very difficult for me when we are not connecting on the intuitive feeling level, which is basic to my being able to work.

J (MALTA): When you cannot get the couple to listen to each other, there is a lot of anger and it is hard for me. I set ground rules, put a stop to abuse. As time goes by, I take a stand more and more.

Many of these therapists feel exposed to aversive interactions between partners or between the couple and the therapist. Sometimes they feel useless. Some refer out; others try to limit the problematic interactions. Some label the couple as having personality difficulties, while others blame themselves. It is indeed a profession rife with challenges and struggles – to remain neutral and to absorb anger, pain and fear in the room. This quote sums up a universal reaction to negative couple interactions.

S (ISRAEL): I can't see humiliation. I feel like pulling inside of myself. I see how a soul is destroying itself and if I don't stop it, I am a part of it. It's common in clients who want love so much but never experienced it. Sometimes there is competition for the therapist's love. This makes me feel physically sick.

J (MALTA): It is difficult for me to deal with abuse without taking sides. It is hard for me to stay neutral.

Compared to the space given to difficulties, there were only a few statements of clearly enjoying the work.

S (TURKEY): I like working with couples rather than alone. What I like is people's communication and how people chose each other. I like teaching new things to the couples.

When allowed to ponder therapy without a protocol for the interview, spontaneously the therapists gave far more attention to the difficulties they have than to the pleasures they gain.

3. Use of theory in practice

Few of the therapists (five) were loyal to one theory. These 'loyalists' worked exclusively with: Imago therapy (Canada); Satir therapy (Turkey); emotionally focused therapy (Turkey); psychoanalytic-oriented couple therapy (Turkey) and a specific protocol developed by the therapist herself (Turkey); as we see here four out of the five came from Turkey. These therapists traveled to continually acquire more training in their method of choice. All the others used a wide mixture of theories. For example:

C (MALTA): I use a lot of Winnicott, emotionally focused therapy and show people it is ok to be angry. I use communication training.

C (UK): I like Winnicott's model because it creates a space for thinking about countertransference. The therapist's role is to be a safe base.

This is interesting in light of the fact that most of the therapeutic literature on couples focuses on one theory. In the field it appears that therapists are probably eclectic. There also exists a professional literature on integrative therapy with couples. However, except for one therapist, who had invented her own integrative model (Turkey), the rest talked about using their intuition and their own experiences to help them choose a method with specific couples. They did not use any preexisting integrative model.

S (TURKEY): I use different theories with different couples. Imago therapy cannot be used with each couple. Not with non-communicative men. With them I would use more cognitive stuff. I use my own experience. My own marriage changed how I relate to couples, not books.

D (UK): I do family therapy because some people don't like psychodynamic (especially men). I use social constructivist, Milan school of strategic questions. Often I start with behavioral methods. It puts me in charge. A lot of couples respond well to circular questioning from the Milan group. But my real knowledge is my experience, which has taught me not to be rigid about methods.

M.(CANADA): I think intuitively not systematically. I do look at the forms of attachment of couples and I ask myself where they are in the developmental stage, things like object constancy. I was a snob about CBT [cognitive behavioral therapy] as well as medication to modify thoughts. But I realized there really are these thoughts that are destructive, and I don't want to go there. With couples I intuitively think unsystematically.

The importance that most therapists give to intuition, personal experience, and fit of the method with the therapist was surprising to me. Yet after reading the interviews I realized that I too rely on intuition, personal experience and methods that fit me the best. There is a conceptual messiness about the work in the field as opposed to the clean use of theory in the literature or at presentations at conferences. This messiness can undermine a therapist's confidence, summed up by the poignant statement by one therapist, 'I think ... what would a real therapist do?' I see Winnicott chuckling at that.

Unfortunately there is little written about the frustration couple therapists feel when exposed to master therapists of a particular theoretical base. Therapists who are actively working in the field know that no theory encompasses everyone. There were a few therapists who were clearly anti-theory and sounded a bit angry at the models presented by conference presenters.

M (CANADA): I ask myself what would a real therapist do? I don't know what I am doing in many situations. We don't really know what couples should do. These theories are maybe making things worse. We need lower expectations in the field, to be good enough. Most people have good enough relationships.

4. Therapist goals in couple therapy

There is recognition that often the goals that the therapist has are not the goals of the clients. Accepting that gap is seen as moving towards good enough, even though the difference might remain at the end of therapy.

J (CANADA): The therapist has different goals than the clients. For the couple it is accepting that marriage isn't like in Hollywood. The ability to tolerate the failure in expectations (both the clients and the therapist) is important.

C (MALTA): There was an unaffectionate husband. He became abusive and accused his wife of not being good enough. In therapy he felt safe to tell me about his depression. He got medication for that. They were not sexually satisfied, so I suggested they buy a book about sex and it helped. But he said that is enough and didn't want to do anything more for her. He couldn't empathize with her and didn't want to work on their relationship any more.

Most of the goals for the client couple seem to focus on the therapist herself and her development and not on the couples. Moreover there is a decided rejection of having goals for the clients. This is surprising in light of the strong emphasis in the couple therapist literature on goal attainment of all kinds, whether emotional, behavioral, or cognitive. We coded goals, but did not find therapists talking about client goals. Rather they talked about what they themselves get from therapy and how therapy has changed them.

J (UK): The older I get, the more accepting I become. A therapist must beware of ambition. Accept what they say. I used to be more black and white. This has to do with my own personal life. Can someone who does not have one primary love relationship do this work? I am not sure.

C (MALTA): In time I have become more direct. I am surer of myself and I have a wider repertoire. I draw more from my own relationship with my husband.

R (CANADA): I had an early career crisis about what my passion is. I came to creativity. I started to study this on my own. Best way to learn is to teach, so I am planning on giving an extension course on creativity at the university. I need to learn not to be afraid when things aren't going well. I constantly have to learn new stuff. A year and a half ago I wouldn't have known what a transgendered couple is. I had to learn about transgendered health problems. I don't like learning on the backs of my clients.

S (ISRAEL): A good enough therapist hasn't too many ambitions – no narcissistic need to succeed. We need to work on not trying to be someone else. I need to find what I am good at, like empowerment. I talk to people and make them feel fantastic, instead of trying to set goals in areas I am not good in.

Therapists interviewed seemed to really enjoy the process of the interview. Quite a few said that they never had this chance to talk about themselves. I assume that their focusing on themselves comes from a need to do this that might not be met in their training. A few said 'This is really like a good supervision' and seemed to be very happy to have a good listener for their own dilemmas.

5. Countertransference

The focus on the self of the therapist also led to most therapists talking about their own reactions to their clients.

E (ISRAEL): There is a big part of me wanting couples to leave the session happy. When I meet couples for the first time, countertransference is activated. To become more attuned, I need to address this countertransference in me.

J (UK): Sometimes I feel burned out, tired; after a while I can't be good enough. It is because I get attached to people and I want to save their marriages more than they do. Sometimes I have an overwhelming feeling of responsibility for failure. It is not clear who is to blame.

A (MALTA): I am sensitive to particular things like women getting hysterical because of my own mother who shouted too much. On the other hand my mother gave me the basic altruism required to be a therapist. After my mother's death I am able to make this a coherent story. I should remain neutral, not emotionally involved. Not to get caught up in anxiety. My becoming attached makes me avoid them when things get uncomfortable. I may not give them regular sessions. Countertransference is a challenge to authenticity and empathy. I know that in therapy the first thing that worried me is what about the children. What they will experience. This has to do with my own history of parenting. I always question if I am projecting my own bad experiences onto them.

N (CANADA): Working too hard is a bad sign. Means I am more invested than the couple. You have to be aware of your own processes. A way to train yourself to do this is to read a book and document your individual processes while reading.

S (TURKEY): Working with a problematic couple, I felt I would hate to be in that relationship. I am very conscious about my countertransference. I shut that part of me that is prejudiced. I open a third eye or a fourth eye to really get interested in the non-communicating husband.

Some mentioned being aware of their own body and what it was telling them about what was happening with the client.

K (ISRAEL): I feel problems physically. I feel the stuckness. My pulse is racing, I sweat, and then I try to understand what is happening in the room and make it happen in a different way. I try to pay attention to physical pains – noticed when my back is hurting. I had a couple with a really difficult situation around betrayal and adultery. I felt physically sick from it and had to figure out what was happening to me.

C (UK): Countertransference is a challenge. You need to think about how things happening to you may be a reflection of them. How to use the body to understand. Our sense of ourselves is in the body.

The focus on countertransference had no connection to the theories used in treatment. That is, not just psychoanalytically trained therapists focused on themselves and their countertransference. The focus on themselves is also echoed by cases that they discussed with me. Many talked about their difficulties with certain types of cases and they tended to put the responsibility on themselves for the failures to connect.

E (UK): One woman came who complained that her husband did not put the kids to bed. He was a good father, but he had to be exactly as she wanted or he was useless. I had a hard time with her. I was angry with her and she didn't like me. They split for a while and got back together. He bailed her out of debt. She wasn't managing finances well. She was mad at him for his lack of faith in her and she had only faith in her father, who never said no to her. I didn't try to change her but helped him hear the difficult things she had to say. He surrendered and gave her everything she wanted. My problem was how to be angry at her without alienating her.

N (CANADA): There was a couple in which she complained that there was no family time, but when they were together she just went into the kitchen. Then something happened in therapy; she wanted therapy but then she didn't show up. She felt I was not giving her enough time in therapy. I just didn't fall into her definition of how things had to be.

Clearly the therapists were using themselves as the major tool in their work.

6. Use of self and support

There is a decided tendency in all interviews to focus on therapist issues. But in looking for solutions to their own issues, 10 out of the 42 therapists mentioned seeking support from others. In three of these cases the support came in an imaginary form.

R (ISRAEL): I always think, 'What would Michael White do here?' When I am stuck I just ask how is this conversation going for you, which direction do you want to go? The worst situation is the borderline and I always ask others for peer support.

N (CANADA): Even after 33 years, I still say to myself, 'What would a real therapist do?'

J (MALTA): At times I am not sure of myself in therapy. I imagine all the teachers I had in life supporting me to be good enough.

Use of real life outside support was mentioned in seven of the interviews.

E (ISRAEL): I need to see how we are all connected. The baby can feel when his mother is sad and when she is in tune with him. I use the safety need of connection. As a therapist you must work on yourself rather than adding another type of treatment. I have learned how to use my connections with other professionals to help me.

J (UK): When I am confused I call a friend or colleague and talk about what went well and what didn't.

M (CANADA): I grew up with shame as a Jew and I experienced anti-Semitism. I also had a clinically depressed mother. Cognitive workshops helped me.

J (MALTA): Sometimes I am burned out and I need support from whatever possible … my supervisor … I lead a group of parents with stillborns and sometimes I feel that I can't protect myself there.

Not one talked about going to therapy, although they might have used therapy but not mentioned it.

From this material we do not know if professional support is seen as important or not. Although only 10 out of the 42 therapists talked spontaneously about professional support (and three of those were imaginary), we do not know if the reason was that only a minority saw this as important. Perhaps the rest just assume that professional support is important and therefore did not mention it. Since these therapists were forthcoming in talking about their own personal issues as well as the difficulties of doing couple therapy, the relative lack of citing supervision or therapy is interesting. Most talked about working on themselves. How and where do they do this work? Perhaps relying on others feels to them like revealing a lack of experience or security?

7. Transitional space

While only a few therapists talked specifically about transitional space, many of their quotes seem to me to indicate an awareness of the therapy space as a crucial transitional space as discussed by Winnicott. I might have called this category the therapeutic alliance, but the responses indicate a concept broader than that.

T (ISRAEL): Intuition is a transitional space. I can see where the energy is stuck and free it. Emotions are energy with a name. How do I move a couple in the therapy space away from aggression? The turning point has to do with connecting them to their parenting selves. Them as parents, or thinking about their own relationships with their parents. For example, when the husband's parents did not allow crying, he was reactive to his child crying and hit him. Seeing this in the session is what makes him move away from aggression.

N (CANADA): Attunement, awareness and honesty are the basic components to facilitating my relationship with the couples. Apologizing as a therapist is powerful as well. Sometimes waiting for a week before you apologize is more powerful because it suggests that I thought about them, they are important.

D (UK): Curiosity is important for both the therapist and for the couples. If a couple is puzzled, that is a step in the right direction. How to create an atmosphere of play? For playing you need to be secure. I like the idea of the capacity to be alone with their experience with the other (e.g. the therapist). The therapist's role is to be a safe base.

S (TURKEY): I always try to reconnect with the couple if there has been a disturbance. I show them I am trying to understand them in a different and new way. You need to think about the sessions in between sessions to come to new understandings. If the therapist is stuck and the client is stuck, this is where the transformation really happens.

Many therapists mentioned the therapeutic alliance and linked being good enough with creating this safe place for themselves with the clients. These therapists mention good enough, but later in the interview. I coded the good enough category only for the answer they gave to the initial question. When good enough came up spontaneously in the interview, it is included alongside the topic being discussed.

M (CANADA): I met a couple and created a good alliance with them. Once when I was upset I said something that sounded like I support the husband. I had a good enough relationship with them to cushion this incident, a good enough alliance. It was forgiven and we moved on.

K (ISRAEL): Good enough is the creation of a good chemistry between three people – the couple and the therapist. Honesty between the couple and the therapist is important. It is a process, not reaching specific goals. Attunement is important because it creates safety. Good enough is not harming the clients and the good enough therapist is willing to learn new things.

The majority of the therapists mentioned the therapeutic bond as crucial to success in therapy. They seem far more concerned with this than specific tools or theories.

I especially liked this response:

D (UK): It is good enough to give something useful. Making a therapeutic relationship of respect, connection and understanding. Only then can mistakes be forgiven. Show that you are genuine and that you care.

Cultural differences

I find it very easy to be culture-blind, especially coming from a dominant group in a culture. That is, as a Caucasian Ashkenazi from the USA working in Israel, it is easy to be culture-blind when your ethnic, racial background is considered modern and in the forefront of professional discourse. It was by interviewing the couple therapists from around the world that I came to see culture more clearly. First I saw the differences between the Maltese interviewees and the others. This is presented next. After recognizing the unique aspects of the Maltese therapists, I re-examined the other groups for aspects unique to them.

Malta

Malta was unique in the tendency for therapists to mention children as very important in couple therapy. A review of all the other interviews shows that children are not mentioned at all. Children are sacred in the traditional church-oriented Maltese culture. Here are some responses that reflect the importance of children in this culture.

A: Couple therapy is especially difficult when there is a childhood trauma. … I try to imagine them as wounded children to contain their emotions. … You are like the mother bird digesting the worms (emotions) for the young.

E: There was this woman who didn't take care of her children because of the relationship with her husband. This was very hard on me.

C: I get very upset when the father is abusive without thinking of the children. I cannot work alone with these cases.

C: I know that in therapy the first thing that worried me is what about the children? What they will experience.

R: There was this couple who were not married but had a child. They had cases and arguments against each other about the child. I said I cannot continue working with them until they develop a dialogue.

In my brief visit to Malta I was impressed with how traditional the family structures were, despite a great deal of modernization. Adult children are expected to live at home until marriage. One of the interviewees from Malta had forgotten to wake her adult son up for his university studies and she was hardly able to do the interview without finding out whether he had made it to classes. The fact that this son was 30 did not mean that his mother did not feel responsible for getting him up. The family met every evening for a meal, which was considered important for quality time in the family.

Divorce was only one year old in Malta, and while couples in the past separated there was no legal support for this. The Catholic Church is a strong factor in their traditionalism: it runs many of the counseling services for couples. It is possible that as divorce becomes increasingly prevalent, therapists there will have to find ways of coping with contradictions. The couple therapist is often an active part of a divorce process, especially by empowering women to reject abuse. On the other hand there might continue to be pressure on therapists from within themselves or from clients and agencies to keep the family together at all costs. As one Maltese therapist said about a husband in her treatment 'He couldn't understand how a family therapist can break up a family.' How Maltese therapists cope with these issues will determine the shape of Malta's couple treatment in the next few years.

Istanbul, Turkey

My first surprise in Turkey was learning that there were many different official family therapy associations. Coming from Israel where there is one such association, and any attempt to create another one is almost unthinkable, I was surprised at the ability of the therapists in Istanbul to create professional associations according to their needs. I was visiting just at the time when another such association was being founded. I asked how the associations got along with each other and my questions were met by surprise. Why shouldn't they get along? So something absolutely forbidden in my culture is not just allowed but embraced. I was told of the advantages of having different family therapy associations so that you can pick the one that fits your professional identity best.

The existence of multiple associations was also mirrored in the diversity of types of therapy being done. Some therapists strictly followed object relations, some were strictly Satir-oriented, and some had made up their own format, while others preferred listening to their gut instinct. Turkey is a place of multiple identities and pluralism. There are therapists who were influenced by the more liberal times of the previous government and find the current fundamentalism about religion and women's roles difficult to adjust to. But mostly there was an acceptance of the ethnic and religious diversity that makes up Turkey. The city of Istanbul is a symbol of this diversity, with part of the city being seen as European and the other as Asian. Apparently the Turkish population is used to diversity, and different groups of people and professionals live side-by-side.

Vancouver, Canada

One theme that seemed most prevalent in Canada and not so much in the other countries was an emphasis on not taking the emotional baggage of clients home. I heard many different expressions of the same thing, specifically statements like 'I do not want to work harder than my clients.' Or 'I see the problems they have as their problems and not mine, although I always try not to do any harm.' It seemed to me that the professionals in Vancouver were concerned with the boundaries between them and their clients. Part of this has to do with the fact that many worked for governmental agencies that put a limit to the number of sessions they could have with a client. If they saw a couple, they used this to have twice as many sessions, but it seemed that they were unhappy with these limitations. I stayed in touch with some of the therapists and after a year many had left the governmental agencies to strike out on their own. The context of having only a few sessions with a couple undoubtedly created a certain distance in the relationships and in the goals for therapy. It seems likely that in such a situation goals have to be scaled down: the client is seen as temporarily in treatment, which might create more rigid boundaries in the therapeutic relationship.

London, UK

It appears that one aspect unique to this professional group is their connection with an umbrella organization called 'Relate'. Although most of the therapists I interviewed were in private practice, many had been trained by Relate, which has a psychodynamic orientation. This orientation, combined with the fact that most of the therapists were self-employed, results in a dynamic that appears the opposite to that in Vancouver. The London therapists were willing and able to see therapy as potentially a long-term endeavor. The development and strengthening of the self, as well as awareness of psychopathology, was unique to these therapists.

It also was common and acceptable that the couple therapy might turn into divorce counseling. That might be because divorce is fairly common and also because the emphasis is on the mental health of the individual in the couple system. For London therapists working on their own, therapy moving from couple therapy to divorce therapy was not unusual, nor was it seen as a failure. As in Canada the therapists had fairly strong boundaries with their clients. They mentioned that the client is the most important aspect of change: how willing they are to invest, how much psychopathology there was, and the potential for divorce as an acceptable outcome.

Israel

Seeing what is unique to Israel is the hardest for me. Like a fish not aware of the water, I have been trained and have trained others for 40 years in Israel. I was better able to see the unique aspects after looking at the other cultures.

One special aspect of the Israeli professionals was the presence of trauma in the histories of the clients they see. Some therapists feel comfortable working with couples where trauma is also an issue. Others seem to think that when trauma is an issue a specialist in trauma should be consulted. Trauma is a fact of life in a country always at war and dealing with terror inside its borders. In truth there have been more deaths from traffic accidents in Israel than from terror attacks. But traffic accidents are also viewed as often resulting in trauma.

Another issue that profoundly affects Israeli therapists is the rigid and difficult route to becoming accredited by the Israeli Association of Family and Couple Therapy. This organization has a lot of power in Israel to determine who is given accreditation and which programs are acceptable for accreditation. The fact is that the government has not stepped into this question and the rules of the Association and their level of demand have no legal backing. But most therapists who do one of the several family and couple therapist programs in Israel also want to be accepted as a member of the Association. This shapes the career paths of many therapists who are willing to volunteer in order to gain supervised hours. The issue of acceptance as a certified family and couple therapist has resulted in high standards and continuing education as the norm.

In Israel the ending of a marriage through the process of therapy is felt by the therapists to be a kind of failure. Although they understand that some people really do better after divorce, they have a hard time accepting that they were not able to save the marriage. Most therapists I interviewed believe that family-of-origin issues are crucial to family and couple therapy. Divorce is viewed in the context of family-of-origin issues and often as an attempt to solve these issues by leaving the family (instead of staying in therapy and working on their own self issues). Many of the therapists themselves have been in therapy, both individually and with their partners. Going to couple therapy is widely accepted and encouraged as a way to try to save family unity.

Similarities and differences

Overall I have a firm sense that there are far more similarities between therapists in different cultures than differences. The therapists have all been influenced by the same master teachers, the same professional literature and similar workshops and conferences. There are international associations of family and couple therapy that allow a cross-fertilization of ideas and dilemmas. The similarities are strengthened by the internet, with courses running on the web.

Also, the literature on family and couple therapy does not pay a great deal of attention to culture or ethnic differences between larger groups such as countries. While there is a literature on ethnic or racial differences in treating couples within a country, that literature focuses on what to do with differences between the therapist and the couple in background variables. The literature examining the differences between countries that does exist does not come from the field of therapy. Rather the literature on differences globally comes from sociology and anthropology. There is a real lack of knowledge about how couple therapy is similar or different in different countries.

Interconnections between categories

The categories found included: good enough as applied to couple therapy; difficulties in doing couple therapy; use of theory in practice; goals in couple therapy; countertransference; use of support; transitional space and gender issues. What might be some of the interconnections between these categories?

I will look at interconnections by focusing on the prevalence of the category of difficulties in couple therapy. This is important as most therapists mentioned it, especially the problem of being exposed to fighting, aggression, abuse or humiliation in the therapy room. We can see this as a real problem, but also as an opportunity. The problem is of dealing routinely with aversive interactions, but the opportunity is that this throws couple therapists back to themselves. After all, they have to deal with the immediate problematic interactions in the room far more than the therapist working with individuals. I assume that therapists working with individuals are less exposed to aversive interactions and also that they are routinely expected to be in supervision and therapy.

It is possible that because of the real difficulty in doing couple therapy there is a natural emphasis on the process of the therapy sessions. After all if the negativity is not changed, the therapy will not succeed because the therapist is unable to connect to both partners in a positive way. Therapists focus on themselves because they need to be able to deal with split alliances, betrayal, lying, and secrets as well as out-of-control escalations in the room and all the other challenges. Couple therapists are routinely exposed to situations where they might naturally favor one spouse over another or be perceived to do this. The criterion for success with couples is not clear. What is a successful couple therapy? What is a successful couple? Expectations are high for happiness in couples without realistic goals for what they consider happiness in their marriage.

Lack of clarity on couple goals seems to have led to a rejection of goals for couples and more emphasis on the therapeutic transitional space and countertransference. Therapists working with couples have to manage the interaction in the room to be able to work productively with the couple. The therapist has to become aware of their own impediments to the connection with both partners and have the ability to see the relationship as a separate entity. The challenges are great and demand a high level of responsiveness on the part of the therapist. The passive therapist is lost in the turmoil of an escalating fight or the differences experienced by men and women. Gender is mentioned as something to overcome. That is, therapists, especially from traditional cultures, are aware that gender differences between them and the couple add to the difficulties of doing couples work.

In the couple therapy literature there is a lack of stress on the needs of the therapist. So on one hand the couple therapists deal with an especially difficult form of therapy and on the other hand they do not get a clear message from the prevailing literature and training that they need to work on themselves or how to do this. They seem to know that they have to work on themselves. Despite the literature on different methods for treatment, the therapists talked mostly about their own development and interaction with couples. There was a decided silence about the tools of therapy other than the self of the therapists. They are very aware of countertransference and problems in the transitional (therapeutic alliance) space. How to work on these goals for the self of the therapist is not specified. The clear happiness expressed at having a chance to do the interview and to be listened to seems to reinforce this idea. It appears from these interviews, and future research can follow this up, that these therapists are stressed by their work, focus a lot on difficulties and perhaps feel too alone in their work.

The concept of good enough therapist was eagerly embraced by the interviewees, who often used the phrase throughout the interview. There was a definite sense of relief in some of these therapists about reducing their own expectations for perfection. They remembered the importance of play, of intuition, of creativity, and of their own bodies.

The interviews and Winnicott

I wonder what Winnicott would have made of these interviews? I can only guess that he would not be surprised by the focus on the self of the therapist. The good enough mother is indeed the focus of most of his work. I imagine he would be happy to hear of the importance these therapists give to their own self-awareness and reflexivity. After all, maintaining a good enough relationship is mostly the work of the mother in interaction with her infant. Maintaining a good enough role in couple therapy mirrors this. It is up to the therapist to gradually adapt to the couple, leading them from their projection, negativity, and problems to a better way to relate to each other. The infant in this case is the couple relationship and the child inside of each partner.

Intuitively many interviewees focused on basic therapy goals, such as genuineness, trust, and creating a safe place for the couples. These were mentioned more than interventions to change couples. Issues like not being anxious when things aren't going well occupy these therapists more than how to be better change agents. As a matter of fact there was an unexpected rejection of goal attainment (seen as ambition) for the couples.

The therapists seem to know that their job is to hold and contain negative feelings, but they found doing this difficult. Therapists from around the world seem to be aware that overcoming perfectionism is an important personal goal to help them adequately contain so much negativity in the room.

However, some see the models and teachers as demanding too much perfectionism. We see this directly in some statements, and in their lack of mention of therapeutic tools. They seem aware that they cannot be as amazing as the masters who trained them and in their rejection of perfectionism as well as specific couple goals they are directing us to a different kind of training. They are telling us that training has to take on the self of the therapist as a major issue in couple therapy.

I am left wondering about the possibility that couple therapists do not have enough social support for their own issues as practicing therapists. The combination of facing aversive situations between couples and perhaps towards the therapist as well combined with lack of social support would indeed make couple therapy very difficult. To help, they seek additional training in different theoretical models. Adding more models to their work does not seem to result in more focus on professional tools as an answer to the difficulty of doing couple therapy.

Despite their rejection of perfectionism, these therapists focused on difficult-to-achieve goals for themselves. Being accepting, genuine, trustworthy, and other self-goals are not easy to attain. There is recognition of the importance of the therapeutic encounter between them and the couple. Are they actually being perfectionist about these goals? The interaction between high emotional demands on the therapist with not enough social support could lead to eventual burnout. We who teach and give workshops need to wonder about the messages we are sending in our training. Do we imply that we have found what 'works' with couples, rather than what is needed by the therapist to keep up the transitional space for their rather difficult couples?

The fact that so few of these therapists use only one model seems to imply that we need to focus on how individual therapists go about integrating theories and on the self of the therapist as the key to this integration. Adding more models (even models of integration) seems not to be the direction these therapists really need. Rather they seem to need attention to themselves as the major tool in working with couples. This focus cuts across differences in therapeutic models.

If the therapist's self is the central agent of change, how much concern should we give to how therapists are taught? Perhaps we need to rethink how we present theories and models. If the self of the therapist is truly the major factor in helping couples, we need to encourage therapists to integrate their professional roles with their true selves. We can use Winnicott to think about how we 'present' theory/practice as objects to our trainees and supervisees. Do we reflect enough with them about their feelings about the theories and case material? Could we be impinging on therapists in training without noticing the effect the material they must ingest has on them?

Do we give enough emphasis to the transitional space that is the working medium for change and learning? The transitional space exists between mothers and infants, between husband and wife, and between teacher and student. Whenever two or more subjectivities intermingle, we have the transitional space as the meeting place. Winnicott's ideas about object presenting and handling help us to focus on how ideas (as objects that are played with) are introduced and offered to our clients and students. If we are truly interested in reaching for their true selves rather than compliant false selves we need to remember the concepts of good enough mothering and bring them to bear in the intersubjectivity we inhabit.

4 The process of good enough in therapy with couples

The depth and richness of Winnicott's ideas, concepts, and theories is remarkable. In this chapter I will lay the foundation for thinking about couple therapy using Winnicott's ideas. We return to some of these ideas in the chapters that follow, but we can see this chapter as a pivotal one in linking Winnicott's good enough mothering processes, couples and their therapy. Of all the many processes Winnicott proposes as significant, the issue of hate and aggression is important enough to warrant a separate chapter.

I have not come across any one book that focuses on Winnicott and couple therapy. Yet Winnicott is often mentioned in a variety of articles and books. His ideas appear in a myriad of places in the professional literature. For example, Coleman (1995) looks at the concept of projective identification in couples and proposes that there is a more positive idea that Winnicott proposed: that of a shared unconscious field. In my attempts to pull together Winnicott's ideas and couple therapy, I had many diverse places to look for material. Winnicott clearly made his mark on psychoanalysis, on child therapy and even on thinking about institutions like academia. Other writings mention Winnicott's ideas as helpful to couple relationships. Few of them focus on how these ideas can then be used in therapy with couples. As I will show in this chapter, it is an obvious next step to see as many of his ideas as possible as having a potential contribution to couple therapy.

The only other book entirely based on Winnicott and couples relates specifically to sexuality of the couple. McCarthy and Metz (2008) proposed a model of good enough sex that can help couples struggling with perfectionist ideas about sex. Couples often hold perfectionist beliefs, such as that sex should always result in erection for men or orgasm for women. They relate performance anxiety as a major cause of distress in couples who are married and especially for long-term marriages. This performance model amplifies fears of inadequacy and predisposes to life-long sexual disappointment. The good enough mothering concept certainly would be helpful in reducing perfectionist goals in sex. But Winnicott has much more to offer couples.

Winnicott

Winnicott rose to prominence just as the followers of Anna Freud were battling those of Melanie Klein for the right to be called Sigmund Freud's true intellectual heirs. Winnicott was trained by Melanie Klein but became increasingly independent in his thinking over the course of his career, ultimately contributing original ideas of his own. Winnicott used writing and lecturing to polish and develop his own ideas. He was not concerned if his ideas mirrored those of others at his time. He once introduced a paper of almost revolutionary ideas, presented at the British Psycho-Analytic Society, with the words:

> I shall not first give an historical survey and show the development of my ideas from the theories of others, because my mind does not work that way. What happens is that I gather this or that, here and there, settle down to clinical experience, form my own theories, and then last of all, interest myself to see where I stole what. Perhaps this is as good a method as any.
>
> (Winnicott, 1945)

Except for one book published in 1931 (*Clinical Notes on Disorders of Childhood*), all of Winnicott's books were published after 1944, including *The Child and the Family* (1957a), *The Child and the Outside World* (1957b), *The Family and Individual Development* (1965e), *Theory of Emotional Development* (1965b) and *Playing and Reality* (1971a). This is a very short list of Winnicott's writings. Those readers who would like to go into greater depth than possible here are referred to two excellent texts on Winnicott, his life, and the evolution of his ideas: Davis and Wallbridge (1981) and Rodman (2003). Winnicott used his extensive case histories (his estimate is 20,000 cases) to work on his theories.

An introduction to a process view of good enough mothering

People misread and misunderstand the way Winnicott meant 'good enough' – which does not mean just settling for anything. There is really no such thing as 'a good enough mother', but there are mothers who are sometimes good enough and sometimes not. It is the balance between these two that led to thinking of processes and not just outcome.

Misreading Winnicott is a phenomenon known with regard to other psychoanalytic thinkers. For example, Ogden (2001) makes the point that Winnicott has a unique way with words. He uses words more to *create* an experience rather than just using words to describe an experience.

Our conventional use of language is partly to blame for reifying concepts – that is, making them appear to exist on their own. To reify is to regard or treat an abstraction as if it had concrete or material existence. Our common use of language invites us to concretize nouns as if they exist in real life. It is hard to overcome this. Even the words 'good enough' could theoretically suffer from the same problem – how much 'good enough' is good enough? So we need to be aware that applying Winnicott to couples is not to add another diagnostic term. We might easily find ourselves thinking about a couple and saying to ourselves 'They really don't have a good enough relationship' or 'They do have a good enough relationship'. Good enough is not a noun and certainly not something one can have. It is more a verb and as such it denotes a process. While grammar-wise the following sentence is incorrect, it is more in line with what Winnicott would have wanted: 'This couple held each other while angry by good enough(ing) each other.'

To see the good enough parenting that therapists do for couples and the couple do for each other is to view good enough as a development that increases over time. That is, we can think in terms of increasing good enough mothering between us and the couple and the couple with each other. This idea is similar to Murray Bowen's idea that we never get to 100% differentiation of self (Skowron and Friedlander, 1998). We are all a work in progress.

Winnicott and perfectionism

Winnicott (1956) located our drive for perfection as a central problem in early mother–child attachments. Rather than attempting to be a perfect mother (or wife), good enough is an idea that promotes balance between failures and their repair so that the outcome is good enough to continually adapt and change according to the ability of the infant to cope with the environment. Here are two examples from therapy:

> In working through the genogram Rob realized that he did not know anything about comfortably being with someone while alone as well. He did have one memory of playing contentedly under his mother's sewing machine while she worked. She had a wonderful (for him as an infant) box of buttons, which he never tired of playing with; this box was a source of magical excitement, which was contained by his mother's quiet work at her machine. It was a good time and it was a memory that he could access to help him think about being differently with Marilyn.
>
> Marilyn herself had the same kind of genogram in which there were severe cut-offs and too much enmeshment; however, with her these might both be true in any relationship, which might careen between too much distance and too much closeness. Her father used to walk out of the home when he was mad, but he also was very demanding of her mother to relate to him when he was there. This volatility was part of her anxiety upon being alone together with Rob. When he talked with her, she felt pushed to converse. However, when he went into his study, she felt abandoned. She could not find a place of peace unless he was either at work or abroad. Her only memory of finding a place of 'continuity of being' was when she was in the garden of her childhood home. The garden was close to a forest, where she often roamed freely. The best feeling she remembered was sitting in a little nook

> next to the garden while knowing that her mother was home. She could not play in the forest unless she was sure her mother was there, although she hadn't thought of this before. In therapy she tried to figure out how such a peaceful yet alert experience could be had with Rob. She was able to make some suggestions, one of which he accepted. This was to help her return to her hobby of painting on porcelain while he was nearby but not in the same room. For her this was a significant move. She had given up her hobby because she felt too much anxiety in the home to be free to be creative. The therapist worked on how far Rob could go away from her in the house while she worked on her hobby, without the anxiety starting. Finding this comfort zone was a kind of repair for her. Careful with the details, the couple decided he could be in his study (which he loved), but he would come and check on her at least once every half hour.

We can see in this case a combination of family-of-origin work with some behavioral contracting. Both of these theories have generated useful tools that the good enough therapist can access. The importance is to remember that any method or tool has to fit the spouses and the relationship.

Help from Piaget

I would suggest that there is a conceptual connection between Winnicott's ideas and those of Piaget. Piaget, like Winnicott, came upon his ideas of accommodation and assimilation as the twin processes for growth and development. He too watched his own children carefully and came upon his ideas from careful observation.

> Assimilation is a part of Piaget's theory that is evident in the way children perceive the outside world. This part of his theory suggests that a child may change or alter what he perceives in the outside world in order to fit his internal world; the result of assimilation is that 'complex and familiar external objects are simplified to fit pre-existent categories in your head,' and this may cause stereotypes and 'pigeon-holing' for children. Assimilation occurs when the child does not change the internal world to suit the object, and this is a simpler but less realistic form of perception.
>
> Accommodation may be a more complicated and challenging form of perception and learning for children. Piaget's theory on accommodation asserts that the internal world must change to be able to fit the outside world. Accommodation occurs when a child perceives information that can not fit into any pre-existing category; the child must then create a new area of intelligence, perception, and thought in order to process the information gathered from the outside world. According to Piaget, accommodation is when a child must alter the ideas in his head in order to 'fit the realities of external objects'.
>
> (Atherton, 2013, p. 7)

Although assimilation and accommodation are very different processes, they both deal with ideas about perception and reality. Piaget's theory on accommodation is interesting and important to understand when dealing with children and adults. It is also important to understand that although assimilation or accommodation may predominate at any one moment, they are inseparable and exist in a dialectical relationship. Piaget's theory asserts that accommodation and assimilation occur at the same time, and both are constantly in use when perceiving the outside world.

Applying Winnicott to couples and couple therapy

Winnicott believed that every person has an inner capacity to feel integrated and disintegrated:

> It is sometimes assumed that in health the individual is always integrated, as well as living in his own body, and able to feel that the world is real. There is, however, much sanity that has a symptomatic quality, being charged with fear or denial of madness, fear or denial of the innate capacity of every human being to become unintegrated, depersonalized, and to feel that the world is unreal.
>
> (Winnicott, 1945)

The infant needs to feel omnipotent in the beginning. Feeling at one with the mother allows the infant to thrive. But to grow the infant needs a gradual introduction of the environment to start to realize that they are not alone. The good enough mothering process looks mostly to feedback from the infant (or partner or couple) to judge if a stimulus is felt as an impingement. If so, the baby is threatened with feeling overwhelmed and disintegrated. And the outcome depends on the fit between the infant's need for growth from impinging stimuli and the mother/therapist recognition of distress and return to equilibrium. Thus the stimulus is just enough of an impingement and is coupled with material reaction to help the baby recover.

This crucial process is taken on by all mothers. When the mother is depressed or experiencing marital problems, she might be less attuned to the infant's signals of distress and might thus keep on impinging upon the child. The therapist is also asked in this model to watch for signs of positive or negative reactions to statements or even to lack of reaction. We are not, as therapists, expected to sense exactly what the couple needs. If we were magically somehow able to do this, we would be sabotaging the couple's own need to figure things out for themselves.

So there are two intertwining questions here. One is to what extent does the baby perceive the mother's intervention (feeding, holding, playing) as matching the level of development of the child? And the second is, if there is a momentary mismatch, how fast does the mother recognize an impingement has occurred and how fast can she help the baby recover from its own fears of disintegration?

Piaget was interested in education. He used similar ideas about fit and lack of fit from stimuli from outside to understand the process by which an infant or child matches himself to the environment (accommodation) or how far the infant/child makes the environment match him (assimilation). Both accommodation and assimilation are needed for both and both processes are intertwined. If the child can not assimilate stimuli from the environment, the attuned (good enough) environment accommodates to the child. If the child accommodates to the environment there has to be enough repair by the environment to help the child change.

This is very similar to the notions of Winnicott which question to what extent the environment fits the child (omnipotence in the child and assimilation of the environment) and to what extent the child makes the environment match him/herself (temporary disintegration and repair by the environment similar to accommodation). While Piaget was interested in this dance of matching, mismatching, and change as it applied to learning, Winnicott developed very similar ideas related not to learning but to emotional development. Together both theories can shed light on the interweaving of cognitive development with emotional development. In Winnicott's thinking the perfect match of environment to the child's emotional state results in a continuation of being and a sense of omnipotence of the child.

When the child has to adjust to the environmental impingement, the child must accommodate rather than assimilate to the environment. This latter process involves rupture and repair. If the mother (the environment) notices and responds to rupture (disintegration, impingement) in an appropriate way the child recovers from disintegration. Also, along the lines of Piaget, we would expect that an emotionally secure child would learn better and thus signal the mother that new and more challenging stimuli can be offered. Impingements do occur but lead to increased individuation and sense of self.

When the environment impinges on the child and causes the child to adapt, the major issue is how much does the child have to adapt/accommodate? If the movement towards accommodation is a step too big to take, there is a dangerous explosion of anxiety without response from the environment. This is the beginning of the false self. The false-self child only adapts (accommodates) to the environment and the balance of these two movements is too much in the direction of demands on the child.

This dance between the child and the environment is echoed in many theories of development, growth, and change. For example, narrative therapy asks the clients questions to help them create their own new narrative, and talks about the ability of the client to answer questions. If the questions demand too much understanding from the client, the therapist is trained to ask questions that are easier and closer to the problem narrative that the client is used to. These more problem-oriented and, for the client, easier questions are called 'scaffolding' (Lundby, 2011). This process describes the same dance noticed by Piaget and by Winnicott. In narrative therapy the use of questions more adapted to the way the client views the world is used to help move on to greater ability to deal with change-oriented strategies.

These two fundamental moves, detected by Piaget, White, and Winnicott, are the crux of the process of growth and development. Systems theories of all kinds note these same two intertwining processes they call homeostasis (keeping the old balance) and morphogenesis (adapting to new stimuli) (Bateson, 1971).

We can be fairly secure in taking onboard this fundamental dance because it appears in so many different ways in the thinking of different theorists. It is for humans in the process of change, growth and development; the fundamental building blocks of the move to and from change. It is the fundamental dance between the baby/client/couple and the mother/therapist/couple therapist. The balance between the demands for change and growth and the ability to match where the baby/client/couple are at the present moment.

Application to couple therapy

To return to Winnicott, we realize that a stimulus presented to the child can be judged to be an impingement if there is protest or cutting off on the part of the child. No mother/therapist can predict 100% accurately whether what is offered is going to be taken in happily (but without growth) or is an impingement and needs repair (which is tied to change). There can be no change without enough matching and there can be no change without rupture and repair.

For example, if a couple is at the beginning of therapy they might not be ready for connecting their problems to family-of-origin issues. They might need encouragement and connection to their original love for each other. If they are starting to feel the pain of uncovered wounds, they might need an intervention that links their pain to their history.

This idea can be linked to feeding an infant. An infant cannot tolerate food other than milk. Yet at a later stage solid foods are necessary to keep the child growing.

How does a therapist move in this dance with minimum distress for the couple but with increasing doses of change asked from them? Here we return to the therapist's own self-awareness. The change process is the dance between support for what is balanced and support for change. How can a therapist know how to do this dance? Each couple and each partner is different. The dance is the matching of what the therapist has to give along the way and the reactions and responses of the partners and the couple. The importance of the therapist's own self-awareness is crucial in the movement through this dance. Since Winnicott did not list a series of stages or a list of questions to ask, what does he offer us in dealing with what appears to be a universal human struggle? Winnicott is asking the mother/therapist to be self-aware. Each 'change agent' (mothers, educators, therapists) have their own internal reactions that are a mirror of what is going on (in the child/student/couple); we might call these intuitions, but we can learn about them as part of a self-reflective process within the person involved in change-making.

The importance of reflexivity to the good enough process

This book places the reflexivity of the therapist, the ability to introspect and reflect on what he/she is thinking, feeling, and doing, as central in doing good enough couple therapy. For couples themselves, becoming more reflective helps partners to bridge an important paradox that is fundamental to the experience of 'we-ness'. The paradox involves the challenge inherent in the partner's attempt to reconcile the simultaneous separateness and interconnectedness of his/her own mind and the mind of the other. The difficulties that can emerge in attempts to fully engage with the mental states of the other may be related to one's struggle to fully appreciate the strength of the self in partner interactions while at the same time remaining aware of the other's separate self.

Reflexivity or self-reflection is both an outcome of good enough therapy as well as a major tool used by the therapist. The therapist uses reflexivity to stay attuned with their own intuitive knowing and resonance with the couple. The reflexive therapist encourages the partners to reflect on each other and on their own inner processes. Good enough couple therapy creates a container or holding environment for reflecting on the pain, anxiety, and distress of the couple without causing increased suffering. The therapist (like the good enough mother) gathers up all the spilled emotionality in the room and mirrors it back to the couple in a way they are able to hear. The therapist also uses their own reactions openly to share their reflections. It is when the therapist is able to model a sense of calm reflection, and comfort with difficult material, that partners have an experience of being held themselves. Furthermore, when partners encounter a supposed expert in couple relationships who can acknowledge that there are no simple answers when it comes to marital relationships, it frees them from the belief that they should always immediately know what to do. In couple therapy each partner learns to increase their capacity to tolerate and regulate their own internal affective reactions, and that allows them to do so for their partner. Increasing this reflexivity on the part of the couple relates directly to how the therapist can hold their own emotional reactions. Therapist reflexivity is crucial to creating the holding environment for partners' reflexivity.

Good enough marriage

Winnicott himself was married twice. His first wife, Alice, was apparently eccentric, extremely difficult and demanding. According to Winnicott's biographer Rodman (2003), his marriage was never consummated. The stress of his first marriage led him to have several serious heart attacks over a period of 20 years. Throughout his two marriages he was always in psychoanalysis, often with well-known analysts such as Melanie Klein and Joan Riviere. In addition, Winnicott was constantly analyzing himself. He used drawings and his wealth of written papers to help him develop a theory based on intimate knowledge of himself. He left his first wife after realizing that the strain of being with her was going to kill him.

His second marriage was indeed a 'good enough' marriage. Rodman conducted an interview with Winnicott's second wife, Clare Britton, in 1981. He writes that during World War II Winnicott was engaged as a consultant in Oxfordshire, where difficult children were housed in staffed hostels as part of the evacuation scheme for their protection from the bombings by Germany. Clare Britton was a social worker there and the two fell in love while working together. Together then and for the rest of his life, Winnicott would develop his ideas alongside his work together with Clare. Apparently she was an outstanding social worker who supported and challenged his thinking. She was apparently a very strong woman who pushed him to clarify his ideas. Clare's assertiveness and insistence led to his eventually leaving his first wife and marrying her; she was not willing to accept his inability to 'be a man'.

Clare was not intimidated by Winnicott's stature and expertise. She thought about their ideas and they 'played' constantly with his thinking and hers. Together they developed many of his most important contributions. Here is a letter she wrote to him, showing how they were lovers both in body and in mind. The combination is an ultimate experience creating the good enough marriage, which has the characteristics of the good enough mothering experience.

> April 2, 1943
>
> About the existence of good. To make it clear to myself I must sum up a bit first –
>
> The ultimate 'good' thing = the experience in which the inner good world unites with the good in the world of reality through some relationship – as you said for a baby this happens when the inner good mother unites with the real mother.
>
> It is only possible to attain this experience of the existence of the inner good world because only in this way can the belief in the goodness be sustained through periods of doubt in the reality situation – you said that for the baby it means that a relationship with the real mother is only possible because of the existence of the inside good mother. So far so good? Now the importance of these experiences is that they are the only proof there is that one is good oneself. In these moments one is entirely good and entirely safe.
>
> (a) Difficulties arise if there is a lack of good relationship ones good world and oneself never become good: lack of reality. This is a dangerous situation.
>
> (b) Only in certain moments is the inner good linked up with reality – so that mostly reality does not really satisfy. And you said that this is the great problem of living and perhaps something which must be always reconciled with (i.e. the hate engendered by frustration).
>
> You said – that in facing this problem one must be scientific and say that a good experience happened once and may happen again (I said this sounded hopeless) but there is nothing to say that it will.
>
> Now I want to say it differently (and please tell me if you think I am wrong); if one has a good experience once – it never ceases to exist, it is

> dynamic and creative and enters so deeply into the fabric of the personality that it is independent of time and place and of individuals even and simply cannot pass like any ordinary event. It is not only made up of eternal reality.
>
> I think that these experiences form part of the background of one's faith in life – one's religion in other words. In this way they are stored up and preserved against the 'evil' days and surely this faith does help in dealing with reality – it is not an escape from it. For one thing there is not the same anxiety about the existence of good and of being good and one is freer to hate and more independent. But this faith comes only to those who utterly trust their feelings and experiences of good. And it is not a blind faith because it has reality behind it.[1]

Clare apparently was a force to be reckoned with. In terms of their relationship, she was adamant that he devote himself to her and leave his first wife. With regard to his ideas, she fully understood the essence of his idiosyncratic way of thinking and was able to join his thoughts and help him elaborate them.

'Why was Clare so important to his work', asks Daniel Berg in his 1994 manuscript 'Why Winnicott?' (Berg cited in Rodman, 2003). Berg and Rodman saw his love for her as enabling him to be creative to his greatest capacity. Winnicott apparently described his love for her as towards a transitional object, a girl doll. One aspect of their relationship therefore was that in her good enough mothering she made herself available to be re-created in the image of his desires and needs in a way that she not only did not challenge but actively encouraged. She also provided him with near-perfect 'mirroring', as can be seen in her comments on how she was shown all of his squiggle productions, the drawing game in which his unconscious feelings could be manifested.

> 'There were his endless squiggle drawings which were part of his daily routine' she later recalled. 'He would play the game with himself and produced some very fearful and some very funny drawings which often had a powerful integrity of their own. If I was away for a night he would send a drawing through the post for me to receive in the morning, because my part in all this was to enjoy and appreciate his productions, which I certainly did, but sometimes I could wish that there were not quite so many of them.'
>
> (Rodman, 2003)

In these short vignettes of their life together several important ideas for the good enough marriage are set forth. I will elaborate on them here and then talk about my own marriage of almost 40 years.

The couple relationship as a good enough internal object

The idea proposed by Winnicott and elaborated by Britton is that if at some point in the relationship there are good moments, these are never destroyed but remain available if the couple wants to use them. This way of thinking becomes an essential part of Winnicott's ideas, in which the earliest of good moments do remain as resources for later use. There are many examples of this way of thinking in his writings. For example, when he analyses delinquent behavior, he is seeing it as a protest against the loss of something good that was once experienced.

In intimate adult relationships there usually are moments at the start of the relationship that bind and connect the couple to move to later stages, such as marriage, having their first child, buying their first house. These good moments feel to the couple as lost to them forever when they are in the misery stage of their relationship.

Since the couple cannot access these memories, the therapist has to be the one to retrieve them, breathe new life into them, and maintain their existence throughout the vicissitudes of the therapy. Of course a basic action would be to ask about these early memories and to label them so that they can be retrieved again when needed. However, this is impossible if the therapist herself loses contact with the good that existed and still exists in the couple relationship:

Ruth and Sam are a couple in their sixties, a second marriage for each of them. Sam is a famous doctor, while Ruth has no career and spends most of her day with her grandchildren. They have been married for 5 years, all of which were marked by stressful repeated fighting, separations and cruelty to each other. I, as therapist, worked hard to retrieve their earliest memories of meeting for the first time. Something must have brought them together, and I searched for those defining moments of their bonding. Each had a vision of the other that was originally complimentary. For example, at first, Ruth was very impressed with Sam's work and reputation because her first husband was, as she saw it, a 'loser'. At first, Sam was impressed with Ruth's devotion to family because his first wife had been career-oriented. However, within months his devotion to work was felt by Ruth to be an abandonment of her and her interest in her grandchildren appeared to him a life not worthy of respect.

The problem for me the therapist was in the degree of cruelty I encountered in this couple's interaction. Each told revealing and unpleasant stories about the other, sometimes with intimate details that were humiliating for each to hear from the other, especially in front of another person. The stories were hard to hear, even embarrassing.

Their black-and-white polarized way of seeing each other (once all good, but now all bad) was hard for me as a therapist and as a person. I felt silly reminding them of their early positive perceptions because they were equally cruel to me when I tried this. For example, I asked Ruth what she now could get from his career that might warm her heart. Ruth snorted and laughed at these whimsical phrases and imitated it in a nasty way. I felt silly having even brought it up.

It seemed to me that it would be important to hold the negative aggressive feelings this couple engendered in me. I sat quietly with them for a while before intuitively coming up with: 'You know, when you make fun of me it feels like you are showing me how you feel in this relationship. It must feel humiliating to be in the relationship and still care so much. And this is so different from what you once felt coming from each other.'

Holding to this way of using myself as an object was at first startling for the couple and then calming. At one point Ruth started to cry, saying that she so much missed the respect she once felt from him. Sam at first could not relate to this in a positive way, saying 'Well, respect has to be earned and you (the therapist) haven't earned my respect.'

Once again I sat with the feelings his comment triggered in me. I was able to locate feelings about trying hard and getting nowhere – with my parents especially. I remembered how hard it was to win their respect and how frustrated I was that I followed their rules (high grades, doctorate, etc.) and still never got their acknowledgement. Once again the space this reflection created allowed me to use myself as a good object by saying: 'I guess Sam that you might have been disappointed in others, maybe other therapists, maybe your parents, maybe Ruth. You want to be very careful before you place your trust in someone new. I can see how that would be important to protect you from further disappointment.' Sam shifted in his seat and was silent. He seemed to know the role of adversary, but did not appear to know what to do with a discussion of vulnerabilities.

I thought it might help him to disclose some of my life experience. I said: 'I think I might know what you are experiencing. You know I had parents who were achievement-oriented. But even when I did achieve a lot, they did not really recognize it. It was very frustrating for me and I kind of lost my trust in people for a while. Is that familiar to you at all?'

Sam then expressed his exhaustion with keeping up his role as head of a hospital. He mentioned here that he would have preferred to be a practicing doctor, but Ruth was so impressed with his role that he did not want to rock the already rocky boat by changing career directions.

I felt a connection between the two of us. I think that my body language and facial expressions showed Sam that I knew where he was coming from. I said: 'Perhaps you are showing us how hard it is to trust that Ruth wants you for who you are and not for your role. When she cries, maybe you feel she is trying manipulate you, to try to get feelings out of you that you don't feel right now.' Sam could take this in and stopped challenging or attacking.

As their therapist I realized that their original bond has elements of a false self. Reconnecting to the reasons they first married only intensified their awareness of the false self underlying their marital contract. Winnicott insists that the pain or anxiety felt by the baby occurs only when there is something that was lost. I wondered what they had seen in each other that was special, that did not relate to a false-self persona. I decided to share this line of thinking with them:

'You know, the amount of anger, frustration and pain you both feel seems to tell me that once you two found something very precious in each other, something that now seems lost. Maybe it feels lost forever?'

Ruth, crying silently, started to grope for words. I felt she was heading for new territory, not something she had thought about over and over. Knowing that she might come up with a 'spontaneous gesture' from her true self, I positioned myself close to her and looked patiently in her eyes. Sam found it hard to stay in the emotionality of the moment and tried to help her. I used my arms to block his input and circle Ruth as if holding her. He went silent and waited, listening.

She finally said: 'My father ignored me as a girl. In our house it was the boy children (she had several brothers) who got attention. I guess I was looking for someone worthy who would also listen to me. So I got the worthiness, but Sam didn't listen to me any better than my father.'

I asked: 'Did he never, ever listen to you?' and she said: 'No, you are right. At first I got a lot of attention from him. He liked my knowledge of history and society, my intelligence, and also my good nature. I could tell him about acts of kindness I did in the community or for my family and he seemed impressed. I don't know when it changed, but I lost his respect somewhere along the way.' She started crying loudly. Sam looked very uncomfortable.

I reflected back: 'To have finally found that person who could give you exactly what you needed but then he stopped must have been so painful.' She nodded and continued crying. I let the moment build without any response other then eye contact with both of them.

Sam seemed alone and sad. I turned my chair and asked him how it felt to hear about her loss. He said: 'I feel guilty actually. I didn't stop respecting her really. I still respect her. I just got so hurt by her I had to withdraw.' I said to both of them: 'You know, it must be so painful to feel like you have found exactly what you were looking for and then feel you lost that good feeling you once had. It feels as if it never happened. Somehow all the good gets contaminated by all the negativity that exists now. But what if those good feelings were still there, somewhere, just waiting to come out again?'

In a later session I worked more with Sam. He had found a solidly good person in Ruth. His childhood and his first marriage were based on his achievements and getting the rewards society gives for highly achieving people. But in Ruth he experienced at first a sense of love for him regardless of his status. Because she was a giver to so many people, she was comfortable in the role and did not demand performance from him to get her warmth. When they started fighting during the stage of disillusionment, he lost something very precious. She stopped giving to him unless he complied with her demands. While familiar with this achievement-oriented approach, he mourned the loss of an accepting person.

We can assume that many of the feelings that couple therapists feel in the presence of the partners reflects the emotional state of the relationship. In the above example, the couple has lost touch with the good enough relationship they had once experienced, if only for a few months. The idea that these good feelings are always there to be used is a matter of faith on the part of the therapist, who sees no evidence of this in the current interaction.

Recently there has been an interest among psychoanalysts in 'gestational psychology'.[2] The idea here is that all humans have experienced oneness with their mothers *in utero*. We all carry with us the template for this first experience and always know later on that things were much better when in the womb. The idea here is that the couple experiences disappointment in each other from the start of the relationship, although it is hidden at first. The disappointment goes beyond anything in the actual couple's relationship but speaks to our ubiquitous sense of disappointment upon leaving the ideal womb experience.

Some of these ideas about the feelings the fetus might have in the womb can help us understand the universality of disappointment in one's partner. Using this interpretation of Winnicott would allow us to see Sam and Ruth's disappointment with each other as more related to unconscious knowledge of pure bonding in the womb than to loss of the honeymoon stage of the marriage.

Rather, the honeymoon stage is a creative reconstruction of what we once already had. This fits Winnicott's way of thinking, such as when he writes about fear of breakdown as connected to already having experienced breakdown and how unconscious knowledge of this affects us in our lives. Here we are taking this way of thinking to the positive experiences in the womb and the sense of loss we all have after birth.

Using these ideas means assuming that the couple already know oneness and have been mourning its loss all their lives. This means that therapist and couple are united in their human disappointment with life. Many of these feelings can pop up suddenly in a session. When a therapist sensitively notes that feeling disappointment may have more to do with being human than a specific relationship, there is a potential for deep empathy and bonding for all involved.

Winnicott and projective identification

While the therapist feels what the partner might be feeling, there need not be an explanation such as 'projective identification'. Winnicott only used this term infrequently. He called projective identification 'unconscious communication', which he believed to be going on all the time between partners as couples as between infants and their mothers. While projective identification is a defensive maneuver, unconscious communication is a prototype of the original mother–infant bond. It is an elasticity of boundaries that couples need to feel connected. It was clear to him that we are always acting out what we feel to be our feelings but that are also the feelings of the people close to us. Since he put so much emphasis on the therapeutic relationship, his interest in unconscious communication was mostly about the countertransference of the therapist. Countertransference in the context of couple therapy is more complicated than in individual therapy. It will be discussed further in the next chapter.

Holding

Winnicott's famous quote 'there's no baby without a mother' was his way of helping us see the mother–infant bond as an object in itself. From birth to death, there's no person without reality, and only a holding, providing, and facilitating reality will create the conditions for human experience as the basis for a life that is about more than just survival. The mother's goals include holding, providing, and facilitating. At first these are purely physical, but as the child grows the task widens and deepens.

Holding includes empathy, containing, and mirroring and requires fine tuning to the baby's needs. By holding, the baby spends more time in the integration phase and develops a 'going on being'. Holding allows the baby to move from 'I' to 'I am'. That movement is a frightening moment, and the baby can take that step only if there's someone to hold him in her arms and comfort him in this terrible moment of survival anxieties.

The baby can enjoy the feeling of being alone only if it's for a short while and if he knows the mother and her loyal commitment to him. These conditions are necessities to get back to the integration phase; such phases should normally appear in adulthood as a firm sense of self. Good holding needs to fit the baby's physiological needs (there's not yet a distinction between physiological and psychological) and to be empathy-based. The holding is never identical for two different babies, if it's empathic. It changes according to tiny changes in the baby every day. When the holding is successful, one does not feel the presence of the holder.

Good holding creates a 'psyche dwelling in the soma' – a psychosomatic existence. The baby lives in the body if there's a strong connection between the motor, sensory, and functional and the emotional state of being. The psyche that is dwelling in the soma means that the infant's raw emotions are filtered primarily through the body. It is the attunement of the mother that turns what could be undigested and overwhelming feeling states into manageable signals. A good description of this process is offered by Stolorow *et al.* (1987). They write about the function of the caregiver in developing affect tolerance and the capacity to use affect as signals to oneself.

> These developmental attainments require the presence of a caregiver who can reliably distinguish, tolerate and respond appropriately to the child's intense shifting affective states. It is the caregiver's responsiveness that gradually makes possible the modulation, graduation and containments of strong affect. … this modulation and containment of affects make possible their use as self-signals. Rather than traumatically rupturing the continuity of self-experience, affects can thereby become employed in the service of its preservation.
>
> Holding thus is far more than a physical act but a basic route to self-knowledge and reflection, as well as having the ability to use affect to preserve the sense of going on being.
>
> The therapist's job is to hold each partner and the relationship at the same time. The therapist's ability to have multiple viewpoints that even contradict each other creates a sense of security in the couple and of being held. Being held is not the same as taking responsibility for the couple. It is the therapist's job to stay in what is often known as the 'I' position, i.e. 'I noticed just now that you (the wife) are breathing very quietly. While you (the husband) seem to be almost hyperventilating. What is going on with each of you just now?' Staying close to the physical is one way that holding feels concrete and real. The idea that holding is fundamentally a physical act (with the infant) that is transferred into a moment-by-moment awareness of the body language of the partners.
>
> (Stolorow *et al.*, 1987)

Holding in couple therapy

The therapist starts by holding the volatile feelings of each partner. It becomes important to link the negative and the positive feelings so that what is held by the therapist at the start is a *whole* baby.

I was taught about holding in the year I spent learning about Winnicott from Rusty Palmer. He developed an exercise for training that was extremely helpful in understanding the delicate aspects of good enough holding. In pairs the therapist trainees took turns holding each other (sitting on the floor with one therapist sitting up and the other lying down in the lap of the first). The exercise was done silently for about 10 minutes for each person to experience being either the holder or the one held. Seemingly a very simple task. However, the feelings that were expressed in the feedback stage showed that holding is a powerful and important therapeutic concept. In analyzing each person's reaction to being held or holding, an entire lesson on Winnicott's ideas was taught. The emotions that arose were those of mother and infant. For example, one man said that he felt too big for his holding partner. This led to a discussion of how the infant may feel too much for the mother. Another example of post-exercise feedback led one holder to express having felt ashamed to have her 'infant' partner hear her stomach growl. This led to a discussion of how the mother shares or doesn't share her physicality with the baby. It appeared that all the responses to the exercise could be useful in understanding the complexity of the dancing of holding an infant. The profound sense of importance that each person expressed (Freeman and Combs, 1996) highlights how much information we can get about an adult's experience from such a basic unit of the mother holding the child.

Holding the couple: an example from couple therapy

Here we hold the relationship for the couple who have metaphorically 'dropped the baby' (relationship). We are providing a holding environment and do not forget the baby nor do we drop the baby. We hold the baby for the couple so they can recuperate and start to remember that there is a baby and that that baby is loved and cherished.

The language used here is from narrative therapy and 'externalization'. We can hold the relationship by talking as if the relationship existed on its own. While the couple is aware that their children are entities, they usually do not see their relationship as an entity, and certainly not their own baby.

THERAPIST: I hear how angry and disappointed you both are. What do you think the relationship feels when so much rage is directed at it? Does the relationship feel ok with it?

PARTNER 1: The relationship is not a thing itself; it is just the two of us.

PARTNER 2: I think she is right … the relationship used to be a happy one and now it is a sad one.

THERAPIST: What does the sad relationship look like to you?

PARTNER 2: I see a little girl sitting in the corner wishing someone would do something, but nothing good happens. … It is so strange; when we met I did feel a bit like that little girl, but I thought I had found someone to hold me. I don't mean physically. We used to have a sense of humor about things. That felt like holding me and I felt like I could have fun. Now everything – well the relationship actually – is so heavy. Sometimes we get a laugh or two out of it though.

THERAPIST: Can you share those moments now, even angry feelings? The other parts are still there?

There are many situations in which the therapist holds the couple's relationship while they are locked in battle or are trying to decide whether to stay together or separate. This holding can be talked about openly, as when a therapist says:

> Right now you are both not sure if this relationship will last. So I will try to hold the relationship for you while you work on deciding. If you want me to do this, I will remind you about what you have said about the relationship, I will take the voice of the relationship so that neither of you forgets how precious the relationship once was for you.

Or holding the relationship can be done while not discussing it openly. For example, when the couple are overly optimistic, the therapist might remind them that it is possible they will still have a few fights to get through. Or when the couple seem to have forgotten what they have together, the therapist might remind them of positive feelings and behaviors the relationship once generated.

Holding has many potential levels of expression. It may mean giving support and encouragement to one or both of the partners if they need it. It means backing off and allowing silence for a couple who have become passive and are waiting for the therapist to speak. Holding may involve making sure the setting is not violated by missed appointments, lateness, problems with payment, or other aspects that hold the couple in the lap of the therapy.

Creation of the baby's separate self

The baby creates a membrane to separate Me and Not Me. The membrane is gradually formed through 'maternal preoccupation'.

The 'primary maternal preoccupation' is the mother's state of mind of being empathic and sensitive to the baby's needs. Winnicott says it has biological origins. The mother can imagine what it is like to be the baby. She used her experiences as a baby, and so she's in a very dependent and vulnerable state herself.

The mother continually adapts to the baby's changing needs. The primary concern is that the mother won't disappoint the baby, although she may frustrate his physiological needs. Also it is crucial that the failures and disappointments fit the growing abilities of the infant and that recovery from disappointment or rupture between the infant and mother are mended quickly.

For the couple therapist, the creation of a separate couple identity is a major goal, just as the mother has to help the infant sense their own separate self. By talking about the relationship and making comments to each partner about the relationship, the therapist continually fosters an awareness of the separate sense of the relationship as a type of object on its own. Of course, this sense is bolstered by continuous awareness of what each partner is feeling and contributing to the couple awareness.

We can also look at the way therapists undergo 'primary maternal preoccupation', which is much like Bion and others' views on reverie. Bion's concept of maternal 'reverie' as the capacity to sense (and make sense of) what is going on inside the infant has been an important element in post-Kleinian thought. Reverie is an act of faith in unconscious process ... essential to Bion's alpha-function. It is considered the equivalent of Stern's attunement, or Winnicott's maternal preoccupation (Jacobus, 2005).

The therapist goes into a state in which he/she is conscious of both internal emotions and a joining and attunement with the couple's emotions. This is a passive but also active state of consciousness in which the therapist (like the mother) is entirely focused on sensing unconscious communication. In couples work there are three people involved and all three are being sensed by the therapist.

It is a huge challenge for any therapy to stay in a state of reverie while also aware of the couple. This is a basic skill that doing Winnicott-directed therapy with couples demands. That is, we have to learn over time to stay in tune with our own reactions (through the state of reverie) while staying in tune with each partner and the relationship. No wonder therapists find this form of therapy the most challenging. In a good enough model we don't expect to be continually in touch with ourselves and the couple/partners. All we can hope for (and which is good enough) is to move between these different positions in a flexible and relatively relaxed state. When we do feel this balance between our own musing and what we sense from the couple, the chances are that either we will come up with something useful, or we can more clearly see where we are out of balance.

Continuity of being

A beginning sense of self fosters the feeling of continuity; the baby can feel relatively continual well being. This is the beginning of the development of a true self in which the infant's spontaneous gestures are recognized and continued by the environment. This allows a sense of 'going on being' in the infant, a melding together of all kinds of dissociated feelings and fantasies. It is the holding by the mother that allows the development of a sense of continuity of being.

If the mother cannot hold adequately and thus she cannot help the infant create this feeling, the baby will experience unthinkable anxieties related to annihilation. The baby can develop reacting more than initiating – he develops behaviors that suit and comply with the environment, and not his internal needs and wants. He changes for others. The adaptation is made by the baby, not the mother. This is the beginning of the false self.

Disturbances in holding, which lead to the failure of the mother to adapt, are felt by the child as impingements. When a child has to react outwards too much of the time, all that's left of him is a collection of reactions, so he has no ability to integrate. Since the tendency towards integration is a potential we have from birth, it can be lost and then found again through good enough mothering.

Similarly to mothering, the therapist has to foster a sense of continuity of being in several ways. One way is to be consistent in their own behavior by remembering what was told and connecting the dots for couples who don't see connections between different feelings or actions. I always take notes because I want to increase a sense that I am interested in everything going on and also that I remember what was said. I will sometimes reflect my notes back to the couple so that I make sure I have written the notes accurately.

A wife seemed annoyed when the phone rang in my office. I asked her if the ringing did not feel good to her. She looked surprised at my sensitivity and smiled. I physically took the phone off the hook. She also turned to her husband and said 'You know, I think that is what I need more of from you too ... it would feel so great if you noticed what was bothering me and would try to do something about it.' Her husband was defensive at first. He said 'I am always trying to make things easier for you!' I asked him if her request felt like a criticism to him and he nodded. I said that we change by noticing differences. 'When I took the phone off the hook this seemed to her different than what she experiences with you. But you feel you are already doing these things for her. Would it interest you two to explore this more?'

Another way that therapists foster continuity of being is by naming impingements coming from the therapist as much as possible. This takes sensitivity to what is going on and having the ability to be wrong and accept that. There are very different reactions to therapists' interventions. Sometimes the partners argue with the therapist. Sometimes they appear disturbed by a therapist's statement. We can have a hunch that an intervention is an impingement when there is arguing or body language that appears to be resisting. Silence and changing the subject might be another way that impingements are handled by the couple. Asking them about it is the best way to go. What is important is to say something like 'That doesn't feel right to you?' Sometimes the statement by the therapist is right, but the timing is wrong. Whatever happens when we try to name an impingement is more 'grist for the mill'. If they agree that an intervention did not feel right, or one of the partners agrees while the other doesn't, or they both clam up, we have information that we can reflect on. Perhaps the intervention came too early. Maybe it was right but scared them. They won't always know what was wrong.

It is our job to help train our couples in giving us honest feedback. That might well be the beginning of learning to deal with pain between them. For example:

> Jan and Ted have been in couple therapy for 6 months. Many things changed in their relationship but also there were problems that seemed resistant to change. They had come to therapy because Jan had an affair and it took months for them to get over the crisis and down to business about what had been going on between them to lead to her having an affair. With affairs there is often a traumatic experience with the one who has to stop the affair and with the other who has been deeply hurt and lost trust. For about 6 weeks we did not talk about why the affair happened. Rather we spent most of the time getting over the anxiety, anger and aggression that was their relationship. We used different tools to deal with their high emotional reactions: narrative therapy with externalization of the feelings, dealing with different parts of themselves which were activated, relaxation techniques and individual sessions were all used to calm things down.

How can the therapist know when it is time to move on to an examination of the relationship they had that gave birth to an affair? The literature says that it usually takes 4–6 months until the crisis has settled down. But the literature does not tell us how to know moment by moment what is needed now.

Using the ideas of Winnicott around rupture and repair, as well as thinking of impingements and change, I offer a transcript from a pivotal session with the couple. The session was after 6 months of therapy (both couple and individual sessions).

TED: We had a really good week for the first time in ages. We decided to put a hold on our feelings and take time off like you advised. We went to the country this weekend and found a really nice bed and breakfast. We got closer, although I still saw images in my mind of Jan with Peter. But I really tried to keep those fantasies out of my mind.

THERAPIST: Sounds like you were aware of anger and rage just waiting to ruin this weekend, but you managed to keep them out. How did you do this?

TED: I just did, I guess I stopped myself from elaborating on my images. I remembered that Jan has been so open about loving me that maybe I can take a break from what happened.

JAN: I can even tell you when you were struggling and when not! You get this look on your face and I see you aren't with me, you are somewhere else. Now I guess you were thinking of me and Peter, right?

TED: Right….

THERAPIST: Jan, do you agree with Ted that even if there were images and you both knew it, the weekend was good?

JAN: Yes, it was. I was worried that Ted might get upset, aggressive again or cut off and go off on his own. But he didn't and I respect that a lot.

THERAPIST: Jan, what did you have to do to cope with knowing he was going off into his fantasies?

JAN: I guess I just trust him a bit more now. I know he will come back because he knows that basically I love him and that thing with Peter was a stupid mistake.

TED: A mistake? You call something that almost destroyed our family a mistake?

THERAPIST: I wonder if it isn't time to start to look at why 'the stupid mistake', or whatever we might call it, happened.

TED: No, wait a minute. It was not a mistake. Tripping up and twisting your ankle is a mistake. This was a catastrophe and not a mistake.

THERAPIST: Good, we have two ways of viewing what happened here. One is to see it as a stupid mistake and the other to see it as a catastrophe. Do you want now to try to get to agreeing what we should call what happened? Or would you both like to get into how come 'it' happened, no matter what we call it?

Jan and Ted were silent for a few minutes.

JAN: First of all, I agree it was a catastrophe. The entire family has been in crisis for months, so Ted is right. I would much rather get into why it happened than what to call it.

TED: I agree … it is time we examine ourselves. Just the fact that Jan knows it wasn't just a mistake is enough for me to let it go.

We can feel more sure that an intervention is not an impingement by seeing positive results. We see partners relax, go silent, or nod in agreement. Or our statement causes them to turn to each other and increase their dialogue. An impingement can be located when the partners ignore what was said, fight it, argue with each other about it, stay silent, and all the myriad ways that body language shows discomfort.

The ability to locate impingements is crucial to the success of couple therapy. It is also extremely difficult to be attuned with both partners at the same time. One partner may not experience our intervention as an impingement. One partner says: 'Oh that is so right … I have been thinking that for a while'. But the other partner says: 'I don't think so … he has been saying that for a long time, but I don't agree.'

Therapists need to study each couple anew as to what constitute impingements and what helps the couple going on being. The good enough mother does not make assumptions based on another baby. Each infant arrives as a unique universe and needs to be learned anew after each birth. This can be learned but is fundamentally based on getting feedback from the people we are learning from. One couple may enjoy a joke, while another seems put-off by humor. Each couple and each partner has their own 'going on being', which it is the therapist's duty to learn.

While being attuned to two people at one time does appear a difficult task, it is also the basis of understanding couples and helping them understand each other. If they did not have these different emotions, thoughts, beliefs, values etc. they would probably not need therapy. When the therapist can hold both partners' experiences (even when they contradict each other or contradict what the therapist has said), the couple has the opportunity to see how seemingly opposite differences can live together. If the therapist is sensing one person better than another, this can be a cue to what could develop into a major impasse in the therapy. The therapist has to have the ability to hold in mind opposite realities at the same time. This ability is healing for a couple who have been at odds about whose version is more truthful.

When the therapist feels impinged upon, it is likely that unconscious communication is showing the therapist exactly where one or both partners are stuck. The therapist has to learn their own language, so as to be able to notice impingements from the couple. I have learned that when one or both partners laugh sarcastically at something I say, I feel impinged upon. I have also learned that my body reacts first to impingements and then only later do I understand what is happening. My body tenses up, I sit up a bit and often don't look the partners in the eyes. Sometimes what I feel is what one of the partners feels and this can become a useful intervention. Or other times I need to go inside and work on my own reactivity, either during the session or afterwards.

Fear of breakdown

In infancy the baby feels breakdown or death. The baby hasn't got any ability to cope with these feelings. If the mother is gone for a long time, the baby can't digest these feelings, he can't contain the idea that the mother will return. Her return can't fix this trauma. Years later he will cope with fear of death, a death he already experienced.

Everybody has a universal fear of breakdown, fear of past experiences. In psychotherapy, fears of breakdown can arise because the nature of the therapeutic relationship brings up dependency feelings. Dependency is feared because one fears not having the internal powers to resist breakdown. In the good enough therapeutic environment restoration of fears does not lead to breakdown, Thus in good enough therapy the patient can recover from the past trauma. Therapy allows flooding of past pain within the holding of the facilitating environment.

Fear of breakdown is most often evident when partners either try to gain control of the interactions in therapy or when they distance themselves and cut themselves off in the session. Gaining control may be shown by interrupting, fighting, correcting the other or any behavior that shows the therapist that the partner is trying to make sure things go his/her way. The opposite is also true. When partners cut-off, stonewall, forget what was said and remain silent, they might be struggling with underlying anxiety and fear of loss of control. Either way it is the job of the therapist to create a sense of safety so that controlling behaviors are not needed.

Often the sense of anxiety gets picked up by the therapist who feels anxious without knowing why. Catching the anxiety of a person afraid of breakdown is actually an excellent (although difficult) way to understand what is going on.

In couple therapy there is often a powerful anxiety around loss of control that might lead to potential breakdowns. If the therapist can see this fear as normative, help comes in the form of deep empathy, creating boundaries and demonstrates positive results from bringing the anxiety to the surface to be named and dealt with.

Couples are often frightened of the powerful urges in each towards destruction. When in a fight, they each fear falling apart and losing the relationship along with their sanity. The therapist who is aware of this anxiety arising and being warded off can hold it and bring it back to the couple in a form they can cope with, using statements such as 'It is so hard to fight because sometimes we are all afraid everything will fall apart. Have you ever thought of this?'

The outside world

The mother brings the world to the baby. It's important that everything will appear to the baby as its own creation. The baby feels the world is in its control. From this state he learns to give up his omnipotent being and move to the other side of the spectrum – understand that he was created by the world. The importance of the omnipotent feeling is not to feel he is the creator of the world but to prevent the feeling of need from the baby. He does not yearn.

To yearn is to experience separation. It's important that the mother will only be good enough and not perfect, it's important that she'll fail at times, so the baby will not be deprived of the feeling of yearning altogether. He needs to yearn sometimes, and then be satisfied. The baby needs to preserve the feeling of yearning as something of his, to feel the connection between yearning and an action being taken. This will mean preserving the feeling of self.

The therapist brings the outside world to the couple in the form of knowledge, ideas, interpretations, musing and other reactions to what is going on. The therapist is the outside world to the couple and needs to remain somewhat outside their interactions. A therapist who has become too enmeshed with the couple does not challenge them to react to the therapist's interventions. Bringing the outside world can take the form of teaching a theory or idea, giving a homework assignment, asking for an enactment in the session or taking on the role of one partner in role playing with the other. Any tools that the therapist uses can be seen as bringing the outside world to the couple. We try not to be too smart so as to challenge the couple's underlying sense of omnipotence. Yet we need to challenge their ways of being in order to create the material with which the couple have to interact. A balance that is good enough finds ways to change couple knowledge and behavior while also allowing them to be themselves with each other and with the therapist.

Mirroring

The baby sees himself in the mother. The mother is mirror for the baby. A good enough mother mirrors a feeling of love and omnipotence. If the mother is not good enough she will mirror her own moods and the baby will learn of his separate self prematurely. That is, the infant needs a certain amount of omnipotence even though the truth is the infant is helpless. If the mother does not mirror his emotions back to her child, the child will learn of the need to fake his true self and adapt to the external reality.

This is still better than a baby who lost all hope and doesn't look for mirroring anymore. If he looks at his mother and sees nothing, he will not connect at all.

The mother's role is to reflect to the baby whatever she sees in his self. Psychotherapy aims at the same process by holding in treatment. It reflects back to the client himself – what he sees and hears and feels – so he can take back control over the different parts of himself. This way he will feel complete.

It is the couple therapist's task to process the experience and offer something back that will mirror what they as a couple cope with in their relationship rather than the individual preoccupations of one or other partner. The mirroring can be verbal or nonverbal. In its verbal form the therapist says something like 'You, Joan, seem frustrated and maybe also discouraged? While you, Jake, seem to be trying harder and harder the more Joan seems discouraged? Does this feel accurate to both of you?' Accuracy in mirroring is crucial, misunderstandings need to be at a minimum. It is the activity of mirroring itself that opens the door to reflexivity. Joan may say, 'No, I am discouraged. I am just a bit tired of it all'. Jake may say, 'Yes, I do try harder the more I think she is giving up.' Here Joan says, 'I am not giving up at all. You can relax. We are in this together for the long haul. I just get tired sometimes.'

This interaction shows mirroring that is both accurate and inaccurate. The repair comes when accuracy is found by the couple and given to each other as a kind of gift. Even mirroring the worst feelings can feel supportive. It has a sense of having been seen and that is crucial to our sense of going on being and aliveness.

Wedge (1996) has pulled together concepts of mirroring, play, and transitional space:

> The act of mother mirroring her infant is what Winnicott called play, which he viewed as the wellspring of all creative and meaningful experience, the only sort of experience that makes life worth living. Play begins when the infant sees himself in his mother's eyes as in a mirror. This early experience of play opens the realm of what Winnicott calls transitional phenomena, an area of experience that must be classified between subject and objective. This transitional realm is not the experience of permanent objects, nor is it merely an unconnected flux of purely subjective sensations. It is a realm of experience between the factual and fictions … it is an area whose central truth is that paradox must be accepted. It is the realm of the mirror. We cannot resolve the question of whether we make the world or find it there. The object bears within it the image of the beholder, just as the mother's eye reflects the image of the child. But the beholder is also shaped by the object, as the mother sees herself in her child.
>
> (Wedge, 1996)

Mirroring is the mode of relating that begins a process of differentiation of self and relationship. The therapist would try to mirror the pain, helplessness, and hopelessness that are engendered by this way of seeing things. If we think of both the couple and the therapeutic relationship as infants, these are both intricately bound to their context. That is, just as there is no infant without a mother, there is no couple relationship without the partners as mother. Just as there is no infant without the mother, there is no therapeutic relationship without joint caring by both partners and the therapist.

This way of thinking does not privilege any one type of feeling over another. The danger in that is creating a false self in which the partners learn to talk about pain or sadness instead of anger or hate. But angry and hateful feelings are real and have a vibrant function in keeping the relationship alive. Mirroring would mean that the couple therapist is comfortable with all kinds of feelings and mirrors them back respectfully. It is the couple therapist's task to process the experience and offer something back that will mirror what they as a couple have to manage in their relationship rather than the individual preoccupations of one or other partner.

THERAPIST: It sounds very frustrating for you. Is that what you feel?

PARTNER 1: No, not really. I am just sad about how things are turning out …

THERAPIST: So what is that like for you to feel so sad?

PARTNER 1: It makes me kind of angry. I am missing so much from life spending my time being sad about her.

THERAPIST: So the first feeling is sad, but there is also anger? Any hate?

PARTNER 1: Hate? That is a bit much … well, sometimes.

THERAPIST TO PARTNER 2: What is it like for you to hear your partner express sadness, anger, and even a bit of hate?

PARTNER 2: Strangely I feel relieved. He is depressed a lot but I knew he was angry inside. He never talks about that, but I find myself angry all the time. But he is angry and I have to hold all that for him.

THERAPIST: So there is something relieving about naming the experiences you have together. You both have strong feelings about the relationship and it is hard for both of you to say out loud what the relationship is like for you. It seems that to be in the relationship right now brings up many different feelings. Is that true for both of you?

Partners 1 and 2 agree.

PARTNER 1: I am a bit worried about having talked about hate, seems a bit harsh.

PARTNER 2: No, I feel like you do, I feel relieved. Hate comes and goes; I don't think you always hate me. Rather you hate me than be indifferent to me. At least I know that you also love me.

PARTNER 1: Yes I do, and it feels a relief you know that after talking about all these harsh feelings.

THERAPIST: So you both are able now to see the relationship as having both good and bad sides?

The therapist is using mirroring without privileging one emotion over another. The mirroring is meant to help each partner think and feel about the other and themselves. Therapist interventions help the couple see their relationship as an entity that they co-create moment by moment.

Increasing independence

Development is a gradual adjusting to failure by the good enough mothers. The mother de-adapts to the baby. She doesn't answer his needs as quickly. The baby learns to cope without his mother and, using his developing mental capacities, turns a good enough environment into a perfect one.

The baby becomes angry and hateful and enjoys these emotions. Through it he begins to create a relationship with his mother as a separate being. If the mother is too protective and doesn't give him any reasons to be angry, she will not allow him to integrate love and hate.

The baby begins to experience a world beyond his control. This is a painful realization, but the urge for separation makes it easier. Both differentiation and integration begin in this stage. This stage is called relative dependency because in the previous stage it was absolute dependency, in which he wasn't even aware of the fact he had needs that had to be fulfilled.

Therapists have to answer to the couple's dependency needs as well as their need to become independent from the therapist. A therapist who says 'I never accept phone calls from my couples' worries me in that some couples need more than the sessions. They might need to know that the therapist is there when things go wrong at home. A therapist who is afraid of dependency will prematurely push the couple to being more independent than they really are able to be.

On the other hand, the couple has to gradually be let go by the therapist. Just like parenting a child, there are times when the child has to try themselves to do something even with fear or without quite knowing how. The therapist who notices signs of the start of independence from therapy can foster more of this behavior or feelings without too much enthusiasm. That is, we are not trying to get rid of our couples and give them a sense that they should be going it alone. But we do want them to know that we celebrate even small attempts at independence and are willing to openly acknowledge these attempts. This is especially true when the attempts go wrong and our support is crucial to recognizing underlying bids for independence.

False and true self

The false self is experienced as a real thing. The baby loses connection to anything in himself. The false self defends the true self by keeping the true self out of the interaction with a nonresponsive environment. Later on, the person acts completely as false self, but knows that this isn't the whole truth. Perhaps he doesn't know what he wants, but he knows there's another true self. The false self defends the true self but searches for places the true self can express itself. This can lead to suicide because the person wants to express himself, but may not find a place (Winnicott, 1971b).

For Winnicott it is the failure of the environment in the earliest stages of life and the subsequent accumulation of painful, traumatic experiences that will lead to the individual organizing primitive defenses in order to protect the 'isolated core (true self)'. And to emphasize his point, that the violation is psychological more than physical, he writes that, 'Rape and being eaten by cannibals are mere bagatelles as compared with the violation of the self's core true self.' He poses the question 'how to be isolated without having to be insulated?'

Couples have to deal with this question all the time. They can respond instinctively to empathetic sharing by therapists. For example, a therapist might say 'It is such a dilemma. How does one stay true to one's real self and still stay in interaction with your partner?' Often couples are fighting around these basic concerns. The sense of helplessness and being overwhelmed is met by the good enough couple therapist with understanding and holding of these powerful fears. The therapist might focus on a specific fight and say 'You know, when I was listening just now I felt that you were both dealing with a life and death sense of urgency. I wonder what that is about?' Or the therapist might say 'You know, it is so important to us humans to be real and when we don't feel accepted in our real selves, we move away. But then we become isolated and lonely so we move back. When we move back sometimes it feels good but plenty of times it feels bad. We don't necessarily get the acceptance we are looking for.'

The capacity to be alone in the presence of others

The baby internalizes mother not as an object but as an environment including the baby. Being alone in a containing environment allows the baby to play. If the mother can't be a quiet presence two things will occur: he will not develop the capacity to be alone and he will become addicted to external objects. The person always will try to integrate and express the true self in some ways.

The baby's anxiety when the mother is not around tells us he knows how essential she is to him. At this point the capacity to be alone develops. The most important aspect of it is the capacity to be alone in the presence of another. This is a state of being that's quiet and undemanding in the presence of another. Only there can one discover his private life. These ideas are typical of Winnicott's paradoxical thinking, which is that the capacity to be alone can only develop within the relational context.

When the baby understands there's a relationship between his parents, emotions like jealousy and hate arise. If he has a good capacity to be alone, he will cope with these emotions without problems.

For couples there is always a need to know that they can be alone while being together. The couple that clings to each other rejects the alone part of this equation. The couple who distances rejects the together part of this equation. Couples talk about being alone while together, although they might not label their behaviors this way. They will talk about intruding on each other's privacy, resenting time spent with the computer, work or with the children. They may have to actually leave in order to get alone time. The model here is that alone time can be had with the other like a supportive parent in the background.

The therapist can bring these issues up because they are universal for all couples, even if the specific couple have not mentioned it. The togetherness and aloneness of couples' lives is an ever-changing kaleidoscope of interactions. We can ask couples how often they check in with their partner when they are busy doing their own thing. Often couples are experiencing profound loneliness when in the company of the other, sometimes even more than when truly alone. These are basic existential issues for all of us and need to be tackled even when unrecognized by the couple.

The right not to communicate

In his later writings about the true self, Winnicott said that at the core of the true self is silence. In an almost Zen way of thinking (arrived at on his own) is the idea that the true self can be 'incommunicado' and needs to be forced not to communicate.

Communication can be either direct or silent. Winnicott wrote:

> When I look, I am seen, so I exist. I can now afford to look and see. I now look creatively and what I apperceive I also perceive. In fact I take care not to see what is not there to be seen unless I am tired.
>
> (1971b, p. 114)

Winnicott outlines five different classifications of the false self across a spectrum spanning from the pathological to the healthy. The false self is set up in the individual to protect the true self. At the pathological end there is a total split – the false self is not connected to the true self – but at the healthy end the false self is a necessary boundary between the outside world and the inside. We could call this a healthy split, because it protects rather than dissociates. There is a link here with his 1965 paper, 'Communicating and not communicating leading to a study of certain opposites' because it is in this paper that Winnicott takes the model of the pathological basic split in the individual (whose pattern of relationship is distorted), and states the corollary:

> In health there is a core to the personality that corresponds to the true self of the split personality; this core never communicates with the world of perceived objects, and [that] the individual person knows that it must never be communicated with or be influenced by external reality. Although healthy persons communicate and enjoy communicating, the other fact is equally true, that each individual is 'an isolate, permanently non-communicating, permanently unknown, and in fact unfound.'
>
> Rape and being eaten by cannibals are mere bagatelles as compared with the violation of the self's core [...].
>
> (1965d)

He poses the question 'how to be isolated without having to be insulated?'

Most couples do not directly feel cannibalized! But too much communication and pressure to communicate may result in a sense of intrusion that is very uncomfortable. While women may be guilty of pushing their partner to interact more than wanted, men also pressure women to reveal themselves more than they want. For example, a man may want to know all the time where his wife is. His partner may not feel like being overtaken this way. She might want times when he doesn't know where she is, and not because she is having the affair he might fear, but because she too has a need not to communicate. The need not to communicate is a fundamental right to have self-sovereignty and couples might have to negotiate this issue.

Healthy withdrawal

Let's consider withdrawal in its healthy and its pathological forms. In health, the withdrawal from life and relating is a resting place – a place to 'be' and 'feel real' (something that dominated Winnicott's thoughts in his last decade of work). The baby is resting in a state of un-integration. In health the mother is in a state of primary maternal preoccupation, which in Winnicott's words is the precursor to enjoyment of both mother and child. Maternal preoccupation is like Bion's idea of reverie. It is a relaxed state of reception, being able to relate without any impingement on the other. Therapists can often feel when they are in such a state of active/passive receptivity. In this state the other is absorbed in a way that allows and encompasses all behavior and feelings.

Pathological withdrawal, however, is one that is based on the experience of gross impingements from the environment where the baby, who is not being held, is forced to react – interrupting the continuity-of-being – so that the place that should be for rest becomes a place of retreat from persecutions.

Winnicott states that the impingements that are not met by the infant will get through to 'the central core of the ego' and this he adds 'is the very nature of psychotic anxiety'. So it would appear that the core self, which must be incommunicado, is in fact itself made up from accumulated memories of violation (Winnicott, 1965c).

Miscommunication isn't a passive state but an active state whereby the environment lacks understanding of the baby, who develops a split – not real communication, but just expressing what others want to hear.

For couples, having a resting place in the relationship is crucial to feeling comfortable with each other. Of course, too much resting place and one of the partners becomes anxious. The therapist can help by making resting from interaction a positively viewed state for connection. This is one of Winnicott's many paradoxes. The therapist promotes rest because the relationship is meaningful; without it demanding our attention and being meaningful, we would have no reason to rest. Giving each other rest is a gift that can either feel supportive or threatening. In either case, the need is there and the fears underlying giving each other this rest need to be discussed.

Unifying experiences

Unifying experiences are moments when the baby's experience is whole – an integrative experience of a whole baby. This collects the baby's broken experiences. These experiences create a feeling of self. But there must be a feeling of dispersed, un-integrated baby from time to time, to collect mental resources and creativity.

Disintegration, on the other hand, is a state of terror.

The first disconnection that concerns Winnicott is that between calmness and excitement. A baby, who hasn't got a firm sense of self when he is given food or warmth, cannot know he is the same self when he's angry and unhappy. He needs to learn to play with his repertoire of responses.

For couples the sense is having the knowledge that we are the same couple whether interacting, withdrawing, or bringing others into the relationship. I like to call this being able to connect the dots. That is, the couple may feel that the partner is a different person when the partner is being alone or being angry. The very same couple may have moments of love or passion, hate or disinterest. It is very hard for couples who have not had good enough mothering as infants to see the connection (connecting the dots) between the relationships in all its many forms.

The therapist can directly talk about this. 'You know sometimes people really feel that they don't know who their partners are. Sometimes the partner is so loving and sometimes so hating and it is the same partner'. Most people have some sense of these splits, although they differ greatly as to their capacity to hold all the different masks their relationship wears. Here the ability of the therapist to connect the dots in his/her own life is often evident. Doing therapy is one way we therapists practice connecting the dots in our own lives.

Notes

1. Printed by permission of The Marsh Agency Ltd on behalf of The Winnicott Trust.
2. Cohen, T. (2013 personal communication) Gestational psychology and Winnicott's ideas.

5 Hate and aggression in couple therapy

One of the central ideas in Winnicott's writings is the importance of hate and aggression in a real true-self relationship. Aggression in the child is seen as a natural part of development as they test out the limits of their personality. They kick and scream in rage. People who have not extended in this way in childhood may be repressed. Aggression also tests their environment and helps them to relate to it.

The coexistence of love and hate

Winnicott believed that only by a sequence of events in which the object is aggressed against and survives it can the object then be useful for the infant. The sequence is: '(1) Subject relates to object. (2) Object is in process of being found instead of being placed by the subject in the world. (3) Subject destroys object. (4) Object survives destruction. (5) Subject can use object.'

When the object is the mother, this is a very trying time for her. She acts as a 'container' for the child's aggression and, if maintaining calm, helps the child to get over the aggression. For Winnicott, the therapist's task thus becomes to provide a holding environment for the client so they have the opportunity to meet neglected ego needs and allow their true self to emerge. One of the most important attributes of the therapist is simple patience. Winnicott (1969) advises therapists to be patient as eventually the individual will reach the same conclusion on their own, with far more joy than if the therapist had rushed to a premature interpretation.

The notion of surviving aggressive attacks is extremely important and central in couple therapy for the very reasons that Winnicott talks about with regard to the infant–mother dyad as well as the analyst–patient dyad. In those two cases the container object has to survive the attacks to be of use to the other.

Couple therapy can make use of these ideas, but they need to be tailored to having two people in the room who are also currently aggressing against each other as well as the therapist. As I found in my interviews, many couple therapists find this constellation difficult to deal with. Aggression is not just discussed as in therapy but is acted out in the room in couple therapy.

Therapists' reaction to hate and aggression in the room

Hate and aggression are pivotal concerns in Winnicott's writings. They are also among the most difficult aspects of couple therapy for the therapist. Couple therapists I interviewed said that coping with anger, aggression, and hateful feelings in the room make couple therapy the hardest kind of treatment. Is this a coincidence? I will propose here that because of the overlap between the mother–infant dyad and the couple dyad, aggression is crucial and difficult in both relationships. Thus the way aggression is handled in relationships will predict the mental health of the participants of both types of dyad (mother–infant and couple partners).

There is no relationship that so mirrors our original mothering experiences as our intimate couple experiences. This is true because the importance of sex (physical touch) creates overlapping between the two sets of dyads. Mothers touch the body of an infant as lovers touch each other. Touch is primal to words and essential to well-being of the infant. In both types of relationship there is a real physical holding response that is crucial to the tone of the bond. Touch and sexuality is a primary element in the couple bond. While there are indeed some couples who are happy without sex, the majority of couples place touch, sexuality, and erotic interactions as critical to their couple happiness.

Beyond sex there is the centrality of the two types of dyads to our mental health. It is accepted knowledge today that the infant–mother dyad sets the stage for all relationships for the rest of our lives. Our lifetime mental health is interwoven with our mother's good enough holding, handling, and object presenting. In the transitional space between the mother and the infant, the self of the infant is not only expressed but is elaborated further, giving the infant's ego a mirror and response that carries it along to greater differentiation and articulation. Winnicott is only one of many theoreticians to make this point and to focus on the mother–infant dyad.

Similarly the state of our intimate relationships is crucial to our mental health. Apparently this is truer for women than for men. With regard to women, Diane Kirschner writes:

> Bad or unsatisfactory marriages may contribute to health and psychological problems while a good marriage may protect a woman from certain diseases or help her to recover faster if she does get ill. We can't go into all of the studies so here are a few. A study of long-term marriages in which the partners were unhappy, showed that women more than men were likely to suffer from high blood pressure and obesity. Other studies have showed that poor marital quality was associated with depression, worsened physical health, poor sleep and metabolic problems.
>
> We've also already showed that once a woman is divorced or widowed that her economic, health and general well-being are all adversely affected. In other words, there is a severe marriage penalty for being in a bad marriage or getting divorced that never-married singles don't pay. In fact, singles with

> strong social support have been found to be nearly as well off as married women in good relationships. That's because social support and love are probably the key drivers behind many of the positive findings in comparison studies of singles, married, living together and divorced gals.
>
> So what about women in satisfying marriages? In comparison studies, they had the least atherosclerosis in their arteries and lived much longer if they did have heart disease. They had fewer doctor visits, lower blood pressure than singles or women in unhappy marriages. Studies of long-term couples showed that they report fewer headaches and back pain. Happy couples healed twice as fast from flesh wounds than those who demonstrated hostility toward each other. In NIMH studies of the brain, men and women in long-term marriages showed activation in the areas of the brain associated with dopamine, that is, the passion centres, as if they were newlyweds. There is no question then that the social support of a loving partner contributes to having a healthier, longer and happier life.
>
> (2010, no page)

Men benefit from good marriages and both sexes have better physical health when there is a good marriage. Bookwala completed a study showing this connection:

> This study examined the role of marital quality in the physical health of mature adults. Participants were from the National Survey of Midlife Development in the United States aged 50+ years who were in their first marriage. Five dimensions of marital quality and four indicators of physical health were used. Results: Regression analyses indicated that marital quality indices accounted for a significant amount of explained variance in physical health. Most notably, higher levels of negative spousal behaviors uniquely contributed to physical health, predicting more physical symptoms, chronic health problems, and physical disability, and poorer perceived health. The occurrence of negative spousal behaviors was consistently associated with poorer physical health.
>
> (2005)

Reparenting in couple therapy

Many couple therapists intuitively know that couple therapy is an opportunity for reparenting both partners as well as supporting the health and development of the relationship. What is the focus here is not this developmental aspect of couples' relationships. The reparenting aspect of couple therapy has been dealt with extensively in the marital literature in methods such as 'Imago' (Hendricks, 1988).

Here we will focus on the importance of aggression and hate in both mother–infant and couple relationships. This aspect of the former has been proposed by Winnicott as primal to the development of the ability of the infant to see the mother (and eventually the self) as a separate entity. With regard to intimate relationships I will propose here that an understanding of Winnicott's ideas about aggression and especially hate can help us better understand the development of couples' relationships.

There is considerable overlap between what Winnicott offers about handling aggression by the good enough mother and what we therapists can do about aggression in couples' interactions. It is also essential that therapists know how to handle aggression, especially in the countertransference. This goes beyond having technical skills in conflict management. Rather, the couple therapist needs to work on their own internal reactions, defenses, and countertransference responses to aggression in the room. We as therapists have to acknowledge what Winnicott liked to call 'hate'.

Winnicott's views on hate and aggression (Winnicott, 1949)

Winnicott was interested in the shift from the infant's fundamental omnipotent and narcissistic attitude towards objects as extensions or projections of the self, to what most would regard as a more advanced kind of relating. In this more mature relating, the object is recognized as separate and distinct from the self. This can be viewed as moving from narcissistic to healthier object relations. Winnicott was especially concerned with the process whereby the subject (infant) comes to place the object (the mother) outside the area of the subject's omnipotent control.

The originality of Winnicott's contribution lies in his recognition that:

> This change … means that the subject destroys the object … that after 'subject relates to object' comes 'subject destroys object' (as it becomes external); and then may come '*object survives* destruction by the subject'.
>
> A new feature thus arrives in the theory of object-relating. The subject says to the object: 'I destroyed you.' 'I love you.' 'You have value for me because of your survival of my destruction of you.' 'While I am loving you I am all the time destroying you in (unconscious) *fantasy*.' Here fantasy begins for the individual. The subject can now *use* the object that has survived.
>
> (1949, p. 71)

It is important to note that it is not only that the subject destroys the object because the object is placed outside the area of omnipotent control. It is equally significant to state this the other way round and to say that it is the destruction of the object that places the object outside the area of the subject's omnipotent control. In this mutual circular and systemic interaction, the mother also reclaims her own autonomy and life, while contributing to the mental and emotional development of the infant.

Because of the survival of the mother, the infant begins living a life in the world of external objects, and so the subject stands to gain immeasurably. Winnicott believed that there is a price in this normative process. The price is in accepting the ongoing destruction in unconscious fantasy with regard to object-relating. This is a position that can be arrived at by the individual in the early stages of emotional growth only through the actual survival of objects that are at the time in the process of being destroyed. Winnicott links the mother becoming real to the infant (and the infant becoming real to itself) through fantasy destruction and the safety of survival of the destruction.

According to Winnicott, the subject is only able to achieve mature relations with objective objects through a process of separation from the subjective object. This is a process entailing both the 'destruction' of the latter and, at the same time, a giving up of the illusion of omnipotence and the need for omnipotent control. The illusion of omnipotent control underlies both subjective enmeshment with the object and resistance to recognizing the 'otherness' of the objective object.

> 'It is generally understood that the reality principle involves the individual in anger and reactive destruction, but my thesis is that the destruction plays its part in making the reality, placing the object outside the self.'
>
> 'The assumption is always there, in orthodox theory, that aggression is reactive to the encounter with the reality principle, whereas here it is the destructive drive that creates the quality of externality.'
>
> *There is no anger* in the destruction of the object to which I am referring, though there could be said to be joy at the object's survival. From this moment, or arising out of this phase, the object is *in fantasy* always being destroyed. This quality of 'always being destroyed' makes the reality of the surviving object felt as such, strengthens the feeling-tone, and contributes to object-constancy. The object can now be used.
>
> It will be seen that, although destruction is the word I am using, this actual destruction belongs to the object's failure to survive. Without this failure, destruction remains potential. The word 'destruction' is needed, not because the baby's impulse is to destroy, but because of the object's liability not to survive, which also means to suffer change in quality, in attitude.
>
> So not only is there 'no anger in the destruction of the object to which I am referring', but the destruction is only potential and only becomes actualized if the object fails to survive. This idea is quite distinct from any simple notion of a primary destructiveness.
>
> In this vitally important early stage the 'destructive' aliveness of the individual is simply a symptom of being alive. I realize that it is this idea of a destructive first impulse that is difficult to grasp. It is this that needs attention and discussion. To help I wish to point out that I am referring to such things as *eagerness*. Hence, the infant's eagerness – perhaps its 'ruthless' love is felt by the infant to be destructive if and when the object fails to survive. However, when the object does survive (and without retaliating or changing its attitude), then such eagerness and 'ruthlessness' are not felt to be destructive.
>
> (1949, pp. 73–74)

Winnicott is making an interesting point about reality, using his paradoxical language to touch upon an old philosophical question. Is there destruction of the object if the aggression is handled well? It seems to me he is saying that aggression and destructiveness only feel such when they succeed in destroying the object. If the object survives the attacks, the feeling is one of excitement, eagerness and even joy – certainly not of aggression or hate.

Winnicott proposes that the mother who turns away from the aggressive child or retaliates has not survived the child's aggression and to the child has not survived. This is so dangerous to the child that the child will develop a false self to attempt to comply with rather than aggress against a mother who is not capable of surviving the infant's attacks.

In later writings Winnicott took an advanced view of the question of reality. That is, he proposed that only when the mother cannot handle the child's aggression does destruction occur. Earlier he seemed to take a more pragmatic view of destruction. Thus Winnicott changed over the years. At first he pioneered the frank acknowledgment (not necessarily expression) of a therapist's anger at and hatred of a patient. Illustrating his themes with what must have been difficult, perhaps courageous, self-disclosures, he wrote that therapists 'must not deny hate that really exists'. The denial of hate led to 'therapy that is adapted to the needs of the therapist rather than to the needs of the patient' (Winnicott, 1958, p. 418).

In later papers he developed the idea that anger, aggression, hate, and destructiveness exist so long as they are impulses not well dealt with. If the mother or the couple therapist cannot stand the negative affect of the infant/couple, the experience is one of anger, aggression, hate, and destructiveness. If the aggression of the child or couple is handled well (survived) by the mother/therapist, the experience is not one of destructiveness.

Young has written about Winnicott and continued in disclosing his own destructive countertransference.

> My patients do project extremely aggressive and sometimes hate-filled feelings into me, and they evoke such feelings from an ample reservoir within my inner world. The trick … is to retain the ability to think under fire – to contain and detoxify and eventually make sense of what is happening and give it back in a helpful, digestible interpretation and not as a retaliatory re-projection.
>
> I want to say first that I increasingly believe that containment and demeanor can be as important, and I suspect often more important, than anything clever we might say in interpretations. Winnicott thought this, too. Surviving murderous, demeaning, sarcastic, insulting, humiliating attacks assuages the patient's primitive anxiety.
>
> Sometimes we fail. I can think of two patients whose violent feelings exceeded my capacity for containment. One, an obese, miserable and deeply embittered school teacher (the daughter of an abandoned and wretched mother), did finally exceed my ability to contain what she projected into me. I learned this the hard way by acting out. I unwittingly walked right past her sitting in her car a couple of minutes before her session and went off to a pub to have a good-bye drink with

a departing colleague. Though I was quickly fetched back and although we did have several more sessions, this rejecting re-projection could not be repaired.

Another, who claimed to detect all sorts of unforgivable true attitudes beneath my surface Politically Correct ones, e.g., sexism, chauvinism and anti-Semitism, also eventually left after the break at the end of a year's work. Before that I twice found her unbearable enough to convey that I was prepared to let her leave. I wish I had been able to acknowledge more fully to myself the truth of her charges. Not that I was in my day-to-day life a Ku Klux Klansman or abuser (her best goading word) but that racist and sexist feelings were detectable in me, as they are in others and in her, and the problem was how to mitigate, sublimate and suppress them by means of principled behavior, while addressing her primitive anxieties at another level. Her anxieties about not being held were always on the surface, and her distrust was ever-present, urgent and insistently accusing. No one could be trusted, so she goaded until she was satisfied that she had elicited proof that her fears were well-founded, and she was very talented at doing this.

(Young, no date)

Over-emphasis on positive feelings in couple therapies

What is going on with couples when their interaction becomes angry, hateful, aggressive, defensive, and attacking? Are these interactions by definition always destructive? Using Winnicott's thinking about destructiveness of the infant towards the mother, we might propose that it is the difficulty each partner has in handling the other's emotions that determines whether excitement and arousal become anger and hate. If we think along Winnicottian lines, the crucial issue is the absorption of the destructive impulse in a way that does not destroy the partner and therefore does not destroy the relationship. Turning away, retaliation, and cutting-off are typical couple moves that turn what might start out to be a bid for connection to a destructive sequence. Like the tree falling in the forest, whether there is a sound (in this case destructiveness) depends on the listening (or lack of listening) by the other. Here are two different examples of destructiveness that give cause for concern – both coming from the same situation.

Example 1 (destructiveness)

Alan comes home from work at 9 pm. He usually comes home at 8 pm. He did not call ahead to say he would be late. Elaine greets him at the door with an angry face. 'Where were you?', she asks. Alan envisions a fight coming up. He moves past her, leaving her standing alone. She is furious at his lack of reply and storms into their living room, shouting 'You could have called, you know'. Alan is silent and refuses to talk about it. She goes upstairs to their bedroom and slams the door. They do not have dinner together and when he comes up to bed he finds the door locked.

Example 2 (bid for connection)
Alan comes home from work at 9 pm. He usually comes home at 8 pm. He did not call ahead to say he would be late. Elaine greets him at the door with an angry face. 'Where were you?', she asks. Alan envisions a fight coming up. He moves past her, leaving her standing alone. She is furious at his lack of reply and storms into their living room, shouting 'You could have called, you know'. Alan points out angrily that she could have called as well. She says 'You are the one who was late ... don't you even think I was worried?' Alan says he did not think about it. 'I would have called if it had occurred to me you would be worried, but one hour late hardly seems like a problem'. She says 'It is a problem for me.' Alan replies, 'Ok ... ok ... let's not ruin our whole evening over this. I had a meeting with Tom and he was late ... that's all.' To which Elaine responds, 'Yeah, I guess he is getting it at home now too'.

The two similar incidents end differently. Holding the anger and allowing it to be expressed is part of the process where they can hear other things as well. This couple had to move beyond the anger but had to dwell there before they could move on. People will always have anger in their lives as they disappoint each other or distance each other. When there is no anger there often are no other feelings either.

However, there has been a definite trend regarding these issues in the couple therapy literature. Today there is a privilege of 'good' communication over 'bad' communication between partners in intimate relationships and an a priori description of what constitutes good and bad communication. Couples are trained or taught to match their behavior to the 'good' communication behaviors. Today the basic message coming from much of the couple therapy literature focuses on getting couples to treat each other better.

There does not seem to be overall acceptance that good communication skills reflect and predict good relationships. For example, research has looked at two overlapping longitudinal samples of US couples with children, covering a period of 15 years after the first child's birth (Hirschberger *et al.*, 2009). The first sample extended from the pregnancy with a first child until that child was 5.5 years old; the second from ages 4.5 to 14.5. Growth curve analyses revealed that marital satisfaction declined over 15 years for both husbands and wives. Attachment security measured in the second sample was associated with greater marital satisfaction, but did not buffer against declines in marital satisfaction over time. Husbands' lower initial level of marital satisfaction measured around the first child's transition to school was the only significant predictor of marital dissolution.

The findings of the extensive literature on marital satisfaction were analyzed in an important paper by the family studies researcher Frank Fincham and his colleagues (2007). They cite findings that emerged on the behavioral correlates of marital happiness that can be summarized in a simple ratio: the ratio of agreements to disagreements is greater than 1 for happy couples and less than 1 for unhappy couples. But observational research documented that the behavior of happily married couples is less predictable (structured) than that of unhappy spouses who tend to reciprocate one another's (negative) behavior. Although seemingly obvious, such findings contradicted the long-standing belief that happy couples are characterized by a quid pro quo principle according to which they exchange positive behavior. Also, both observed and self-reported behavior account for approximately 25% of the variance in marital happiness. Something other than behaviors seems to account for the remaining 75% of happiness.

These findings hint that couple therapists' fascination with skills training 'good' communication may be somewhat misguided. Failed attempts to teach couples to behave more positively led to an abandoning of the change aspect of behavioral couple therapy in the 1970s and a renewed interest in getting partners to accept each other. But what must they accept? It is self-evident that it is easy to accept one's spouse when they are being nice. Acceptance is only a powerful predictor of marital happiness when it involves accepting one's spouse when they aren't being so nice.

Object relations couple therapy

Closer to Winnicott than communication therapies are object relations couple therapies as practiced by Scharff and Scharff (2000) and Clulow (2001). As discussed by these and other object relations couple therapists, a focus on the therapeutic alliance and the creation of a safe containment is crucial to good therapy and not taken for granted. Object relations therapy is interested in the inner world of the therapist, in the meshing of the inner world of the therapist with the inner worlds of the partners in couple therapy. Transference and countertransference are both expressions of idiosyncratic ways people have of filtering reality and interpreting it.

In analyzing the proverbial couple from hell – George and Martha from the Albee play *Who is Afraid of Virginia Woolf?* – Clulow (2001) shows how their 'games' are so different than the playing that Winnicott believed was essential to creative and healthy interactions. Just as the research mentioned above shows unhappy couples to be more patterned and structured than happy couples, George and Martha have defensive games that seem to have their own script played out over and over. There is no real playfulness or spontaneity, although there is an amazing amount of pure hate. Although there is a cat-and-mouse kind of destructive verbal battering, there are few interactions showing love or intimacy. Mostly there is violence and we have a sense that (as do the other couple invited to witness George and Martha's passion play) of the next potential explosive violence lurking in the background.

Winnicott believed in real spontaneous play. He probably would not have been surprised that later research shows happier couples are less predictable than unhappy couples. He used his squiggle games daily to play on his own. His relationship with Clare Britton was often based on their playing with their ideas about good enough mothering. Object relations couple therapy also seems to advocate helping couples give up their narcissistic defensive system and learn to play spontaneously with each other. The importance of play mirrors Winnicott's emphasis on transitional space where there is no danger to the child who is then free to become absorbed in being.

Object relations couple therapy focuses on the ways that individual defenses intermingle with each other in the couple relationship. The major dilemma for adults is how to maintain a sense of self while being intimate with another person. The therapist creates a safe base in the room for the couple to have spontaneous gestures that are picked up and elaborated by the therapist. Over time and with correct interpretations, the partners can begin to relate to each other as 'other', but as also connected.

Many of the various streams of object relations couple therapy touch on psychoanalytic ideas that Winnicott also included in his writing. Although he had a unique paradoxical style of writing, he essentially agreed with some basic ideas that today are fundamental to object relations couple therapy. These include importance of the transference and countertransference phenomena; splits and parts of the psyche; and above all the long-term effects of the mother–infant dyad on one's lifetime relationships. Many theories have intermingled with Winnicott's ideas in a pool of interrelated thinking, such as holding, transitional and potential space, and the importance of playing.

Creativity and hate

Winnicott especially hated compliant behavior in children and adults. His focus on insanity might have come from his work with psychotic patients, but he saw coming and going to the insane places inside all of us as the basis for both health and creativity (both of which he believed were related to each other).

Schwartz, speaking at a symposium about Winnicott, stated:

> Winnicott says and he is quite explicit about this, if I believe in primary creative and there is creative, destruction is right next door. It's right there. Then madness sort of weaves its way in and out, like flotsam. In work with patients we have to sort of befriend one's own rhythm. Winnicott was interested in madness all his life. He believed that everyone has creativity. And that is what makes life worth living. The concept of the use of the object is an integral part of destructiveness and an integral part of creativity. He saw creativity as based on destructiveness and on madness. He believed that his hate was a key to these three – that there is something about hate that allows creativity, destructiveness and madness to rise to the surface and allow a sense of aliveness when these feelings are adequately held within oneself and by another.
>
> (2009, p. 3)

Winnicott offered his ideas about the therapist experiencing hate towards the client and the working through of hate for the therapist and the patient. He proposed that both need to make contact with hateful feelings. What is it about hate that Winnicott sees as reparative? We know he saw excessive compliance as the false self. He believed that real therapy (in his case analysis) begins when the true self can express itself. Something has to happen to allow the expression of the true self.

Winnicott proposes that the experience of hate is a freeing of powerful emotions. What is it about accessing hate (in the therapist as well as the client) that Winnicott sees as so important and liberating?

In an interesting paper, Green proposes that

> Hate can serve as a form of self-delineating. Through the experience of hating we are able to relinquish the expectation that the person change to meet our need. We are then free to accept the other as separate, rather than as 'a recalcitrant part of an expanded self.' Thus, while rage is indicative of unmet or frustrated dependence, hate facilitates differentiation, the precursor of genuine recognition. The way I am defining hate is related to what Fonagy, Gergerly, Jurist and Target (2002 p. 76) would refer to as mentalized anger. Rage is unmentalized and pre-reflective. Hate is the affective experience of aggression that is reflected upon. For Fonagy and his colleagues affect regulation does not mean the expunging of negative effects, but relates instead to the capacity to reflect upon the affective state and stay simultaneously in contact with the full emotion of the state.
>
> (2006, p. 189)

In this paper Green proposes that in Winnicott's thinking, hate is the 'destruction' used to break through our internal object world. It opens us up to see the outside other. Hate divests the other of power and appropriates it to the self. In this way of thinking, rage represents the helplessness of needing the other's responsiveness and not getting it. Hate represents the acceptance of not getting what we need from the other and no longer depending on that other to meet that need. Yet, many people are not free to feel hate because as children they had parents who could not tolerate their hate. A person has a second chance in psychotherapy if the therapist can accept and interpret the hate rather than unconsciously avoid or disavow it. In a similar way, a therapist may need to delineate his sense of self through hate. Without the ability to recognize hate, the therapist may be unable to break out of a countertransference reaction that could then manifest in the form of pathological accommodation to the patient's needs, or in attempts to maneuver or push the patient in a certain direction.

Here is a letter to me from a client who had decided on divorce:

> I know that I was very convinced in our last couples session that I indeed want a divorce. But at home I started to feel bad, strangely enough, that my husband did not fight for me. He behaved himself very well and was polite

> to the extreme. It is insulting that he doesn't protest more. Also I realized that this was a problem all along the way. He doesn't protest, he doesn't let me fight him. He is so nice it is like I am all alone in this relationship. If he would at least fight back I would feel there was someone out there.

The idea of protesting is related to anger and to hate when anger is not recognized. Can we love another and be loved without any anger? So much of the communication literature wants to tame anger so that it no longer feels angry. This opens the way for feelings of hate; if anger is threatening, hate is even more so. Winnicott sees hate as the destruction of the false, making way for the creative finding of the true self. My understanding is that hate is the final outcome of a rejection by the other of negative feeling states. In order to have a relationship, hate has to be recognized because it is a red light that when ignored can doom the relationship to emotional deadness.

The basic idea here is that to be creative, spontaneous, and true while in a relationship with another, we need to experience and reflect upon anger and hate. This is an internal process. It does not mean spewing forth angry, hateful feelings without control or emotional regulation. It does mean, however, that that part of ourselves which can hate is a friend to other parts that are creative and life-sustaining.

The fact is that many couples who come to therapy feel that their relationship is a kind of dead thing. They will often talk in metaphors that resonate with death and dying, such as:

> I cannot feel towards her anything any more.
> I cannot breathe when I am with him.
> I have this heavy feeling in my chest when she reaches out to me.
> I feel smothered in this relationship.
> This relationship is killing me.

For many couples (and perhaps for couple therapists), this death knell feels final. All that remains is to have the funeral, bury the body (the relationship) and move on.

But what if feelings of anger and hate have been buried so deeply that they are unrecognizable? Hate is a very difficult feeling to experience. Robert Young wrote that it is hard to stay with the feeling of hate … the mind wants to run away from it. Yet if Winnicott is right, hate might be the key to the doorway of a new relationship and a different one. Hate might thus be a sign of life from someone inside the relationship.

Here is an example of the use of hate in couple therapy:

Jacob and Leah are both in their mid-forties. They came to therapy as a last resort before divorce. Both had already consulted lawyers and it was one of the lawyers who actually suggested they get a 'second opinion' from a couple therapist. They actually planned for only one session but after the first session they began a course of couple therapy that lasted two years and resulted in their decision to stay together.

When they came to therapy, they both used the death metaphors for their relationship. Leah had been the first to notice that her feelings for Jacob had 'died' and that the relationship felt like living in a coffin. Jacob objected to this type of talk, but unconsciously he also used death metaphors in the first session. He said that being in the relationship felt like he was buried in a deep dungeon and could hardly breathe ... the air was running out.

Using their metaphors, I asked when the relationship became terminal. They both agreed that they had gone through a terrible trauma and never really recovered. They had been involved in a terrorist attack that killed two of their four children. They had been on a bus going to Jerusalem when a suicide bomber blew himself up, sending the bus into a ravine. Their children were twins aged 8 and the youngest of their four children.

Both partners had a lot (several years) of therapy for themselves as part of the trauma treatment given to all victims of terror attacks in Israel. They had used many different methods (EMDR, relaxation, meditation, support groups, paid holidays, long-term individual therapy, etc.) by the very competent trauma teams attached to the government. Each remained in individual therapy because it was paid for and each felt that they needed it. However, they both commented that they felt closer to their individual therapists than to each other.

But while focusing on their own grief and trying to stay connected to their other two children, they had lost the connection to each other. As a matter of fact, they both felt that being together brought back the trauma and that in order to move on they had to leave each other and either live alone or find someone else.

When couples reach such a dead-end position, most therapists do not see how to help them find a way back to each other. It was so awful that the terrorist attack killed not only their children but their marriage. In getting a history of the family, I noted the multiple traumas running through the genogram of both partners. Both had grandparents who were killed in World War II and thus had parents who were parental children who had grown up far too early. Both had learned at home not to rock the boat so as not to cause their already overburdened parent any more grief.

The couple seemed relieved to have a place to talk about their marriage. They both said that divorce was inevitable but they needed help regardless. They needed help in how to talk to their children, how to disengage from each other. Even though they said that they had no relationship, there still seemed to be a lot of eye contact, mutual mirroring of body language and asking each other questions. They appeared very connected, but subdued, overly polite and careful with each other.

What was significant in its absence was any expression of anger. They seemed to be proud of that. When they talked about their parents, they mentioned that they had to take over a lot more responsibilities than other children. But there was no anger about this. Also when they talked about the terrorist attack and the loss of their connection, there was no anger. The major affect in the room was grief and pain. I felt it and found myself also having a hard time breathing. There was no space in the room. I started dreading the sessions and even forgot one of them.

I had a dream one night in which I was shooting the husband of this couple. He also had a gun, but it was malfunctioning and I realized in the dream that I could have killed him. In the dream I also realized that I was dreaming. I was having a dream about dreaming, which made me very angry. There was a feeling of frustration and helplessness. I couldn't shoot him and also couldn't not shoot him. I woke up with this feeling of anger, although I did not know why. During the day after that dream, I actually allowed myself to fantasize and reflect on this couple, the lack of anger and the dream, which was so aggressive but only almost violent.

I wondered if what had died was their ability to hate each other. Had they ever allowed themselves to hate each other? The hatred that they might have felt towards the terrorist might have been projected on each other, and such powerful feelings might have felt far too destructive to process. Did they perhaps blame each other for the trip to Jerusalem and their children's deaths? Were they guilty about it? What were the couple dynamics around the trauma?

My next step was to go through the trauma story again. The couple had been adequately briefed about the trauma and did not protest talking about it. However, they both said there was no point in it; they had grieved enough and finished that work. Yet they said that they trusted me and if I was asking about something so sensitive maybe I was right. I thanked them for their vote of confidence, and mentioned that I did do some thinking about it. However, I could not promise that it would help, but wanted to know if they think it could hurt them. They both felt that they had been over that territory so much that there was no danger. I asked if they would be willing to signal me if either felt any feelings of wanting to stop. They agreed to that.

As they talked about the events of the day leading up to their trip to Jerusalem, the wife said 'I often go over and over the sequence of events before the bus trip. Jacob had insisted we show the twins the city of Jerusalem again, even though they had already visited it many times. I often thought afterwards why I had agreed to go when it seemed so unnecessary and I would have changed the history of our entire lives … our twins would be alive today if I hadn't gone to Jerusalem.'

I asked her if she often complied with his wishes and she said yes, and not just his wishes, everyone's wishes. I asked: 'Do you even feel angry at Jacob for insisting on going?' She said she was only angry at herself for agreeing. But while she was talking, she looked away from Jacob and actually moved her chair so that her back was more towards him than before. He suddenly said 'I feel a little annoyed with you'. Leah was shocked. She said they had never talked about angry feelings since the event. There was a silence in the room and I wondered what the next step would be.

I tried to access what I was feeling. I suddenly remembered the dream as well. I felt fury that the turn of events that day had ruined these gentle people's lives. I thought deliberately about the suicide bomber and felt hatred both to him and to the climate of terror in our region. It seemed so unfair that we had to live with years of fear and also that we learned not to hate in order to survive. I felt the hate and actually began seeing other terrorist events in my imagination. My feelings of hatred grew, but I did not share them. What I wondered out loud about was if they ever used to get angry at each other and fight? Jacob said that they had been very proud that they rarely fought and were different from most couples they knew in this respect. I suddenly wanted to tell them about my strong feelings, but wondered if it would be helpful and how to phrase it. There was a lot of silence in the room, which gave me space to think. Finally I said, 'I have spent so many years learning not to hate those people who have terrorized us for decades. But I don't always succeed. Sometime I really hate them.'

It felt like a relief to say this. Also I was not overwhelmed by my hatred; I could see that part of me was just a part and not all of me. But I felt that it was healthy to say it, even if it wasn't politically correct. The couple was quiet and thoughtful; although they did not react to my statements, they looked very curiously at me. Finally, Jacob said that he wished he could get angry. Leah said, 'I am already angry at you, at fate, at everything'. Jacob said, 'What good will that do now?' I answered him by saying that I felt a bit of relief talking about my own hatred (and I used the word hate not anger). I asked them to consider and think about the feelings of hate and see what happened until the next session.

The couple then went into a stage of active crisis in their relationship. Not only did they fight a lot, but there were all kinds of symptoms such as depression, need to drink, inability to sleep, the need to throw and destroy objects. Sometimes I felt guilty about having triggered all this, but also I knew that if there was any chance for their marriage to survive, they needed to process the mutual anger, rage and hate that the traumatizing event had triggered. Also, the event happened to a couple who did not have the ability beforehand to process anger. After the immediate crisis (about 6 weeks) they began to talk about their relationship before the event. There apparently had been plenty of problems that were not dealt with, serious issues that were so hard for them at the time that they did not talk about them.

In the two years of this therapy I became a good enough mother/therapist who invited anger expression in the room and was able to take it when it related to me. I actually tried to find out when they felt disappointed, frustrated, or angry with me. I modeled a person who sought out bad feelings and found them a doorway to truth and reality. I went according to the idea that if they processed angry feelings (to each other and to me), they might not get to hate. This did seem to be the case, although hate came and went occasionally.

The old relationship indeed had died. Like a tree whose dead parts are chopped off, new branches and leaves began to grow in their relationship. They learned how to recognize what they were feeling, especially the 'ugly' feelings that previously had been so hidden from themselves. Together with the ability to openly express anger and occasionally hate, this couple began to laugh together, to find humor in daily life and to enjoy each other's company.

Many feelings were stirred up working with this couple during the course of therapy. Many feelings seemed totally irrational and I never spoke about them. For example, I went through a stage where I was jealous of the intimacy that they were experimenting with. Sometimes they seemed like they had just met each other and I felt a longing for those days in my own marriage.

Sometimes I got irritated when we seemed to be going over and over the same ground. Or I got frustrated when we were talking about an incident at home and one of them closed down and refused to talk. I learned over time that usually this signaled having accessed the trauma and that day on the bus. There were times I felt like stopping seeing them. The events they went through still had to be processed over and over, even though they had done so much therapy about it. I got impatient with them and also found it hard to hear the terrible details over and over. Yet I also felt admiration. They seemed to me to be heroes, so courageous and brave.

In other words, through my clients' experiences I got the opportunity to touch much of the range of human emotion. I did not think it necessary to burden them with my own reactions unless we were really stuck. I think they knew a lot about what I was experiencing, even if I did not express it all in words. They became attuned and even protective towards me. What I wanted to be sure to do was to build a space where a new relationship could be 'played' with.

Infantile needs in couples

The point here is that good communication often does not need to be taught in the same way as a skill like driving. Rather, good enough holding allows couples to care for the other when also asking for the self. If we know, as Winnicott proposed, that the infant needs a few moments of hesitation, perhaps that is also needed and occurs naturally for couples from holding environments. But therapy can interject places where good enough principles are possible.

However, if it were this easy, most couples would have figured it out themselves. The difficulty is that many have experienced the lack of good enough mothering. Perhaps the mother was depressed, didn't want the child, was over burdened in child care, was not given enough support from others and had herself experienced not good enough mothering. She was not able to adequately hold and handle her infant. She was unresponsive to objects he presented to her. She wanted to hold and she did not continue on the child's spontaneous gestures.

Unique to couple therapy is the need for the therapist to pay attention to interactions and feelings on many different levels of reality. These various levels of reality include the interaction between therapists with partner 1; the interaction between therapists with partner 2; the interaction of partner 1 with partner 2; the interactions of all three people in the room with the couple's relationship; the interaction of all three people in the room with the therapeutic relationship. Thus the therapist is the holder of the transitional space encouraging playful solutions and reactions that a good enough mother would do naturally. The therapist also watches how each partner mothers the other and what care they are taking for their 'baby' relationship.

No one can attend to all these levels at once. But over time these divergent aspects become a system, so that change in one area can result in change in another. Increasing levels of reality can be taken in as the therapist tracks their own countertransferences and reactions and learns each partner's ways of being.

These are key elements in sensing what is going on within different levels of reality. Overall the therapy is successful when the partners are increasingly aware of their relationship as an entity (like an infant that needs continual care) and when the therapist is able to hold in mind increasing levels of reality. Similar to the couple, when the therapist sees the therapeutic relationship (each partner and therapist) is an entity, there is a widening of the lens of reality to include the therapeutic relationship as well as the couple's relationship.

In terms of technique, the good enough couple therapist can give the couple an experience of maternal preoccupation, in which the therapist is present for both of them and for the relationship. This demands work on the part of the therapist for countertransference feelings towards either partner or to the relationship. People who were mothered adequately tend to be playful, relaxed, alert, and able to process strong emotion. But they don't often come to therapy. Rather the couples who are distressed come in a state of heightened emotionality, much like an infant who has experienced negative interactions and is expecting more of the same. The therapist as good enough mother lets the partners and the relationship lead, with the sensitive therapist taking up ideas and thoughts for elaboration. This is how communication training done without the awareness of the early childhood environment can feel like an impingement, a new article or food pushed towards the couples as an idea of the therapist. If communication skills are given when one or both partners starts to show a desire for better communication, they are given in a way that feels 'real' to the couple. So it is not what the therapist is giving, but how the therapist is giving it.

6 Transitional objects, transitional space, potential space, and couple therapy

Winnicott introduced the concepts of transitional objects and transitional experience in reference to a particular developmental sequence. By 'transition' Winnicott meant an intermediate developmental phase between the psychic and external realities. In this 'transitional space' we can find the 'transitional object'. When young children begin to separate the 'me' from the 'not-me' and evolve from complete dependence to a stage of relative independence, they use transitional objects. Infants see themselves and the mother as a whole. In this phase the mother 'brings the world' to the infant without delay, which gives them a 'moment of illusion', a belief that their own wish creates the object of their desire, bringing with it a sense of satisfaction. Winnicott calls this 'subjective omnipotence'.

Alongside the subjective omnipotence of a child lies an objective reality, which constitutes the child's awareness of separateness between themself and desired objects. While the subjective omnipotence experience is one in which the child feels that their desires create satisfaction, the objective reality experience is one in which the child independently seeks out objects of desire. Later on the child comes to realize that the mother is separate, through which it appears that the child has lost something. The child realizes their dependence on others and thus loses the idea that they are independent, a realization that creates a difficult period and brings frustration and anxiety. In the end it is impossible that the mother is always there to 'bring the world' to the baby, a realization that has a powerful, somewhat painful, but ultimately constructive impact on the child. Through fantasizing about the object of their wishes, the child will find comfort. A transitional object can be used in this process.

The transitional object is often the first 'not-me' possession that really belongs to the child. This could be a real object like a blanket or a teddy bear, but other 'objects', such as a melody or a word, can fulfill this role as well. This object represents all components of 'mothering', and it means that the child is able to create what they need as well. It enables the child to have a fantasized bond with the mother when she gradually separates for increasingly longer periods of time. The transitional object is important at the time of going to sleep and as a defense against anxiety.

In a later stage of development, the child no longer needs the transitional object. They are able to make a distinction between 'me' and 'not-me', and keep inside and outside apart and yet interrelated. This development leads to the use of illusion, symbols, and objects later on in life. Winnicott related the concept of the transitional object to a more general one, the transitional phenomena, which he considered to be the basis of science, religion, and of all cultures. Transitional objects and phenomena, he said, are neither subjective nor objective, but made up of both.

Transitional object ideas can illuminate different aspects of couple interactions. At the start of a romantic relationship each partner, as well as the new romantic relationship, is often a transitional object from dependency on the family of origin to individual independence. This is of course not unusual and may be highly functional at the start. The relationship can have a feeling of 'coming home', so that the real family home is no longer pulling too hard emotionally on the growing adult. We know today the adult development goes on throughout the life cycle, and couples' relationships can play a big role in the outcome of this process. A secure attachment to a new relationship is truly a safe harbor for continual independent development. In the transitional space of the new relationship great learning and development can take place. It is during this time couples will buy their first home, a step in their independence from the family. They might travel to another country and feel that they are not alone as long as they have each other. They might change jobs or learn a new skill. Romantic relationships are a place of fantasy meeting reality. In this space the couple can try on so many different novel behaviors.

Sometimes the strength of the romantic relationship leads to fighting with the family of origin. The strength to do this might come from the transitional object aspect of the new relationship, which helps face the possibility of becoming more independent. However, sometimes a split develops between one member of the family of origin and one of the partners:

> Ronit and Tom are a couple in their early thirties. Until their marriage two years before the referral, they each lived in their own apartment. Learning to live together was not easy and they had a lot of adjusting to do, since both had been on their own for at least ten years. However, when Ronit became pregnant with their first child, she started to demand a change from Tom. Previously they both had a decent, rather remote relationship with their families of origin. Being pregnant, Ronit started to reach out for her own mother, who responded with great enthusiasm to moves for more closeness. Tom started to resent her being with her mother too much. The two women went together to buy baby clothes, while Tom felt that Ronit should have asked him to do it with her. Tom started to resist Ronit's requests to spend more time with her family. The mother got involved by undermining Ronit's choice of partner. She never had been very comfortable around Tom and now she used the wedge that had been given her to get her daughter closer to her and the family.

Therapy revolved around the so-call 'independence' Ronit truly felt from her family.

When Ronit left her family home and moved into her own apartment, her mother played a major role. They went to get furniture together, and her mother was very instrumental in helping Ronit get her own home. But in reality Ronit never really found her independence together with her mother. She either got very close and they did everything together, like two friends. Or she pushed her mother away and forgot to call or visit. This behavior aroused anxiety in Ronit's mother, who was decidedly in the way at the start of Ronit's relationship with Tom. Delighted to be asked back upon the pregnancy, her mother undermined her relationship with Tom by asking critical questions – how much did he earn and was it enough? How do they expect to have a baby growing up in a one-room flat? Why was Tom not more supportive when Ronit felt morning sickness? It was not hard to shake up Ronit's faith in Tom and make her cling even more to her mother.

The ideas of transitional objects and space were useful in thinking of therapy as a transitional object for both Ronit and Tom. It was a space where they could try out new ideas, think what they really wanted (as opposed to reaction to the families of origin). The fact that the therapist was now in a position to offer a new transitional space meant taking the setting issues very seriously. They had a permanent hour which all concerned kept religiously, despite vacations and sickness. They started and ended the session on time. The format of the session was quite permanent and offered them a sense of security. The therapist always asked about their week and also about homework assignments that they were given. It was agreed that they would not interrupt each other and they would use time out to calm themselves down during a session (one might go out or they took a short break). In other words, like a good enough mother, therapy itself and certainly the therapist became alternative transitional objects and space for them to experiment safely with incremental and agreed upon movement towards both closeness and independence from the family of origin.

Knowing the role therapy played in the couple's life meant that the therapist was especially careful not to take sides as well as to check with them about the effects of the therapist's interventions. They were helped to increasingly create their own rules for therapy, based on experiences of success and failure. For example, they did not like behavioral contracts, but did like behavioral assignments. They did not like the genogram, but did like to draw their feelings about their family.

Also, their needs changed with time. They became more directive about how to use therapy. Sometimes only one of the partners showed up. They worked this out themselves. As the therapy began to have a good effect on the couple, they started to experiment with more distance from the families of origin. There was a definite pulling back from both families, which then had to be negotiated between the partners. This process was mirrored eventually in their pulling away from therapy. They stopped the therapy after a year, which in the last few months had moved to once every three weeks. They made a check-up appointment for three months, which they kept and were happy to have.

A partner's distress is not overwhelming when one can see his/her distress response (fear, aggression) as motivated by underlying thoughts, feelings, or intentions. They gradually learn to hold and contain each other just as the therapist has contained both of them in the therapy room. Recovery from emotional reactions comes about faster through self-soothing and the ability to use the partner as an object for comforting, even if it was the partner who triggered the response. This is very similar to a baby's ability to come back to the mother after screaming at her and use the mother again as a comforting object.

The therapy continued to be available to them, like good enough parenting, according to need. They brought their first child to the therapist in pride and excitement. It was obvious that they were well on their way to independent living. About a year after that, Ronit's mother called and asked for an appointment for herself. Knowing the therapist's role as a transitional object for Ronit, the therapist referred her to a colleague in order to maintain the safety of her work with the couple.

The facilitating potential space

Winnicott introduces the idea of a parent and infant creating potential space, psychological space for play and for discovery. It is play that is universal. In such playing space the infant is relatively safe, but is also exposed to stimuli and to problems. Winnicott proposed the term potential space to characterize this zone between two worlds. To the infant it is very safe and comforting near the breast, at one pole; more and more open and problematic, even challenging and frightening, at the other. As the infant develops, the transitional objects that they find or create in the world of 'not-me', take on special characteristics and functions and embody new principles. A child's brick, for example, may continue to be a 'sucking thing' even after it has started to be an 'elementary geometry thing'. So transitional objects become toys or tools or 'explore-withs' and we – child or adult – will eventually classify them according to how we use them in our practice or our thinking. Winnicott is emphatic: all cultural objects and artifacts need to be understood in terms of how they first appear in play.

The place where cultural experience is located is in the potential space between the individual and the [maternal] environment. … The same can be said of playing. Cultural experience begins with creative living first manifested as play. The child moves on from being largely dependent on the mother; but the polarity of the discovery field and the rhythm of the learning system remain. We play tentatively with a new pattern or idea. We test it, stretch it. If it works we practice with it, internalize some of that pattern as an element in a growing skill or competence. Practice and repetition is the me-strengthening aspect. But we also move from practice and play, out further, towards our exploring margin where we can only just cope. It is here that we sometimes experience the frontier where new forms may break in from apparent chaos. So we may be stretched and fail and suffer.

The mother should adapt both to calm moments and to the infant's stimulated moments. A lot of moments of impingements cause weakening of the ego. At extremes this causes psychosis, and massive anxiety. Normal development leads to integration and living in our body, psychosis is the opposite, being taken to pieces, with no connection to our body and the reality. The personal development of the individual always occurs in an interpersonal context. Within the facilitating environment comes the ability to play.

Therapists create the freedom to 'play,' or 'play along,' with each other's reality, realities that are conveyed principally through language but that also involve matching the affective state of the couple through posture, gaze, timing, and tone of voice. Listening to how partners talk and building on the language and metaphors that they use afford couples a new 'potential' space. Ideas are thrown around like a pillow or a toy (Randolph, 1998). Here is an example of the use of potential space with a couple:

JAN: I cannot seem to understand what I am supposed to do right now.

THERAPIST: Do you mean here in the room, at home, with Ted … .what …?

JAN: I mean here right now. Ted is expecting me to say what I need from him and wasn't getting. What I went to Peter for. But if I start in that direction, I know Ted will become upset and hurt. I love the calm feelings between us. I don't want to take a chance to ruin that.

THERAPIST: So talking about what caused the affair feels like it would ruin the relationship? Do you mean forever, or just now in this room, or this week?

JAN: (laughs) Well, I guess I meant in this room. No, I think probably I am scared we will lose all the good things that have been happening because of therapy and because Ted is being so generous to move on. I don't want to ruin that. I wish we could end therapy now, just keep things the way they are.

THERAPIST: So do you want to cancel your regular hour next week?
JAN AND TED: We weren't saying that.
THERAPIST: Maybe we should move to once a month?
TED: I can handle once a week. I won't ruin things even if I do get upset. I will cope with it. We can always make another session before the week is over. Right?
THERAPIST: (To both of them) Maybe we should set up a meeting for three days from now just in case things get rough. You can always cancel 24 hours before if it looks like you won't need it.

Both partners look relieved, but say that just knowing they could come in was enough to keep the next session for one week's time.

This is an example of potential space; play, transitional objects and how all these are used to remain in a balanced good enough position. The therapist here doesn't get caught up in their anxiety but plays with different time schedules. The actual idea of coming in again the same week was a result of playing with perhaps cancelling sessions or making them once a month. A potential space of play was initiated and led to moving towards having a transitional object (the second session in the week) help in holding the couple. They were navigating the move from crisis intervention to in-depth touching on what led to the affair. That was scary for them, and playfully giving the opportunity to back off led to moving closer to the therapist and using the therapist as a good transitional object.

The facilitating environment tries to capture important moments and elaborate them. Couples who are revealing themselves to each other need a facilitating environment in order to go on disclosing themselves. The therapist creates this environment by being sensitive to moment-by-moment shifts in atmosphere or feelings. The therapist comments with a question such as 'It seems like you two want to go deeper into what led to the affair … am I correct here?' Disagreement or agreement are both helpful in responding to the facilitating environment. The former means that the therapist needs to find something else that is needed. The latter means that the therapist accurately picked up something that needs elaboration. Neither is better than the other and both are needed in the good enough environment. The facilitating environment needs these mistakes to foster the activity and responsibility of the couple for responding accurately themselves.

Transitional objects

What are the parallel elements of couple therapy that reflect the ideas of transitional space and objects? The couple therapist has a complex task in allowing for three different kinds of transitional spaces. One is with one partner, the second is with the second partner and the third is the creation of a transitional space in the therapy room with both partners.

While these tasks overlap in time, there is a sequence that in an overall way is often followed. The therapist first creates and holds the transitional space for each partner. For example, with Sam and Ruth I had to create a place where their intense feelings did not destroy me and in which I could then be creative with each partner separately. The need for two separate transitional spaces parallels the need for the individual partners to feel held and safe before the couple as a unit can be held. After there is a secure transitional space for each partner with the therapist, the therapist can go about creating and holding a larger transitional space including both partners and the therapist. In reality all these actions are going on at the same time, with a shift in emphasis over time.

In the case of Sam and Ruth, each was helped to re-create the good experience in the transitional space between each of them and the therapist. Once they had firmly connected to their original good selves with each other through the work with the therapist, the next stage was approached. In this stage the couple could see what happened to their relationship and they learnt to create a transitional creative space for their relationship as well. Until they can do this, the therapist holds the relationship from the beginning and progressively guides them towards holding their relationship themselves. These concepts will be elaborated in the next chapter. Here there is a short example from the case discussed above.

Sam and Ruth were doing better and were less aggressive in the sessions and at home when I went on a three-week vacation. They mentioned several times that Ruth especially was less upset and depressed and that something in the therapy was really helping her. While presented as Ruth's needs (by both of them), I understood that they were both worried about what would happen while I was gone.

I made a joke at that point that maybe I should create a doll looking like me and give it to them. I meant to be humorous but there was an uncomfortable silence. I realized that I had been kidding them about something serious and perhaps had even hurt their feelings. I was flooded first by guilt and when that calmed down I began to reflect why I had joked about something so important. Memories of my own separations from my family flooded me as I allowed myself to see that I had closed down my own neediness as a child since I realized there was no one out there to hold me. I was then sarcastic about their neediness, even though I had been working towards that exact goal for the months before.

I was silent with them while I gathered up all these feelings and memories and calmed my inner critics and parts that felt threatened. I was able to hold on to all of these without further reaction and when calm decided to offer them a real transitional object. I said that the doll idea was not such a good one. I apologized for suggesting it and asked whether it might help if we decided to communicate by email. It always amazes me how forgiving clients can be when we as therapists are upfront about our mistakes. Sam said 'I don't need email, I can wait till you come back. But the doll idea was kind of insulting. I think it is a good thing that we rely on you.' I was delighted with this response and clearly showed it. Ruth said 'I would like to write to you if you don't mind. Maybe I will sit down and write to you at the hour and day that we would have been meeting?' We went on to discuss the pragmatics of the letter-writing project – would I answer the letters? Would she send a copy to Sam? What would she expect from him?

I realized that my unconscious mocking of their neediness had opened a path for me to apologize and move on. We inevitably make mistakes that we can use. We can view these cycles of rupture and repair as similar to the good enough mother who is not 100% on target at all times. Rather than attempt to be perfect, we can use these lapses as an opportunity for repair and healing. No doubt that the lapses usually have as much to do with our own issues and problems as discussed here. It is not accidental that their neediness and dependency on me triggered my own rejection of dependency from my childhood. There is no way to reach a point, nor should we aim for it, of no triggers in therapy. Rather therapists who work on their own issues are alert to opportunities to bring themselves into the room. Recognizing my vulnerabilities around neediness and being dropped as a child, I could then recognize how I had dropped the couple as well. I don't need to be overwhelmed by this failure but to recognize it as one of the many opportunities offered to make amends. The more I become a secure object who is perceived not as perfect but as good enough and reliable, the more a couple can begin to do this repair work with each other.

Casement believes that, at the end of the day, Winnicott is one of the few twentieth-century analysts who, in stature, breadth (and minuteness) of observations, and theoretical fertility can perhaps legitimately be compared to Sigmund Freud: 'some genius analysts, such as Freud and Winnicott … learned naturally how to learn from their patients. … I believe that the majority of … therapists are more ordinary, sincere hard workers – not necessarily brilliant – who seek the truth with such care as they are able' (2014, p. xv).

Couples with one spouse who had good enough mothering

When either or both partners have had a good enough mothering experience, the early days of the romantic stage of relating are filled with pleasure. If both partners did not experience good enough mothering, the relationship can feel like a second chance. But there are underlying expectations of 'being dropped' and sooner rather than later, the couple experience deep disillusionment, disappointment, and rage.

Contrast theses two couples:

Kate and Bob have been married for one year. They experienced their first year of marriage as building a kind of cocoon. They tended to spend most of their time together and did not feel the need to have close relationships with others. However, Kate was the child of an abusive mother who eventually committed suicide. Bob came from a happy home life and wanted to give Kate some of what he had experienced. Very early on in the relationship Kate experienced disappointment and anger at Bob. Sometimes he was late; he did not always ask the right questions. He did not initiate lovemaking enough. She quickly had a long list of complaints. Bob was a bit shocked by the depth of her anger. However, he never really wavered in trying to re-parent Kate. He truly was a new good enough mother for her. When he found it hard to be responsive (rather than reactive), he would have sessions with his former psychotherapist. Sometimes the two of them came to his sessions and these helped balance the couple. When Kate got pregnant at the end of the first year, they both experienced a renewed burst of energy and of love. Bob had proved himself enough to Kate for her to finally relax and to really enjoy her pregnancy without worrying about her relationship with Bob.

Rena and Yochi were also married for one year but came to therapy to get a divorce. Both had come from abusive and traumatic families of origin. Rina's mother had abandoned the family and gone to live in another country. Her father never remarried and relied on Rina to take on the wife role. This included sexual abuse that was never confronted. She left home at the age of 14 to live in a kibbutz. Yochi came from a religious family where the husband and wife had strict gender roles. He never saw his parents talk. They insisted that the children take on a large proportion of the household work since both parents had physical problems. None of the 13 children got any real attention from the parents. There was also child abuse in this family because the siblings turned to each other for warmth. Yochi not only left the family early at age 13, but he refused to be religious. Thus in many ways he felt cut off from his roots and actually wanted never to think about his old life. This is a couple who argued frequently even before the marriage. The tense atmosphere that was between them from the start was familiar to both of them. Both partners blamed each other constantly for a myriad of issues. Both felt disappointed and disillusioned by promises they felt were broken. Neither of the two partners had the resources to hold the other. They eventually divorced.

Reparenting couples

When there is at least one partner who has the ability to hold the other, and especially with the help of therapeutic intervention, the chances of the couple moving beyond feeling misery and disillusionment are high. This is mostly because adequate holding has a constructive effect, allowing some growth and development on the part of the other. This type of relationship (Kate and Bob) is a reparenting relationship. Bob did many of the functions of the good enough mother figure for Kate. Holding was evident by his listening to her and mostly his ability to not fall apart and retaliate at her rages and hate-filled tirades at him. This helped Kate begin to create the feeling of a separate self with a continuity of being. No matter what she said to him, and she really tried to break him down, he was able to remember his love for her and stay fairly firm.

When Bob was afraid himself of a breakdown, he used the facilitating environment of his individual therapy sessions. By bringing what he learned from his therapist to Kate, he brought the outside world to her. He could have been secretive about what was going on in his own therapy. But his first alliance was to her (perhaps even more than to himself). He thus used things that his therapist said to mirror in a constructive way what she might be experiencing. For example, his therapist had commented to him that perhaps she was testing him to see if she got so hateful he would leave/die like her mother did.

The fact that he used his own therapy to strengthen her, rather than create his therapist (a female) as an object for competition, increased Kate's sense of independence. She had new parenting figures (Bob as father and the female therapist as mother). She felt that they were both supporting her because no matter what she said, they never retaliated. Once she called the therapist and went into a tirade of hate and anger. The therapist remained calm and asked if she would ask Bob to come to the therapy. He was delighted to come in and while she only wanted one session she felt relieved that the focus was on helping her cope.

The other aspect of her life with him that led to growth and strengthening of the relationship was Bob's insistence on having his own space without taking anything away from her. He refused to play the role of the parent all the time. He needed time for himself and he talked openly with her about that. His true self depended on time alone to survive. He was well able to be alone in the presence of others and talked openly with her about having that time alone even when she was in the room.

The right not to communicate was especially important in their relationship. Bob was very much in touch with his need to withdraw and be with himself in order to feel whole. This was crucial to him, but it was also very hard for Kate. She had experienced her mother's suicide as an abandonment. Any distance within the cocoon they had created felt frightening to her. She was afraid of having a breakdown like her mother.

Unifying experiences meant that Kate would have the chance to feel part of the relationship with Bob even though he needed time for himself. He was unusually sensitive to issues of leaving and reuniting. For Kate he was warm and loving and she felt good about herself, or he was cruel and abandoning when he needed his space and then she felt ugly and unloved.

This switching back and forth between feeling beautiful and feeling ugly was incomprehensible to Bob. He felt the same towards her whether in her presence or not. He could not understand why she was so threatened by small events like his going out for a beer with his friends for an hour. He used his therapist to try to make sense out of it all. When he better understood, he asked Kate what she needed to 'hold on to' her beautiful self and his love no matter whether they were together or not. They came up with several strategies. First that he would not go out for more than two hours at this stage, with the hope that in the future she would be able to tolerate more time alone. She asked if he might be willing to come home earlier if she needed it and he agreed. He suggested that he phone her often and share what was going on. They both agreed that if it got too hard for both of them (i.e. Bob might feel resentful about coming home or she would need to talk on the phone more than he found comfortable), they would use her good relationship with his sister as a 'transitional' object. The sister lived very near and was happy to have Kate come over. By widening the cocoon to include another person other than the therapist, both felt empowered and less alone with Kate's volatile emotions.

For both of the couple, the therapist and the sister took on roles of the transitional and the potential space. Neither Bob's therapist nor his sister appeared to lose respect for Kate, and even seemed to think she was heroic in trying to overcome such a traumatic background. Kate was then able to use them to hold on to a sense of continuity of her relationship with Bob even when he was away. What Kate was learning was relating through identification. Over time she was able to feel strong enough not to need the transition objects (the therapist and the sister) and felt identified with Bob. Identifying with him meant that she continued to exist when he was out of the house. She used telephone conversations to help her do this and was aware that she wanted to reduce the number of calls she made. The fact that he was not upset at her calling allowed her to learn to increasingly manage her anxiety on her own.

She herself began to go out for short periods of time with girlfriends she had neglected. She began to understand that Bob's need for other people was not a reflection of something wrong with her or their relationship. This helped her especially when she got pregnant and needed to open up a place for a third person in their relationship. She did this work by fantasizing and learning about pregnancy. For Kate, the dialectic of imagining her new child while also learning about the real child she was carrying helped her strengthen both her love for Bob and her own sense of mental health. Fantasy and reality are both needed for balancing the internal and the external. A real baby that could be the focus of a rich fantasy life helped her learn a healthier way of loving.

Also, Kate and Bob were both able to play the masculine (doing) and feminine (feeling) roles with regard to the forthcoming birth and this helped them both. With regard to the birth, Bob encouraged her to decide on a birth plan on her own. She was very ambivalent since she wanted a home birth, to nurse her baby, and be fully involved with motherhood. On the other hand, she felt extreme anxiety about the home birth and about nursing, which would mean she had to go it alone rather than bottle feed, which Bob could do too.

Here again Bob used his own therapist to deal with some anger he felt about her obsessing about the birth. Everything seemed so significant to her and life threatening. The therapist was helpful in focusing on Bob's own anxieties about becoming a father in a situation where the mother was fragile. It was crucial for this couple that Bob's therapist could hold him and be a transition object for his move to fatherhood. The therapist helped him balance the need to do things to help Kate (i.e. buy the crib, etc.) with the emotional feminine side to his personality (his desire to give a bottle to the baby and to take paternal leave as well). This combination of both doing and being was very supportive to Kate, who needed both from her partner.

Reparenting when both partners did not have good enough mothering

The leap from Winnicott's description of good enough and not good enough mothering to adult couple relationships is not a difficult one. Holding, for example, is something couples do (or refuse to do) all the time. Gathering up the body occurs in sexuality (or it doesn't) as well as in the many ways that couples care for the physical/emotional well-being of each other. If we use Winnicott's ideas we might better understand why coming home to a meal that has gone cold, or to a wife who is sleeping, or a husband who is busy with his phone and computer might all feel like a complete lack in adequate holding, gathering, and presenting.

For example, a wife makes a lovely dinner for her husband and children, but he forgets to tell her he is bringing home some colleagues. The wife panics that she doesn't have enough food. The atmosphere between the couple becomes very heavy. It feels to both like being dropped. While in this whirl of negative feelings, they cannot be creative and humorous about the event, which might have led to some spontaneous gestures (ordering in, going out for food, etc.); what feels like a catastrophe could have been a fun evening.

Many of the interactions between couples mirror and reflect infant care issues. While romantic partners rarely diaper each other, they do care physically for the other and the physical and emotional areas intertwine. A husband who remembers that his wife likes a certain kind of meat and brings it home is holding her. When infant holding had not been well adapted to her needs, she experiences being held again but this time in the right way.

Also when there has been good enough mothering in the childhood of the couple, they do not force changes on the partner. A woman wants to change the date she made with her husband to go to a movie and a restaurant. She can say 'I don't want to go out tonight – maybe some other night.' This could be felt as an impingement without taking care of the other. Or the woman can say 'You know, I got the feeling it is important we go out tonight together … is that true?' When her husband says that it is, she asks 'Is it really important to you that it be tonight?' He says no – he could do it tomorrow. She hugs him and says thanks, since she didn't want to hurt him or miss their night out, but she had preparation for her work to do.

Transferential relating and reactivity

When a couple first come to couple therapy, they have often accumulated a history of transferential interactions. These are expressed as blaming the other ('He is egocentric'), blaming other people (i.e. the partner's mother), blaming the self (self-pity and omnipotent ideas of one's own power). On some occasions the blame can be on the society (too violent, lonely etc.).

In most cases the blame is squarely on the partner. The partner is at fault and the partner is supposed to change. If there is something one feels guilty about, it often is the other partner's fault as well. For example, 'I don't initiate sex enough. But if she wouldn't push me so much, maybe I would' or 'Sure I go shopping too often and spent too much, but if he was warmer and kinder I wouldn't feel so empty inside.'

The therapist is also at the transferential level along with the couple. This has various forms. One is towards one of the partners: 'She is really difficult to be with.' Another type of transference is towards the problem: 'I don't know why they haven't figured out that blaming each other doesn't work.' Sometimes the transference is towards other people in the couple's interpersonal circle: 'It does seem like his mother is too intrusive' or historical events of childhood: 'Seems like he really didn't get enough mothering.'

The point here is that regardless of being right or not, the type of thinking is transferential. It puts one's own feelings out onto another. Within a transferential system there is blame and counter blame. There is a sense of helplessness and confusion. Change attempts don't last. One or both partners leave therapy. The therapist refers out.

Transference, fully established, is a sampling of psychic reality. It belongs to what Winnicott calls the 'realm of illusion', (Winnicott, 1951). He talks of an unconscious agreement between the mother and the infant not to attempt to figure out whether the material is internal or external. Thus the question 'did you conceive of this or was it presented to you from without?' is never to be asked.

In couple interactions with each other and with the therapist, the question of where the material comes from (internally from the individual, between the partners or between the couple and the therapist) should not be asked. That is, the reactivity in the room is from all three sources at the same time and trying to work out where it originated is not just impossible but adds another level of stress to an already stressed situation.

The interactions in the room when relationships are transferential are reactive. There is an automatic kind of thinking and feeling. Most often the focus is on behaviors and not on either feelings or beliefs. Therapists are caught up in this way of interacting, just like the couple. Thus anger is threatening to the therapist as it pulls him/her into a reactive mode as well.

PARTNER 1: I just don't understand why you have to go out almost every day in the week!

PARTNER 2: I don't go every day, just Thursdays and Tuesdays. You exaggerate so much.

THERAPIST: Let's try not to get caught up in the facts … is it really important how many days she goes out?

PARTNER 1: It is important to me.

PARTNER 2: You are just counting days instead of thinking what is really wrong with our relationship.

Responsive mode of interacting: widening the focus

In the responsive mode of interacting the partners and the therapist relate to the relationship rather than to each other. The therapist and the couple relate to the therapeutic relationship as well. It is as if in the reactive form there are only three people involved, while in the responsive form we have two new entities: the couple's relationship and the therapeutic relationship. In this mode the couple's relationship and the therapeutic relationship are both like newborn babies towards which both partners and the therapist show good enough mothering.

PARTNER 1 TO PARTNER 2: Over this weekend I felt that the relationship was really neglected. I felt empty inside, but it didn't feel like there was something out there I could reach.

PARTNER 2: I was too busy with the upcoming school event. I did not invest in the relationship and I guess you felt bad. I noticed it, but I couldn't really change anything.

THERAPIST: How is it for the two of you to think about what the relationship was experiencing this weekend?

PARTNER 1: At the time I was more aware of my own sadness, but now that we are talking about this, I think we both neglected the relationship.

PARTNER 2: I agree, although I am not sure how to do it differently.

THERAPIST TO PARTNER 2: So you feel … sad? Helpless? Do you have some guilt towards your partner or to the relationship?

PARTNER 2: Yes, like we missed out again in relating to each other. It seems that so many things compete with the relationship and the relationship seems to get the short end of the stick.

PARTNER 1: I am sorry I was so oblivious to the relationship. I am glad we are talking about it here at least … that is new, isn't it?

Couples come to therapy mostly in the reactive transferential mode. Anger, rage, disappointment, disillusionment, and hatred are results of this way of relating as well as the cause of this way of relating.

Winnicott's interventions would certainly not try to change all this too early. That would be like trying to get a newborn infant to feed themself. Neither would the therapist necessarily try to get the couple away from anger, even if it is uncomfortable for the therapist. A more coherent way of responding is 'I hear some anger here … maybe disappointment? Frustration? Does that feel right?'

As noted several times in this book, Winnicott does not present us with a unified method of treatment. Thus the next discussion of elements of couple therapy using his ideas does not propose a stage-like method. All these aspects are available at all times. Yet his theories fit a developmental view, with the therapist needed to monitor moment-by-moment interactions as to their level of development. The major question about when to do what is very much like the issues of mothering a growing child. The mother who is 'good enough' starts with total acceptance and moves according to the development of the infant to a more demanding mode of relating. Mistakes in this process are essential and part of the work. Repair can only occur when the mother/therapist has asked too much from the infant/couple. Reparation is a crucial part of the process and can occur at any time in the work with the couple.

Spontaneous gestures in the transitional space

In his writings about infants and mothers, Winnicott placed a strong emphasis on the mother responding to the child's creative spontaneous gestures that come from the infant's true self. His squiggle game was a treatment mode and also a metaphor for responsiveness to spontaneous gestures. One of the elements Winnicott considered could be lost in childhood was what he called the sense of going-on being. For Winnicott, the sense of being is primary, the sense of doing an outgrowth of it. The capacity to 'be', to feel alive … the baby's lifeline, what Winnicott calls its 'going on being' was essential if a person was not to be 'caught up in a false self and a compulsive cycle of "doing" to conceal the absence of "being"'.

Couples often ignore bids from the partner for interaction. Many seemingly 'spontaneous gestures' from one partner go unnoticed and unrecognized by the other. At some point this can also become conscious and useful in a power struggle. That is, deliberately ignoring a bid for contact or any spontaneous gesture can be a way at getting back at the partner for hurts.

In therapy the couple therapist is alert to all spontaneous gestures, both verbal and non-verbal. While one partner is talking, the therapist monitors the other partner's reactions. Looking away, becoming sad or angry are only a few of the ways partners do not elaborate spontaneous gestures. Many of the couples in therapy never had someone really continue their spontaneous gestures, so they don't really know what they are missing.

What is also important for the therapist using this idea is to realize that any behavior can have the function of not continuing a spontaneous gesture by the other. For example, one partner may describe an event while the other tries to discuss another event, or get the facts right or ignore what the partner is saying and start discussing a new topic.

When couple therapists notice the almost inevitable behaviors by distressed couples, they need to respond in a way that is not itself a form of ignoring the spontaneous gestures. That means not to say 'David, Miriam was just talking about an incident with your parents and you now have diverted the conversation to another issue entirely. I wonder what you are both feeling when this happens. I wonder whether it happens frequently.'

Possibly Winnicott was against interpretation because he was primarily concerned with the patients' need to experience an elaboration and relating to of their spontaneous gestures. The most brilliant interpretation, while being right, can give the other a feeling of not being seen.

In couple therapy, as long as the therapist remembers that the client is the relationship (that is, the real baby of these partners) the focus will be on the effects of behaviors and reactions on the entity of the relationship.

For example, to return to the idea that Miriam was talking about one thing and David moved to another, an intervention that does not criticize or take sides would be something like 'I want to discuss what happens in your relationship when one of you is trying to say something and the other doesn't seem to relate to it. What happens then to the relationship?'

The baby of the couple needs to be reassured that spontaneous gestures will be recognized. That means that they both have to come together to parent their relationship in a way that makes the relationship feel continuity of being. When a previously distressed relationship starts to recover, it recovers the ability to respond to spontaneous gestures and this creates a sense of safety and security.

Work on rupture and repair in couple therapy

Perhaps one of the most important functions of holding is the ability to notice a rupture in holding and to repair it so that holding is reinstated. Sometimes ruptures are very obvious. A male partner is talking and his wife turns her back to him and looks through her cell phone for calls and messages. A therapist who does not comment on this and ask them both how they feel is acting out the rupture and participating in it. The therapist who immediately realizes that there is a rupture will find a way to bring the rupture back into the therapy so that it can be talked about and repaired. The woman who is looking at her phone might have felt unheard, might be angry, might feel helpless, or may feel disconnected from the therapy. The most powerful interventions are around rupture and repair. Thus noticing the failure in holding is a major avenue to get to work on rupture and repair.

In a typical paradox, ruptures in the holding environment are failures in holding. The paradox is that these failures are a major route to repair and thus to healing and growth. While most therapists feel bad about ruptures, we can learn much from Winnicott who seemed to delight in fighting ruptures to repair.

The major job of the therapist then, is to be monitoring the holding environment. Much of the communication about the holding environment is nonverbal. A man looks away after a certain comment by his wife. The wife slumps down in her chair with a sigh when her attempt to reach him doesn't seem to work. One or both members of the couple look away when the therapist tries to talk about something. The therapist is interrupted and disregarded suddenly, as if he/she doesn't get it.

It is important to label the rupture as such. This makes continuing as if nothing is wrong or attempting to say the same thing again another way less likely. This is a dialogue about rupture and repair:

PARTNER 1: I keep telling her what I feel, but it doesn't seem to matter to her. I am trying to tell her I am really sorry, but the more I try, the less interested in me she seems.

PARTNER 2: I do hate it when you repeat yourself.

THERAPIST: Is that the problem? That he is repeating himself? Maybe he feels that you aren't hearing him.

PARTNER 2: I have no problem with my hearing.

THERAPIST: I am starting to wonder if maybe you (Partner 2) think that I am taking his side in this?

PARTNER 2: Taking sides? Well, maybe it is like you understand him more.

THERAPIST: Can you tell me what is it I am not getting?

PARTNER 2: I guess I want you to see that the more he talks, the less I feel connected to him. (she turns to her partner) I need you to try harder to condense what you want me to hear … when you go on and on, it just turns me off.

THERAPIST (TO PARTNER 1): So you did get it right when you first said that the more you talk, the worse it gets. If we can find a way out of this loop, would it be of interest to you?

Both partners nod in agreement.

Creation of a separate 'couples' self

Through the sequence of meeting needs and demanding too much, the infant comes to feel like a separate entity. Similarly the sequence of meeting needs and failure allows the emergence of a separate self couple relationship.

THERAPIST: So it sounds like you both had a difficult week … a lot of fighting and arguing?

PARTNER 1: You have no idea … I hardly slept this week and went to the couch to sleep some nights.

PARTNER 2: You only have yourself to blame. If you want to talk to me, don't do it just before we are going to sleep. I am not available and I don't want to ruin my night.

THERAPIST: So it sounds like the relationship can cause you both to lose a lot of precious sleep? How does that work?

PARTNER 2: He brings up the relationship issues just before we doze off. I don't even remember what he is saying, but off he goes in a huff to the couch.

THERAPIST: So the relationship doesn't have its own place and time yet? It sort of barges in like a bull in a china shop and gets you both so riled up that you cannot deal with it?

(Silence as both think about it.)

PARTNER 1: I never thought of it that way. If I had ... perhaps we need to talk about what would be a good time and place for some relationship talk?

PARTNER 2: I have been telling you that for years! What do I say ... I say let's talk about it!!

THERAPIST: So you (Partner 2) feel like you have been in charge of getting the relationship some attention ... You (Partner 1) got a sense just now about trying to make room for the relationships needs?

PARTNER 2: Yes, I feel demeaned that you (the therapist) get to say things that I said and they are like God came down into the room ... whereas now whatever I say, it is like old stuff.

PARTNER 1: She is only trying to help...

THERAPIST (TO PARTNER 2): You know, I can imagine that must hurt. I am sorry that it goes that way. Perhaps I can ask you myself if this is something you have already said? I can check with you first if maybe this is an idea you already had.

PARTNER 2: That would help me a lot, it would validate that some of my ideas were good too, not just yours. I mean, you do have a way of putting it that feels somehow easier ...

THERAPIST: Can you describe what types of statements give you a sense of ease?

Rupture and repair are recognized all the time in a therapy using Winnicott's thinking. It is a central tool in working towards increased responsiveness and healthy development of the couple's relationship through the therapeutic relationship. It is up to the therapist to gently probe areas of potential disappointment. While some couples are able to express their feelings of hurt or disappointment with the therapy, far more are caught up in their anger or disappointment with the partner. They are so negative with each other that they keep trying to preserve the therapist as a positive object. This splitting is a defensive move and to be expected in the beginning. Anger and disappointment with the therapist can be a positive move away from splitting the bad partner and the good therapist. Of course, if the splitting continues with a bad therapist there will be no therapy.

Usually both partners are unaware of more subtle negative feelings towards the therapist, and unsure about their entitlement to comment on something the therapist did. It is very empowering for couples to realize that any or every statement by the therapist is actually a question and not a pronouncement. They have the right (even the duty?) to comment when the therapist's intervention was off target, even mildly. For a therapist working according to Winnicott's thinking, these repairs are the essential act by the true self to reach out to the environment and change it. We seek out even mild situations of disagreement, disappointment, anger, or negative feelings towards a statement. For many people, this willingness not to be destroyed by their negativity but actually empowered by it is a new experience.

Fantasy and reality in couple therapy

The couple's ability to play using their own fantasy life is extremely important in maintaining the sense of continuity of being. Once the honeymoon period is over the fantasy life of the couple becomes more important. During the honeymoon period, many couples act out the good enough mother scenarios. They search for what each likes and tries to get it for them. They are learning their partner's quirks and needs, which in an early stage is often seen as cute.

Often a period of disintegration happens when one of the partners suddenly seemingly out of the blue no longer likes what they previously liked. For example, in the early stages of their marriage a couple liked to play out a fantasy that they were just meeting for the first time. They would go to their favorite bar and 'hit' on each other. They found this playacting fun and sexy. Suddenly the wife no longer wanted to play. She had seen some pornographic pictures on their home computer and she was awash in fear that her husband was a pervert or addicted to porn. Suddenly their game seemed like another potentially dangerous sign.

The couple's ability to play with reality, and to re-experience the fantasy of their honeymoon stage, is crucial in getting through the experiences of disintegration and potential breakdown.

It is the therapist's job to help the couple connect the dots. That is, the couple needs to sense that the relationship can survive their fears, rage, and disappointment, and that there can always be the potential for recovery from breakdowns.

THERAPIST: You were feeling pretty good when you got here today. Am I right?

(Both partners agree.)

THERAPIST: But now you are upset and on the verge of a fight, is that right too? (Again both partners agree.)

THERAPIST: I wonder how that is for the two of you. To have these shifts from good times to bad times, even within a few moments?

(Silence as the couple are thinking about it.)

PARTNER 1: I always feel that it is her that starts these fights out of nowhere. It is amazing. You know we told you about our little game of picking each other up at a bar, as if we were strangers. Suddenly she doesn't want to play and is furious at me … why?

THERAPIST (TO PARTNER 2): So something changed for you?

PARTNER 2: (Silence.)

PARTNER 1: You see, she won't tell me what it is … it is you who start things.

THERAPIST: So what does it feel like to you (Partner 1) to have her change suddenly? And then not to want to talk about it?

Partners 1 talks about feelings of dizziness, tension, stress, hyper-alertness, negative expectations, fear of a blowup, need to withdraw so it won't happen…

THERAPIST: So it is really hard for you? Especially since you don't know why things changed. Are you afraid they are permanently changed? Volatile?

PARTNER 1: I am really worried now.

PARTNER 2: I could tell you, but it might make things even worse for you. I keep silent to protect us. I have some fears and I am not sure about them. Just talking about it may make it worse.

THERAPIST: I hear your fear that talking would just make it worse. What would not talking do?

PARTNER 2: Destroy it all … I cannot talk and I cannot not talk. What a bind.

THERAPIST: What do you think that your relationship wants from you now?

PARTNER 2: No, I know I have to get this out, but how?

PARTNER 1: I agree. I am afraid that the relationship is getting weaker and weaker over time and maybe there will be more and more fighting.

THERAPIST: Yes, I imagine it is sad, especially when you don't really know how long it will take for the relationship to get its act together (laughter). You started off here today feeling pretty good. Is it the same relationship that then gets so stressful? Or do you have two relationships? The good one and the bad one? Or is it the same relationship going through different phases?

PARTNER 2: It feels like a different relationship, but it isn't really. Our relationship always had those moments. I remember a time even before the wedding when I stormed outside and considered calling the whole thing off.

PARTNER 1: So what does it mean about us that we created this monster relationship that turns on us sometimes?

THERAPIST: Do you think that the relationship would agree that it is a monster?

PARTNER 2: No, it isn't really, maybe it is more like a little child who easily gets hurt.

THERAPIST: If it was a child, how do you think it should be treated?

PARTNER 1: I don't know if I can go along with this. The relationship isn't a monster or a child … it is a relationship.

THERAPIST: And what does this relationship need from you both?

PARTNER 1: Patience maybe. Also the fact that we argue doesn't mean that the end is near. If only I could hear what happened without panicking!!

THERAPIST: How can I help with this? How does our relationship here in this therapy help or not help with this important dilemma?

PARTNER 2: Just what we are doing now, I think. We are looking at our relationship from the outside. You help us do this even if it is scary sometimes … It feels real. Ok … what happened is that I was walking by the computer and saw that there was pornography displayed. I got really freaked.

THERAPIST: What was hard for you about that?

PARTNER 2: I connected our little game in the bar and started to get scared that maybe he is a pervert or has some addiction or something. Maybe our games aren't so innocent. I mean what am I dealing with here?

PARTNER 1: Wow, this is a relief! Is that what it was about? Do you think that looking at porn is bad or evil or perverted?

PARTNER 2: Not theoretically … I consider myself an open person, that is how I can play our game. But suddenly I got freaked. I felt I didn't know you … I mean who are you?

PARTNER 1: (laughing) … I am still me … we could look at some porn together! I am not addicted, just curious. Aren't you?

PARTNER 2: I guess so, when I am not freaked.

THERAPIST: So you both like playing around, but fear cut into that?

PARTNER 2: Yes, fear is the monster.

THERAPIST: So the monster is out there somewhere. How does the relationship feel right now?

BOTH PARTNERS: (laugh) … Curious!

Play in potential space

A central theme running through Winnicott's work was the idea of play. Departing radically from orthodox psychoanalytic thought at the time, which held that analysis helped patients mainly by making them more aware of and insightful about their unconscious beliefs and wishes, Winnicott thought that playing was the key to emotional and psychological well-being. By 'playing', he meant not only the ways that children of all ages play, but also the way adults 'play' through making art, or engaging in sports, hobbies, humor, meaningful conversation, etc. At any age, he saw play as crucial to the development of authentic selfhood, because when people play they feel real, spontaneous and alive, and keenly interested in what they're doing. He thought that insight in psychoanalysis was helpful when it came to the patient as a playful experience of creative, genuine discovery. Winnicott saw a danger in psychoanalysis as it was being practiced in his time: Patients could feel pressured to comply with their analyst's authoritative interpretations, whether or not the patient experienced them as useful or enlivening or true to their own experience, and in this way analysis could end up merely reinforcing a patient's false-self disorder. Winnicott believed that it was only in playing that people are entirely their true selves, so it followed that for psychoanalysis to be effective, it needed to serve as a mode of playing.

One example of how Winnicott used play in his work was the 'squiggle game' in his child consultations. He would draw a shape and invite the child to make something of it; or, conversely, the child would draw a shape for Winnicott to do something with. Later analysts would develop the idea in the sense of using these incomplete 'shapes' in our work with patients … a *half-way step to interpretation* – for the patient to do something with – rather than the analyst monopolizing insight in a session.

Another, more famous instance was the 'spatula' game, where Winnicott would place a 'spatula' (tongue depressor) – an object always available in a pediatrician's office – within a child's reach for him to play with. 'You may be sure that if he is just an ordinary baby he will notice the attractive object … and he will reach for it.' Thereafter 'he will suddenly be overcome by reserve ... [then] in the course of a little while he will discover what he wants to do with it'. From this Winnicott derived his idea of how 'the infant needs "a period of hesitation" in which to rediscover' – again a concept transferred to analytic work: 'the analyst needs to tolerate what Winnicott speaks of as "the period of hesitation" ... allowing the patient to use the analyst as someone who is there to be found ... [not] to be shoved down patients' throats' (1971a).

Many of Winnicott's writings show his efforts to understand what helps people to be able to play, and on the other hand what blocks some people from playing. He came to consider that 'Playing takes place in what he called the "potential space" between the baby and the mother-figure ... [T]he initiation of playing is associated with the life experience of the baby who has come to trust the mother figure.' In other words, babies can be playful when they're cared for by people who respond to them warmly and playfully, like a mother who smiles and says 'Peek-a-boo!' when she sees her baby playfully peeking out from behind his hands. If the mother never responded playfully, sooner or later the baby would stop trying to elicit play from her. 'Potential space' was Winnicott's term for a sense of an inviting and safe interpersonal field in which one can be spontaneously playful while at the same time connected to others. Similarly, in analysis, 'Creative play does not necessarily mean always playing alone; and this is the nature of an analysis when all is going well' (1971a).

Increased independence in couple therapy

The infant starts in a state of absolute dependence and moves through the process of rupture and repair as well as attuned mothering to a position of increased independence. The early stage is characterized by omnipotence, which the mother allows. Slowly the infant is weaned away from this omnipotence by experiencing failures in mothering and repair of these failures.

While couples come to therapy as independent and separate people, they regress a lot within the couple relationship. Also the relationship itself is like an infant that at first needs a great deal of tender loving care. However, if the relationship doesn't grow towards more independence, it will suffocate its 'inhabitants'. The sense of omnipotence is a heady, exciting experience for couples in the throes of romantic love. They feel they can conquer the world. Over time their omnipotence is severely tested and begins to change.

Healthy withdrawal in couple therapy

The couple at first often want to spend all their time with each other. Their sense of owning the world and enjoying it is solidified by their developing sexual relationship. Some people stay in the honeymoon romantic stage for months and some even for years. When there never was a romantic stage, the relationship has no dream to fall back on in hard times. While the romantic stage will begin to disintegrate and change, its having been alive means that the couple can revive it occasionally.

Healthy withdrawal means that the therapist gradually allows more free interaction between the couple, especially when they are apparently working in a good enough manner to allow them to take over for a while. In the early stages of couple therapy the therapist is very active and responsive to each of the partners and to the relationship. As the couple begins to focus on the couple relationship rather than mutual blame and seem to rely on the therapeutic relationship to bring their relief, the therapist needs to gradually allow more independent work.

Healthy withdrawal from the relationship as well as from dependence on the therapist allows each partner to reconnect with their separate selves, often felt to have been previously merged with their partner. The couple may come to therapy exactly on the cusp of this dilemma: how to feel myself as a separate person as well as part of the relationship.

A mistake often made in couple therapy is moving too fast towards independence of the partners from each other. Aside from living in an individualistic world where independence is privileged to dependence (which may be seen as a problem), couples reach the point of wanting their own 'selves' back again. However, they do not necessarily want to lose the relationship, although it may appear to them to be a choice between feelings connected or feeling independent. We need both and each fosters the other. It is the therapist's ability to hold both dependency and independency, while modulating the move between them, that allows couples to begin to have both in their lives.

Unifying experiences in couple therapy

Ending the splitting between the good and the bad relationships is similar to the realization that there are many selves and especially that there are true and false selves. Overall the therapist keeps in mind that polarities are actually part of one fabric. It is the therapist's job to hold inside the good and bad relationship and the true and false selves of the partners. This will be covered more in depth in the section on the therapist's inner work on the self.

THERAPIST: So, you had a rather good few weeks and are wondering whether to stop therapy?

PARTNER 1: Yes, well we aren't really fighting anymore. We had some nice times

PARTNER 2: Also, when we did get irritated with each other, we sort of handled it well. We didn't fall into the hole, just sort of walked around it.

THERAPIST: It is good to hear that you enjoyed each other and that the fighting hasn't taken over the relationship. When you talk about walking around the hole, does that mean that you avoided the topic or the feelings? Are you happy with how you handled this?

PARTNER 1: Well, I guess we are so tired of fighting that it was a relief to walk around it. But now that we are talking about it, I think it would be kind of bad to have this all the time. How would we solve any problems? Is there going to be a stage where there are no more problems? Anyway, we won't get there by walking around them.

PARTNER 2: Yes, that is what I saw at home really. My parents never seemed to fight, but there was this sense of walking on eggshells. I actually never saw a fight, so I don't know how I got so frightened of fighting.

(Both couples look to the therapist for the next step. The therapist sits silently and calmly, waiting to see what they will bring up.)

PARTNER 1: I guess she isn't going to bail us out here.
PARTNER 2: Well, what would have happened if we hadn't gone around the hole?
PARTNER 1: You mean if we had fallen in the hole? We would probably be a mess today.
PARTNER 2: No, not necessarily. Maybe we could have had a talk about the problem, instead of avoiding it.
PARTNER 1: Are we talking about the same issue? The thing we had about sex?
PARTNER 2: Yes, that one. Maybe we should talk about it.
PARTNER 1: We've never had a successful talk about sex ... it just feels so uncomfortable.
THERAPIST: Would you like me to help you here. It sounds like you want to stop going around this hole – no pun intended (...laughter) ... would you like my thoughts about this?

(Both partners look relieved and say yes.)

THERAPIST: When you have (in the past) avoided topics that are too hot for you, what does that feel like?
PARTNER 1: Sometimes it is a relief.
PARTNER 2: I don't like it because I feel phony. I act as if things were alright. We are really good at that. No one outside can tell we have problems. We know the act very well.
PARTNER 1: Yes, it feels like a script. It is a relief that we know our parts and won't necessarily fall apart. But we never are really sure we will keep to the script!
THERAPIST: This feels to me like very important stuff. Some people call it a false- versus a true-self experience. Does this talk to you two? Would you like more true-self experiences?

(Both partners agree but also seem a bit bewildered about what a true-self experience would be. The therapist promises to keep on asking and trying to find those times where they feel true to themselves and to the relationship.)

The capacity to be alone in the presence of the partner

Winnicott believed that the ability to be alone was crucial to mental health. He wrote:

> I would like to take up this subject in a different way by studying the words 'I am alone'. First there is the word 'I', implying much emotional growth.

> The individual is established as a unit. Integration is a fact. The external world is repudiated and an internal world has become possible. This is simply a topographical statement of the personality as a thing, as an organization of ego-nuclei. At this point no reference is being made to living.
>
> Next come the words 'I am', representing a stage in individual growth. By these words the individual not only has shape but also life. In the beginnings of 'I am' the individual is (so to speak) raw, is undefended, vulnerable, potentially paranoid. The individual can only achieve the 'I am' stage because there exists an environment which is protective; the protective environment is in fact the mother preoccupied with her own infant and orientated to the infant's ego requirements through her identification with her own infant. There is no need to postulate an awareness of the mother on the part of the infant at this stage of 'I am'.
>
> Next I come to the words 'I am alone'. According to the theory that I am putting forward, this further stage does indeed involve an appreciation on the part of the infant of the mother's continued existence. By this I do not necessarily mean awareness with the conscious mind. I consider, however, that 'I am alone' is a development from 'I am', dependent on the infant's awareness of the continued existence of a reliable mother whose reliability makes it possible for the infant to be alone and to enjoy being alone, for a limited period.
>
> Paradoxically the capacity to be alone is based on the experience of being alone *in the presence of someone*, and that without a sufficiency of this experience the capacity to be alone cannot develop [Winnicott, 1958]. Some people find it difficult to be alone but being with others elicits negative feelings, such as anxiety. This kind of person moves from being too lonely to being engulfed by anxiety in the presence of the other. The ability to be alone with another is a fundamental ability of people who find it possible to create couple-hood with another.
>
> (Winnicott, 1958, p. 417)

For couples the capacity to be alone in the presence of the other is a crucial developmental achievement. While it might have been achieved earlier with the good enough mother, the issue remains one in the background for most people. It is as if couples have to replay that developmental shift in which it is ok for both of them to be alone while in the presence of the other. But those who had a negative experience in infancy will find being in partnership with an intimate partner difficult. A negative infant experience could be either not having enough quiet time with a caregiver or not being allowed to play without impingement. A negative infant experience would be having the mother intrude too much in their space while playing. Or a negative experience might be left too much alone so that when the infant is suddenly needy (i.e. hungry, cold, lonely, scared...) the mother is nowhere to be seen.

Of course those people who had mostly positive experiences with being alone in the presence of the good enough mother had a head start in their intimate relationships. These are people who more easily move from the strong bond of the honeymoon stage to the more contained stage of being together but also being apart. The transition from the first of these to the second is through the ability to be alone while together. This might look different for different couples. For some it means being able to inhabit the same house but be in different rooms. For others it might be having permission from the relationship to be alone while the other is in the same room. Building up these positive steps leads to keeping the other partner internalized and alive while in different physical places. This is one more aspect of the transitional space and is crucial in couple relationships. And as with most of these ideas, it takes time for the abilities to develop.

The right not to communicate in therapy

With all the focus on how to communicate, it is a breath of fresh air to contemplate the idea that we have the right not to communicate. The basic idea came to Winnicott in his later life, when he went deeper into the concept of the true self.

Much like Zen or Kabala thinking, Winnicott came on his own to the idea that the true self can never be totally known. He did not use mystical language but was quite matter of fact about this. From the fact that there is a deep silence in the true self, and that this silence can never be fully known, he evolved the idea that we all have the right not to communicate. If we want to express our true selves and have spontaneous, creative, and playful gestures, we need the protection of the true self, from which all these come. There is a mystery about the source of creativity, intuition, spontaneous play, and feeling real. But they are important to our quality of life. They are also crucial to the success of our intimate relationships.

THERAPIST: We have been meeting for several months now. How would you say things are going in the relationship and in the therapy?

PARTNER 1: I have been thinking that we can take a break, maybe meet in a few weeks or maybe a month and a half?

PARTNER 2: I am kind of worried about doing something so drastic. I feel the need to have these weekly sessions to make sure we stay on the right path.

THERAPIST: How do I help you to stay on the right path?

PARTNER 2: It is true I have noticed that you don't say as much as you did in the beginning. It feels like you trust us to care for the relationship and each other.

THERAPIST: I think that is very true, I do trust you, but actually when I think about it, I started trusting you early on when it was obvious you both were so committed to therapy.

PARTNER 1: I felt that and it helped me feel more trust about this whole process. At first I thought it was kind of mumbo-jumbo. After all, why would someone else know what is good for us. But over these last months it feels like we are closer all the time ...and ... This is also strange, now that I think about it, we are also more separate. Both closer and more separate.

THERAPIST: How does this work in your life ... is it true for both of you? How does it express itself, this closeness and yet also this separateness?

PARTNER 2: I agree we now have both. I guess it is kind of like our relationship with our kids. They are growing and more independent, but we all are still very much connected, maybe just in a different way.

THERAPIST: What allowed you two to combine being together and being separate? They might seem to others as contradictions, but not to you. How is that?

PARTNER 1: It feels to me it started when I felt ok about using the computer for a while without talking to my partner. That used to be a problem. Now, I can disappear in the house for hours and still feel connected.

PARTNER 2: I feel the same. I can be with my friends, but I think about what my partner would say about this or that. I look forward to coming home to tell him about stuff that was said.

THERAPIST: Is there any way that our therapeutic relationship is similar? Or maybe could be similar? Would you like that?

PARTNER 2: I like the thought because I felt scared when Partner 1 thought we should take a break. It was like I was going to lose you. But while we talk about this togetherness and separateness I feel maybe I could feel that way with you. Maybe I could write you emails during the time we are separate?

PARTNER 1: We need to be independent, we cannot keep holding on here forever.

THERAPIST: In this case I agree with Partner 2. You both mentioned your kids and I also have kids who have been leaving home. But it is important to me that we stay in touch, and for them too I think. We find ways and today it is easier with Skype and Facebook. I am comfortable getting emails from either or both of you until our next meeting. I prefer not to answer them, however, because that would begin a whole sequence and I wouldn't know how you are reacting. That feels too much like therapy. But if you could feel free to write to me, knowing I promise to read everything you write, I think it would be a help for all of us. After all, I have become attached to you two as well. I welcome the idea of knowing how things were going.

The idea of having the right not to communicate helped the therapist create boundaries that felt right. The basic 'incommunicado' of the true self can be recognized and used as a way to protect the true self. Winnicott seemed to believe that it was the combination of the false self and the recognition of the right not to communicate that protected the true self.

Since most models of couple therapy emphasize good communication, it is important for the therapist to clarify that good communication includes the right not to communicate. Systems theory couple therapy says that there is no such thing as 'not communicating' and that we communicate in our silences. Making it alright to have silences and that these can be nourishing for the relationship is often met with delight, especially by husbands. The pressure to be seen and known often blocks out the equally strong need to be alone with oneself in one's most true self. Appreciating this needs to be developed to allow real relating and not false-self 'good communication skills' relating.

Imagine a couple who have been struggling with silences between them. It is obvious to them after visiting numerous couple therapists that they are deficient in communications skills. The pressure is on for both to show a new therapist just how terrible their communication is. But this demonstration of closing up is met with delight on the part of the playful therapist. Using Winnicott's ideas the therapist creates a safe place for not communicating. The therapist might make statements like 'We all feel so deficient in our communication with our partners. We might have an ideal of how good communication would look. And that ideal doesn't include silence. What pressure when you have to communicate all the time, and even silence is taken as a kind of (negative) communication.'

Winnicott opens the door to real-life interactions, with all their messiness, lack of control, fears of breakdown and disintegration, feeling inadequate to the job of being a partner and so on. These ideas are a relief to couples who come expecting to find out just how terrible their relationship is.

Potential space and play

It appears crucial that good enough mothers foster their infants' playing and themselves enter into the play as well as letting the child play alone in her presence. This is one of the messages of the Virginia Woolf play, in which there was little spontaneous playing but a compulsive reenactment of a dangerous game. The couple could not handle the separate selves that are the basis of the ability to play.

The idea of the ability to play is summed up in this vignette of a child's play:

> The following is an example of the absence of the state of mind required for playing (i.e. potential space) followed by its presence.
>
> A 2½-year-old child after having been frightened by having his head go underwater while being given a bath became highly resistant to taking a bath. Some months later, after gentle but persistent coaxing by his mother, he very reluctantly allowed himself to be placed in four inches of bath water. The child's entire body was tense; his hands were tightly clamped on to his mother's. He was not crying, but his eyes were pleadingly glued to those of his mother. One knee was locked in extension while the other was flexed in order to hold as much of him out of the water as he could. His mother began almost immediately to try to interest him in some bath toys. He was not the least bit interested until she told him she would like some tea. At that point the tension that had been apparent in his arms, legs, abdomen, and particularly his face, abruptly gave way to a new physical and psychological state. His knees were now bent a little; his eyes surveyed the toy cups and saucers and spotted an empty shampoo bottle which he chose to use as milk for the tea; the tension in his voice shifted from the tense insistent plea, 'My not like bath, my not like bath', to a narrative of his play: 'Tea not too hot, it's okay now. My blow on it for you. Tea yummy'. The mother had some 'tea' and asked for more. After a few minutes, the mother began to reach for the washcloth. This resulted in the child's ending of the play as abruptly as he had started it with a return of all of the initial signs of anxiety that had

> preceded the play. After the mother reassured the child that she would hold him so he would not slip, she asked him if he had any more tea. He does, and playing is resumed.
>
> (Ogden, 1990, p. 15)

What is beautifully described here is the change from conditions in which playing is impossible to a solution initiated by the mother offering to play with the child in a way that made playing possible. The two conditions that Winnicott believed that stopped the ability to play was a dysfunction in the dialectic of fantasy and reality.

Winnicott believed that in a well-functioning potential space, play is always possible. It becomes impossible in different ways, and these all harm the potential space between the couples as the harm was first done between the child and the mother.

The movement from mother–infant unity (invisible environmental mother) to mother and infant (mother as object) requires the establishment of the capacity for a psychological dialectic of oneness and of separateness in which each creates and informs the other. At first the 'two-ness' (that coexists with oneness) cannot be distributed between the mother and the infant in a way that clearly demarcates the two as separate individuals; rather, at this point 'two-ness' is a quality of the mother–infant. This is what Winnicott is referring to when he talks about the infant's development of the capacity to be alone in the presence of the mother. The transitional object is a symbol for this separateness in unity, unity in separateness. The transitional object is at the same time the infant (the omnipotent created extension of himself) and not the infant (an object he has discovered that is outside of his omnipotent control).

The appearance of a relationship with a transitional object is not simply a milestone in the process of separation–individuation. The relationship with the transitional object is as significantly a reflection of the development of the capacity to maintain a psychological dialectical process.

When the process of movement from mother–infant unity to mother as object for the infant is harmed by repeated lack of attunement, lack of mirroring, poor holding, handling, and too many impingements, certain problematic processes are started. Specifically harmed are the capacity to generate personal meanings represented in symbols that are mediated by subjectivity (the experience of oneself as subject who has created one's symbols). The attainment of the capacity to maintain psychological dialectics involves the transformation of the unity that did not require symbols into 'three-ness', a dynamic interplay of three differentiated entities. These entities are: the symbol (a thought), the symbolized (that which is being thought about), and the interpreting subject (the thinker generating his own thoughts and interpreting his own symbols). The differentiation of symbol, symbolized, and interpreting subject creates the possibility of triangularity within which space is created. That space between symbol and symbolized, mediated by an interpreting self, is the space in which creativity becomes possible and is the space in which we are alive as human beings, as opposed to being simply reflexively reactive beings. This is Winnicott's potential space.

This transformation of unity into 'three-ness' coincides with the transformation of the mother–infant unit into mother, infant, and observer of mother-and-infant as three distinct entities. Perhaps here is an oblique reference to the father? 'Oneness' (the invisible mother–infant) becomes 'three-ness', since at the moment of differentiation within the mother–infant unit, not only are the mother and infant created as objects; in addition, the infant is created as subject. The infant as subject is the observer of mother and infant as (symbolic) objects; the infant is now the creator and interpreter of his symbols.

Ogden's development of the idea of the potential space

Ogden believes that Winnicott was on the way to a sophisticated understanding of problems in the potential space. He tried to elaborate on Winnicott so as to extend Winnicott's ideas even further. Winnicott states that it is within potential space that symbols originate. In the absence of potential space, there is only fantasy; within potential space imagination can develop. In fantasy, 'a dog is a dog is a dog', while imagination involves a layering of symbolic meanings. In these very brief statements, Winnicott points to a theory of the psychopathology of the symbolic function, a theory that remains to be filled in.

When there is a good enough fit between mother and infant, in the very beginning (in the period of the invisible mother–infant), there is no need or opportunity for symbols. Within the context of the mother–infant unit, the person who an observer would see as the mother is invisible to the infant and exists only in the fulfillment of his need that he does not yet recognize as need. The mother–infant unity can be disrupted by the mother's substitution of something of herself for the infant's spontaneous gesture. Winnicott (1952) refers to this as 'impingement'. Some degree of failure of empathy is inevitable and in fact essential for the infant to come to recognize his needs as wishes. However, there does reach a point where repeated impingement comes to constitute 'cumulative trauma' (Ogden, 1987).

Ogden connected this third entity to the ability to play:

> Some forms of playing in the analytic setting involve an experience of the analytic third that might be thought of as an experience of the patient and analyst engaged in playing in the presence of the unconscious (jointly, but asymmetrically constructed) mother who facilitates the capacity of the child to be alone in her ('invisible,' unobtrusive) presence. I place emphasis on the words 'to be' because it is the experience of coming into being as an individual with one's own distinct and unique qualities that is of central importance in the experience of this form of the analytic third. One can see and feel and hear and smell and touch something like oneself in the activity of playing. This experience of playful symbol- and metaphor-making allows one to create symbols which give shapes and emotional substance (sensate 'embodiments')

> to the self-as-object ('me') which serve as mirrors in which the self-as-subject ('I') recognizes/creates itself. Other forms of playing in the analytic relationship involve an unconscious experience of the father or the 'father-in-the-mother' whose protectively watchful eye is felt to make safe, for example, oedipal flirtation between analyst and analysand. The creation of various forms of the analytic third which create and preserve conditions in which playing might safely occur evolves throughout the course of every analysis that is 'a going concern' (to borrow Winnicott's apt phrase). Many forms of the analytic third coexist at any moment of an analysis, some of which are pathological in the sense of limiting the range of human emotion and depth of object relatedness into which patient and analyst are able to enter.
>
> (Ogden, 1987, p. 486)

Couples playing in the potential space

The concept of the potential space is especially appropriate for use in couple therapy. Many of the partners were infants who experienced repeated impingement and the trauma of lack of attunement, and lack of repair of ruptures. Many who ask for help have themselves compromised their ability to develop the true self's spontaneous creativity without censoring from false selves (real or in fantasy). Winnicott would have us believe that the majority of mother–child relationships are indeed good enough. Studies on this question, with an emphasis on culture, poverty, ethnicity, and social alienation, would help us understand the conditions under which good enough mothering is not the norm.

Assuming though that the majority of infants do have good enough mothering, what would the couples' potential space feel like? What behaviors would we expect as a result of good enough mothering?

One of the outstanding aspects of happy couples is their ability to play. Many happy couples remember humor as a reason for their falling in love, and also as an outcome of being in love. Research has clearly confirmed that the happier the couple, the more they share a sense of humor.

> Researchers interviewed over 3,000 married couples from five different cultural regions. The team used a questionnaire that gauged the spouses' opinions of their relationships based on humour, satisfaction, closeness, intimacy, and other factors. The study revealed that humour was directly related to overall marital happiness. 'Having a humorous spouse was associated with one's marital satisfaction in all five cultures, and slightly more so for wives' satisfaction,' said the team, noting that humour remained an important factor for satisfaction throughout long-term marriages.
>
> (Weisfield *et al.*, 2011, p. 439)

The return of humor is often a sign that couple therapy is working and that the couple is retrieving its ability to play. They may share intimate jokes that leave the therapist out, or may joke with the therapist – even about the therapist in a playfully kidding way. The ability of the therapist to allow this and to join in with the playful atmosphere helps promote the healing of the couple and a sense that they are invincible and will not relapse. In mother–infant bonding situations we often see the mother picking up the play of the child, whether it is with objects or laughing. We see the mother extending the play and making the smiles and laughter even more potent. This is a role that the therapist can play with couples recovering from distress.

Humor (and thus marital happiness), however, might well be influenced by external social events and traumas. Winnicott's ideas were developed during World War II. And he was especially active in working with children who were relocated and even those who had lost their parents in the bombings. His good enough mother is a gripping idea because it seems to hint at the possibility of healthy psychological development despite environment stress and trauma.

Having worked for 40 years in Israel, I have become aware of intergenerational trauma from the Holocaust. We have a large percentage of people who escaped the Holocaust and came to live in Israel. Many therapists today investigate what were the childhood conditions of the patient or couple. Some are first-generation Holocaust survivors, some second generation. Many of our couples come to therapy with family histories similar to the following vignette. It often appears that parents were depressed, alienated in their new country (without knowing the language and having left behind or lost entire families). I cannot compare what occurs in Israel to what happens in London. But I wonder about the level of trauma that a society can sustain without impinging on the natural good-enough-mother functions.

Saul and Miri are in their late fifties. They remember fighting from the day of their wedding. They both came from parents who were Holocaust survivors and who had each lost another first family in the camps. Both Miri and Saul remember a silent atmosphere in the home. Miri tried to talk with her mother, but her mother said there were many things she would be better off not knowing. In terms of mothering, Miri only remembers her mother working from early dawn till late at night helping her husband: Miri's father ran an all-night grocery store. Saul did not have his own room since the family was so poor that the three children slept on mats on the floor in the kitchen, bathroom and hallway. Saul has no memories of his mother at all and wondered how he was held, fed, or cared, since in his view she was never home. She apparently had many lovers and only returned home when between men.

The fighting that started right after the wedding related to loyalties to each family of origin. Each partner had been a parental child, taking care of their siblings while their mother worked. It would be hard to imagine that these young people could have been able to be good enough mothers to their siblings when it is not clear that they themselves had good enough mothering.

Their fighting had a very familiar sense often seen in couples asking for therapy. There seems to be a very serious tug of war about who will get cared for and who will do the caring. This central issue is rarely stated as such, because it is not just unconscious but generated before language was obtained. The fighting is often around very concrete issues. In their case, they fought about who does the cooking, who cares for the house and child, who has to work more, who gets to decide things, who is viewed as more entitled than the other. The therapist can be lost in the wealth of complaints. But if we go back to the mother–infant bond and hypothesize what happens when the baby is not mirrored, not held, not given the chance to play alone with the mother nearby, not given repairs for ruptures ... all these lead to false selves that learn to do things for themselves. Expectations are low, but so is the vitality of fun, playing, and creation. The baby grows up in survival mode, with the unthinkable anxieties lurking in the corner at all times.

This sense of anxiety and seriousness in all daily life is common to adults who were not given good enough mothering. As they were not allowed to play happily in a protected and safe world, they are non-playful and not creative about their relationship. If both were in such predicaments, we see fighting from the start. But we can also say that hope has not been lost. In fighting with a partner, there may be many sites of renewed hope that good enough caring will be experienced.

Saul and Miri came from extremely deprived backgrounds where there was little time given to just going-on being baby. In the breakdown of the third space that would be created through symbolism, neither of them can break out of their autistic selves. Miri experienced her fantasies as real. If she thought he did not love her in her mind, he did not love her. There was no room for self-reflection, the space of looking upon the situation with a larger lens.

Saul lived totally in reality and did not allow himself fantasies. If the reality meant being at work until late, he never contemplated what this might be doing to his family and wife. His perception of the realities of life was not ever viewed as perception, but as fact.

It might be possible that very impoverished mothers could be good enough with enough mirroring, attunement, and repair for adequate development of the infant. It is also possible that well-established, even wealthy, mothers might have themselves been deprived as infants and have none of the good enough type of mothering. We can make some fundamental assessments about the good enough mothering by thinking of the dialectic Winnicott and Ogdan talked about.

Winnicott believed with Ogden that to distinguish symbol from symbolized is to distinguish one's thought from that which one is thinking about, one's feeling from that which one is responding to. For symbol to stand independently of symbolized, there must be a subject engaged in the process of interpreting his perceptions. If there is a good-enough fit between mother and infant, there is no need for symbols, even of the most primitive type. Instead, there is an undisturbed state of 'going on being' that will later become the background of experience, but at present is invisible because there is nothing with which to contrast it; it is both background and foreground.

Symbols are required only when there is desire; at the stage of development being discussed, there is only need that is met – the satisfied need does not generate desire (i.e. wishing) for which symbols are required. The undisturbed, harmoniously functioning mother–infant unit may be only a hypothetical entity because of the inevitable imperfection of fit between mother and infant. The well-dosed frustration that results provides the first opportunity for awareness of separateness.

At this point, the task for the aspect of the mother that is not a part of the mother–infant unit is to make her presence (the mother as object) known in a way that is not frightening and therefore does not have to be denied or in other ways defended against by the infant. It is this period of the very earliest awareness of separateness, 'beginning at about four to six to eight to twelve months' that has been the focus of Winnicott's work on potential space. He has proposed that in order for this transition from mother–infant unity to a state in which there is mother-and-infant to be non-pathogenic, there must be a potential space between mother and infant that is always potential (never actual) because it is filled in with the state of mind that embodies the paradox that is never challenged: the infant and mother are one, and the infant and mother are two.

> To return to Miri and Saul, we are faced with a difficulty in moving past total oneness with the mother. Psychologically this situation is not uncommon, especially for couples who experience distress over time, as opposed to an occasional fight. The former describes two fused babies trying to create a union of two adults who can both care and are cared for. The difficulty for the couple therapist is that on the very basic level of thinking and perceiving, facts and fantasies are not in dialectical interaction but have hijacked the partners. They are unable to see beyond their fantasies or their idea of reality.

While this might not be such good news for the therapist it does open the door to a way of thinking that is less technique-oriented and perhaps more holistic and comprehensive. The last chapter will look at some potential areas for couple therapists to contemplate. I will also include more about the work of Richard Schwartz and his notions of the false selves and one true self that are congruent with Winnicott. The fact that one theoretician came strictly from family therapy in the 1960 and 1970s while the other came from psychoanalysis starting in the early 1940s makes their convergence that much more intriguing.

An example of self-reflection: a personal experience with rejection

As a therapist working on the level of unconscious feeling, I feel a duty to continually examine my own reactions to hurt, disappointment, and rupture. To be able to give the client couples a feeling that I have been there, I really have to have been there. This kind of self-reflexive attitude is not easy, nor is it easy to expose my own weaknesses. However, I believe that much of what Winnicott is saying is that we professionals need to be in touch with our own craziness, just as others have advised. R.D. Laing, Horney, Whitaker, Jung and Fritz Perls are only a few of the theoreticians who advocated self-analysis and awareness as a fundamental tool in therapy. It is amazing how professionals who come from very different orientations converge on this point.

> Here is a short vignette that includes my reactions to my second daughter and how I came to understand the role of increasing independence in marriage. My daughter, the third of my three children, has often triggered in me former traumas. It was therefore often hard to stay in the good enough mother position to her because I would find myself wanting mothering from her instead of giving it to her. Here is one example where self-reflection and work on my inner pain allowed me to free her from the intergenerational role of parental child.
>
> In this case I found myself very anxious prior to one of my professional trips to a new country where I knew no one. At first I completely blocked how the upcoming trip was worrying me. I had never been to this place, and was diving into cultural waters that scared me. Without awareness, we act out our fears. Thus I found myself turning to friends to come along with me.
>
> When no one could come along, instead of letting my fears come up to consciousness, I turned to my third daughter to come along. Had I not been cut off and dissociated from my fears, I would have reflected on asking her to come along. She and I had been through delicate interactions that had only recently calmed down. If I had been thinking instead of acting out feelings, I would have known that it was not a good idea either to ask her to come and a worse idea for her to actually come along. We were basically just at the end of a long period of rebellion on her part and rejection of me as a way of her differentiating herself. The last thing she would want would be a trip with Mom.
>
> Having cut off from my cognitive mind, the pain I felt hearing her say 'If I go with you it will be the breaking of the relationship' was intense and

physical. I actually felt pain in my chest and a sense of panic that did not fit the situation. A part of me (more mature and adult) could hear that she was trying to save the relationship by not going. But the child in me was stunned. Also she wouldn't talk about it and I was left holding my pain.

The pain was so intense I was shocked. It was impossible to ignore it or to continue looking for people to take the pain away. I was able to recognize a pattern I wanted to learn from. How could it be a coincidence that I felt rejected by my mother, and I rejected her. Now I experienced my own daughter as rejecting me.

The pain I then experienced when I felt rejected was incredibly intense. It was filled with shame at having been revealed as needy and then rejected for that as well. As I sat with the physical and mental pain of rejection, I went through possible routes to take to reduce the pain.

I thought about talking to my husband to try to unload the pain on him. However, he would quickly point out that he had warned me (which he had) and would probably say some version of 'I told you so'. I realized that I quite often jumped into situations that eventually end up not being good for me. I also tended to ignore my husband's warnings and then felt even more rejected when I came to him for comfort and reassurance. This usually made me feel even worse and more rejected.

I was able to see this pattern and decided to try just holding the pain without running to anyone. I did do exercise, because the pain was also very physical and I found that the exercise helped reduce the sense of anxiety and panic. It also helped me not use my usual supports for mental pain – talking with friends, seeing my therapist, and most important running to share it with my husband.

I found that over the period of one day the pain began to subside. I faced the fact that I was basically frightened of the upcoming trip and that I had blocked these feelings by trying to get people to take over and support me. 'Going it alone' began with my journey into my internal world. By not using my usual supports, I was able to handle the pain and let it turn into the fear I had been hiding from. By facing this fear, I was able to reduce the fear of traveling. The internal journey was far more difficult than the actual trip coming up.

What I have learned is to absorb the pain of rejection in a different way. I was good enough in my handling of the pain. First of all the pain was there for several hours. I had to do a repair of my own with my memories of rejection and how I reacted by going back over and over to the place of being rejected. I thought about the idea of being a good enough mother to myself. I could cancel the trip. But by facing the fear and the pain of rejection I felt an opening of a new space that did not frighten me but made me curious about why I had been so scared. This process could repair the pain of rejection.

Amazingly, as soon as I moved beyond the pain of rejection and fear, my daughter came to me with ideas she had about my trip; she had thought about ways I could make the trip less stressful, like shortening it. It seems a bit mystical, but as soon as I handled my own pain she was able to come and offer her support.

One of the teachings this self-reflection gave me was the role of not creating triangles when in a state of anxiety and stress. My usual routine would have been to go to others, especially my husband, to help me not feel so bad. Often this led to feeling worse. Handling my own feelings left me feeling both pride in myself and also a need to share the self-reflexive journey with my husband. This opened up a place of increased intimacy between us because he was proud of me as well as curious about the process.

What can go wrong in the potential space?

Ogden believed that Winnicott meant us to view the potential space as an achievement. It is indeed the place where different subjective experiences interact. He said:

> Winnicott's conception of development can be thought of as a movement from an original state of 'oneness' that is not experienced as oneness because the homogeneity of the situation precludes an appreciation of difference and, therefore, the delineation of meanings. The developmental progression, in the context of good enough mothering, is to 'three-ness' wherein there is a relationship between symbol and symbolized that is mediated by an interpreting subject. The invisible mother-infant has become a mother-and-infant as (symbolic) objects, and infant as interpreting subject. The infant as subject makes it possible for the infant to become aware of the mother's subjectivity. This then allows for the development of 'Ruth' (Winnicott, 1958), the capacity for concern for another person as a whole and separate human being capable of feelings like, not the same as, one's own. With the development of this awareness of the subjectivity of the other comes the capacity for guilt, for mourning, for empathy, for the desire to make reparations as opposed to magical restoration of the damaged object.
>
> (Ogden reading Winnicott, 2001, p. 302)

Ogden's interpretation of the failure of the dialectical process

From this perspective, the breakdown of the dialectical process generating the realm of the thing in itself can be understood as having a specific place in the development of object relations: 'two-ness' (infant and mother as objects in the absence of infant as interpreting subject) corresponds to the realm of the thing in itself. There are only objects and no subjects. This is always a product of the breakdown of three-ness (the dialectic of fantasy and reality, symbol and symbolized mediated by a subject) and not the normative progression from the invisible oneness of the original mother–infant unit.

Winnicott thus implies that he views the normal development of fantasy as being from its inception a part of a dialectical process in which fantasy creates and is created by reality. We thus need both and we need them both to interact with each other inside ourselves.

Empathy is a psychological process (as well as a form of object-relatedness) that occurs within the context of a dialectic of being and not-being the other. Within this context (Winnicott would say, 'within potential space'), one plays with the idea of being the other while knowing that one is not. It is possible to try on for size one identification and then another (i.e. to play with the feeling of being the other in different ways) because the opposite pole of the dialectic diminishes the danger of being trapped in the other and ultimately of losing oneself in the other.

Winnicott's concept of potential space might be understood as a state of mind based upon a series of dialectical relationships between fantasy and reality, me and not-me, symbol and symbolized, etc., each pole of the dialectic creating, informing, and negating the other. The achievement of such a dialectical process occurs by means of a developmental advance from the 'invisible oneness' of the mother–infant unit to the subjective 'three-ness' of the mother-and-infant (as symbolic objects) and the infant (as interpreting subject). Failure to create or maintain the dialectical process leads to specific forms of psychopathology that include the experience of the fantasy object as a thing in itself, the defensive use of reality that forecloses imagination, the relationship to a fetish object, and the state of 'non-experience'. The 'processing' of a projective identification is understood as the re-establishment of the recipient's capacity to maintain a dialectical process (e.g. of me and not-me) that had been limited in the course of the recipient's unconscious participation in the projector's externalized unconscious fantasy.

7 Countertransference in couple therapy

Winnicott's view was that the therapist must come to tolerate his own negative feelings towards patients in order to be effective. Further, the clinician's defense structure, which has so much potential for latent countertransference dislike, requires continual and vigilant self-analysis to clarify and detoxify these aggressive affects. The therapist often likes one partner more than the other and this identification shifts between sessions and even within a single session. If the therapist is having trouble expressing anger, the partner who is more comfortable with doing this may be disliked by the therapist or intimidating to the therapist. Just as in individual therapies, the therapist has countertransference feelings and reactions; the couple therapist has those feelings to each partner and to the relationship as a whole.

A therapist's countertransference feelings of anger, when unrecognized, can impede and eventually derail a treatment relationship. Left raw and unmetabolized, these countertransference aggressions can achieve the status of therapist resistances to the development of the therapeutic alliance.

Winnicott's focus in discussing countertransference was his unique ability to talk openly about hate and the central role of aggression. In Winnicott's theory, hate is paradoxically linked to interpersonal intimacy and true-self development. Winnicott viewed aggressiveness as virtually synonymous with motility and vitality.

In discussing clinician disclosure of countertransference aggression, Winnicott recommended frankness … but only at a point in treatment when the patient had progressed sufficiently to be able to synthesize it. He reasoned that the patient could only understand the therapist's affects on the basis of his awareness of his own affects seen as part of the self rather than coming from some outside figure.

In his famous paper 'Hate in the counter-transference', Winnicott (1949) wrote about his beliefs and thoughts about countertransferences. He wrote primarily about individual psychoanalysis. There is, however, much to be gained in understanding his ideas not just from the point of severe mental health disorders, but in ways that all human beings could react to the therapeutic endeavor.

> Are there not many situations in our ordinary analytic work in which the analyst's hate is justified? A patient of mine, a very bad obsessional, was almost loathsome to me for some years. I felt bad about this until the analysis

turned a corner and the patient became lovable, and then I realized that his unlikableness had been an active symptom, unconsciously determined. It was indeed a wonderful day for me (much later on) when I could actually tell the patient that I and his friends had felt repelled by him, but that he had been too ill for us to let him know. This was also an important day for him, a tremendous advance in his adjustment to reality.

During the Second World War a boy of nine came to a hostel for evacuated children, sent from London not because of bombs but because of truancy. I hoped to give him some treatment during his stay in the hostel, but his symptom won and he ran away as he had always done from everywhere since the age of six when he first ran away from home. However, I had established contact with him in one interview in which I could see and interpret through a drawing of his that in running away he was unconsciously saving the inside of his home and preserving his mother from assault, as well as trying to get away from his own inner world which was full of persecutors.

I was not very surprised when he turned up in the police station very near my home. This was one of the few police stations that did not know him intimately. My wife very generously took him in and kept him for three months, three months of hell. He was the most lovable and most maddening of children, often stark staring mad. But fortunately we knew what to expect. We dealt with the first phase by giving him complete freedom and a shilling whenever he went out. He had only to ring up and we fetched him from whatever police station had taken charge of him.

Soon the expected change-over occurred, the truancy symptom turned round, and the boy started dramatizing the assault on the inside. It was really a whole-time job for the two of us together, and when I was out the worst episodes took place.

The important thing for the purpose of this paper is the way in which the evolution of the boy's personality engendered hate in me, and what I did about it. Did I hit him? The answer is no, I never hit. But I should have had to have done so if I had not known all about my hate and if I had not let him know about it too. At crises I would take him by bodily strength, and without anger or blame, and put him outside the front door, whatever the weather or the time of day or night. There was a special bell he could ring, and he knew that if he rang it he would be readmitted and no word said about the past. He used this bell as soon as he had recovered from his maniacal attack.

The important thing is that each time, just as I put him outside the door, I told him something; I said that what had happened had made me hate him. This was easy because it was so true.

I think these words were important from the point of view of his progress, but they were mainly important in enabling me to tolerate the situation without letting out, without losing my temper and every now and again murdering him.

(1949, p. 70)

A mother's love and hate

Winnicott suggested that the mother hates the baby before the baby hates the mother, and before the baby can know his mother hates him.

> The mother, however, hates her infant from the word go…
> We know about a mother's love and we appreciate its reality and power. Let me give some of the reasons why a mother hates her baby, even a boy:
> A. The baby is not her own (mental) conception.
> B. The baby is not the one of childhood play, father's child, brother's child, etc.
> C. The baby is not magically produced.
> D. The baby is a danger to her body in pregnancy and at birth.
> E. The baby is an interference with her private life, a challenge to preoccupation.
> F. To a greater or lesser extent a mother feels that her own mother demands a baby, so that her baby is produced to placate her mother.
> G. The baby hurts her nipples even by suckling, which is at first a chewing activity.
> H. He is ruthless, treats her as scum, an unpaid servant, a slave.
> I. She has to love him, excretions and all, at any rate at the beginning, till he has doubts about himself.
> J. He tries to hurt her, periodically bites her, all in love.
> K. He shows disillusionment about her.
> L. His excited love is cupboard love, so that having got what he wants he throws her away like orange peel.
> M. The baby at first must dominate, he must be protected from coincidences, life must unfold at the baby's rate and all this needs his mother's continuous and detailed study. For instance, she must not be anxious when holding him, etc.
> N. At first he does not know at all what she does or what she sacrifices for him. Especially he cannot allow for her hate.
> O. He is suspicious, refuses her good food, and makes her doubt herself, but eats well with his aunt.
> P. After an awful morning with him she goes out, and he smiles at a stranger, who says: 'Isn't he sweet!'
> Q. If she fails him at the start she knows he will pay her out for ever.
> R. He excites her but frustrates – she mustn't eat him or trade in sex with him.
> (Winnicott, 1949)

A mother has to be able to tolerate hating her baby without doing anything about it. She cannot express it to him. If, for fear of what she may do, she cannot hate appropriately when hurt by her child, she must fall back on masochism, and I think it is this that gives rise to the false theory of a natural masochism in women. The most remarkable thing about a mother is her ability to be hurt so much by her baby and to hate so much without paying the child out, and her ability to wait for rewards that may or may not come at a later date.

Perhaps she is helped by some of the nursery rhymes she sings, which her baby enjoys but fortunately does not understand?

'Rockabye Baby, on the tree top,
When the wind blows the cradle will rock,
When the bough breaks the cradle will fall,
Down will come baby, cradle and all.'

I think of a mother (or father) playing with a small infant; the infant enjoying the play and not knowing that the parent is expressing hate in the words, perhaps in birth symbolism. This is not a sentimental rhyme. Sentimentality is useless for parents, as it contains a denial of hate, and sentimentality in a mother is no good at all from the infant's point of view.

(Philips, 1988, p. 89–90)

Coping with intense negative feelings in couple therapy

I would propose that experiencing and tolerating negative feelings and reactions from the couple (anger, aggression, rage, hate, revenge, envy, and indifference) is the most challenging aspect of couple therapy. Dealing with the couple's aggression and anger was the most common difficulty mentioned around the globe by the couple therapists I interviewed. The therapist may be exposed to a high level of conflict and often aggression, rage, and hate. They are exposed to lack of congruent communication when there are secrets. They are exposed to grief and loss when an affair is revealed. And partners who withdraw and 'stonewall' (Gottman & Silver, 2012) each other are usually sitting on a powder keg of negative emotions that they are scared to express.

This is very similar to the dilemmas of the good enough mother. Infants' moods and behaviors change very quickly and abruptly. A gentle moment with the infant cuddling in the mother's arms can suddenly move into the crying of a wet or hungry infant who is pushing the mother away or even hitting her. The good enough mother has to adapt quickly to these volatile shifts and move with her child.

Similarly the therapist can easily feel a loss of the holding environment when there are sudden outbursts of crying, shouting, using abusive language, moving irritably in the chair. The fact is that the good enough therapist is (like the good enough mother) willing and able to go with the shifts and change modes when needed. Negative feelings are threatening to a therapist who wants to make everything nice. But to a therapist who is concerned with holding, ruptures, and repairs, these shifts are opportunities to go with the process and thereby strengthen the bond between the therapist and the couple. As these negative emotions become the path towards increasing closeness and intimacy, the couple also learns not to fear them but to use them.

Oedipal dilemmas

Another source of stress for couple therapists is the way couple therapy enacts the Oedipal dilemma. Specifically the therapist, who is supposed to lead sessions, can often feel like a child left out of parental interactions, or used by one parent to hurt the other. The therapist may unconsciously want to get rid of one of the partners to have the other to him/herself. When the therapist has such residual emotions left over from childhood, they may unconsciously be enacted in therapy.

If the therapist was placed in the parental role of caretaking one or both parents instead of being allowed to enjoy the child role, all kinds of feeling arise when (again) the therapist is in the parental role (and now paid for it). I propose that many therapists chose to become therapists out of having played the parental role as a child. The current choice of profession is both a way of staying fixated in that unhealthy position, but also an attempt to overcome it.

Using countertransference in couple therapy

Winnicott was correct in placing so much importance on the rupture–repair interactions leading to increased independence of the child and renewed faith in the mother. If this function is really the crux of change, we need to pay tribute to the importance of working on therapist countertransference. These reactions are places where we will probably need to do repair work if we are alert and aware of our feelings. If countertransference is viewed as a negative event that should be reduced, we lose its potential for healing.

The contemporary understanding of countertransference is generally to regard countertransference as a jointly created phenomenon between the therapist and the patient. The patient pressures the therapist through transference into playing a role congruent with the patient's internal world. However, the specific dimensions of that role are colored by therapists' own personality. Countertransference can be a therapeutic tool when examined by the therapist to sort out who is doing what, and the meaning behind those interpersonal roles. Using Winnicott's emphasis on rupture and repair, we can view countertransference as a chance to see the intersection of the therapist's personal issues with the couple's issues. This creates the potential for growth and development for all people involved.

Countertransference towards the couples includes feelings of hatred to one of the partners or to the relationship as a whole. Here is a case that demonstrates the common dilemma for the self of the therapist, who initially sides with one partner rather than the other. The feelings of the therapist are central in working through countertransference and hate is one of the primary emotions that needs to be recognized and utilized. This case was originally cited by Barth (2012), but has been extended to include feelings of hate.

Barb and Henry had been married for four years. They had one child and were expecting a second. Tensions had been rising since they found out that Barb was pregnant again, but when Henry suggested that his mother come to stay with them after the baby was born, Barb hit the roof. This was the central theme of their first session. 'The woman hates me', Barb said. 'Why in the world would I want her in the house when I'm feeling vulnerable – which is how I'll feel after the baby comes.'

Henry disagreed. 'Mom just thinks you're a little hard on Jake', he said. 'And she doesn't understand mothers who work. But that's just because she didn't work when we were kids. She's old fashioned. But she doesn't hate you.'

Barb laughed bitterly. 'You're her baby. She thinks the sun rises and sets in you. And she hates me for taking you away from her. She would love nothing better than to turn Jake and you against me.'

As I listened, I found myself thinking that Barb sounded paranoid and Henry seemed to be presenting a reasonable concern. I wondered what he saw in her, and why she couldn't hear that Henry seemed to love both her and his mother. I did not feel hatred towards Barb, but I had fantasies about her that seemed to reflect hatred. I fantasized that Henry left her, and that he found someone who could accept his loving feelings towards his mother. I also had a fantasy that she was diagnosed as a paranoid schizophrenic and hospitalized.

I was reminded of my own problems with my mother-in-law and how this issue seriously interfered with my marriage. I felt that Barb was actually lucky compared to what I had to put up with and I found myself feeling jealous. In my home life the problems resulted in years of cut-off between me and my mother-in-law. I noticed that the couple was doing better than I had because there was no cut-off and the conflict was open and on the table.

I felt bad that I had let myself go so far in hating my mother-in-law and also experienced anger at my husband, who did not fight me about this issue but let the chasm develop over years. These thoughts brought me back to the couple from a different place. I realized that I was not neutral to Barb because I had myself acted out some of my hatred for my mother-in-law and now felt guilty about it.

I have learned over the years that when I find myself taking one side against the other, I am always missing something important. Couple therapist Carla Leone (2008) writes that one way to avoid this trap is to 'listen from within the couple'.

What she means is that to help a couple, a therapist has to recognize that both partners have lost something in the relationship and both are looking to the therapist to help them get it back. Leone, who applies self-psychology to couple therapy, says that the problem is often that the very person who once made us feel good about ourselves is now making us feel worse. This idea seems to parallel much of Winnicott's writings, which emphasize the importance of previous experiences and emotions lost and needing to be retrieved. The work for a therapist is to help the couple retrieve the understanding and support, and the sense of belonging that makes it possible for a couple to stay and grow together.

As I listened to Barb and Henry argue about Henry's mother, I realized that both of them were longing to be recognized as good, caring, and sensitive people. I imagined that interwoven in their struggle was Barb's wish that Henry could see her as a good mother and a kind woman, and Henry's wish that Barb could recognize his mother's importance to him. Often these wishes reflect old wounds and unmet needs from childhood.

Barb, it turned out, was the oldest of three. She felt that her mother favored her younger brother and often sided with him against her, and, she said, it felt like she was in exactly the same situation with Henry and his mother. 'It's not fair', she said in a whiny, little-girl voice. I nodded my understanding and said that I could see that she felt that once again she was being treated as the outsider, the bad one. I asked her if at times she felt angry at her mother. She said that she was very angry. I said that sometimes this anger hides a very human feeling of hatred, which we try to deny.

I realized as I said this that I had been feeling like the bad one for years. I had lots of feelings of hatred and then guilt about that. Just talking about it with her made me more accepting of my own hatred for my mother-in-law. Helping her helped me as well ... She relaxed visibly in front of me. It seemed that just having those feelings recognized helped both of us.

Henry jumped in to defend his mother. I held up a hand. 'Tell me about your relationship with her', I said. 'Have you always been very close?' He shook his head sadly. He was also the oldest child. His younger brother had been born with a disability, and had required most of his parents' attention. He had been a helper all of his life – it had been his personality, but it had also been the way he got his needs met. 'I got lots of reinforcement for being such a good big brother.'

As a teen, Henry had rebelled. I asked what he had felt when he rebelled and he said angry. I added 'and I suppose you also felt you hated her ... but then maybe you felt guilty about that?' He was very thoughtful and quiet, listening to new ideas. He was especially aware of the guilt, but had not realized it came from having hateful feelings. But then his mother discovered that his father had been having a long-term affair with another woman and immediately sued for divorce. Henry was furious with his father. 'She was so badly hurt', he said of his mother.

I nodded again. 'So you naturally became protective of her.' He sighed, nodded, and relaxed back into his chair for the first time.

Couples communicate with their bodies as much as with their words. Marriage and family therapist Francine Lapides (2010) has written about the importance of recent neuropsychological research to work with these nonverbal communications. Couple therapy, she says, is about re-wiring brains by helping both partners get their needs understood and admired, and love met.

For both Leone and Lapides, the work of a couple therapist is to recognize and reflect these needs in both members of a couple. But since these feelings are often buried under layers of hatred, anger, and pain, a couple therapist has to find ways to help both clients manage a variety of 'hot' emotions. The therapist is aware that beneath much of our negative feelings of guilt, anger, aggression, and rage lies a more primitive hatred that has been denied for years.

Leone encourages therapists to try to find ways to reflect both partners' 'subjective' or personal experience so that each partner gets a sense of being heard and understood, by the therapist at least, if not always by the other member of the couple. From within this 'holding' space, a couple can begin to explore some of the underlying issues that contribute to the relationship problems.

For Barb, Henry's protection of his mother felt like a repetition of her painful childhood experience. When she heard what he had to say about his own early experiences, she said quietly, 'You know, I think one of the reasons I fell in love with you was that you were so thoughtful and careful with me. I felt that you would be able to take care of things. But now I see that you also need me to take care of you!' As they spoke more about this insight, Henry said in a very low voice, 'Being nice to my mother is taking care of me. I need you more than I've ever needed anyone. But I can't lose her.'

As we untangled many different pieces of their struggle, it became clearer that Henry carried with him a fear that his mother could jettison him, just as she had his father. He also admitted to having feelings of hatred toward her because he felt she had ruined his father's life. He also feared that Barb would do the same. Obviously, these fears made it difficult for him to allow himself to be dependent on his wife. Barb, on the other hand, fearful that she was once again being left out, had been unable to provide Henry with the support that she had given him earlier in their marriage.

None of these things simply untangle themselves; but often when both members of a couple feel that their subjective experience has been acknowledged and understood, the knots begin to loosen and the therapeutic work goes forward. I have found that I can locate hatred when I examine my own fantasies. If I am glad that a client calls in sick, I wonder about my own hatred and who really is the target of all that. It is as if hatred can be a trailhead for examining our own countertransference.

The idea of hate in the countertransference highlights the importance of the therapist working towards being a true self within the responsibility and boundaries of the professional relationship. His paper on hate in the countertransference (Winnicott, 1949) not only created a stir when he presented it, but has continued to be cited, often in many different contexts. My hunch is that his use of the word hatred was meant to jolt us out of our complacency. If he had just talked about anger, we would all nod our heads and say to ourself 'Of course I feel anger sometimes'. But hate? It is impossible to recognize our hate without going deeper into our own true selves. We are left with profound questions: how can we help others be real when we are hiding behind our own false-self professional role? How can we be real in therapy while also maintaining the necessary boundaries?

In reflecting on the case above, the potential space that allowed both partners to begin to process their conflict is crucial. The therapist makes it clear that each partner needs to be heard and understood. What does the therapist need to do and feel in order to create a space of holding two divergent stories? A potential space is the interweaving of all the stories in a whole that becomes something new. It goes way beyond listening well.

Reflect on some essential ideas that we can apply from Winnicott's study of the infant/mother bond:

- The child will develop a healthy false self, depending on the quality of early care from the good-enough mother. Otherwise it will develop an unhealthy false self.
- Initially, the care taker role is to support the illusion of a fused, undifferentiated unity.

- The care taker then gradually and carefully allows disillusionment where the child realizes its (and its care taker's) individuality.
- This separation happens through play and use of a transition object.

Assuming that the good enough couple therapist is thinking developmentally when listening to each person, a process paralleling the growth and development of the infant (relationship) can occur. Partners come to therapy presenting false selves. These selves are their defenses developed throughout a lifetime of interaction first with parents and then friends and partners.

Usually these false selves were helpful at one point in life. They fit the view of a child towards an environment that they felt they had no power over. And indeed a small child does not have the mental and emotional equipment to challenge old defenses. However, as adults these false selves became unnecessary and harmful, especially in intimate relationships. These false selves are often victim roles without a sense of self-determination or independence.

In the example given above, Barb felt like an outsider in her own childhood home and developed a defensive false self that was constantly checking if she was loved and was being included. She always found situations she was looking for, such as feeling left out of Henry's relationship with his mother. As a child, Henry was forced into a parental role that made him care-take his mother rather than focus on his own growth. The false self was a caretaker who did not know how to make boundaries. In interaction with Barb, he experienced the helplessness of the false self. It is true for him that he has no choice about how to react to his mother.

The couple therapist must do more than listen. The therapist is like the good enough mother caretaker. Initially, the caretaker role is to support the illusion of a fused, undifferentiated unity with the mother. The therapist has to create a potential space in the therapy that completely accepts the false selves' versions of reality. In other words, the experiences of the false selves have to be validated as true and real at the time they were used as defenses. This takes time, focus, and patience. Many questions are asked about how these experiences played out in different areas of each partner's life. This process has to take place for both partners.

There needs to be time invested in helping the partners do this kind of fusion with the false selves of their own life and their partner's life. These stories are always about how badly the child was treated by someone else. They are not empowering stories and do not show a more mature view that takes responsibility for what happened. These false-self stories are of being a victim as a child to more powerful adults.

The stage of disillusionment with the false selves' stories can only come through beginning to separate from these old stories. After being held without doubt and disbelief by the therapist, these old victim stories make way for new empowered stories from the true self. Instead of seeing the self as victim, there is an often gradual transformation to a more mature real self that can take responsibility for one's life.

The therapist invites the couple to play with new ways of thinking and being, ways that allow for choices and a sense of personal power. The therapist is in the role of transitionary object because there needs to be a holding of the old relationship and glimpses shown of the new relationship. Gradually each partner becomes more able to show their true selves and recognize the true self of the other. The therapist encourages this by asking questions about the true selves of the partners and the kind of relationship they might have when the true selves are leading. For example:

Barb was fused with a false-self defense of constantly checking whether she was wanted or not. Henry was fused with his false self who was on the lookout for someone needing his care. The relationship that had developed was filled with anxiety on the part of Barb and a sense of burden without thanks on the part of Henry.

If the couple therapist aims to fuse with both false selves, time and attention needs to be paid to all the many ways each partner's life and their relationship were affected by these different false selves. The relationship was often filled with stress and tension as each partner felt the underlying anxiety and anger living in their false-self roles. Barb checked if she was desired and wanted in a myriad of situations. This resulted in many cases where she saw rejection and felt wounded and hurt. Henry jumped in to help with no regard to his own needs and this resulted in anger on his part as well as feeling helpless. The relationship was in a state of hyper-alertness to each partner's particular sensitivity.

The couple therapist needs to be able to grasp these false-self dilemmas and hold them both at the same time. As this becomes internalized, there is a transformation that can occur if the therapist is willing and able to notice and hold the change. In the case of Barb and Henry, after many sessions of exploring each one's false-self reactions and interactions, new material made its way into the session. For example, Barb said at one point, 'I don't know why it is so hard to feel accepted and wanted ... there really are so many people who love me.' Henry said at another point, 'I don't understand why I keep jumping in to rescue people, especially my mother. There is plenty of evidence that they can manage on their own. And there is also a high price I am paying.'

The couple therapist who works through these transformative changes tries to be there when the change is expressed. For example, to Barb the therapist asked about those people who love her and what they see in her that allows that to happen. To Henry the therapist wondered aloud if perhaps letting those people who can manage alone do it, was a way of showing faith and caring towards them.

However, the therapist is good enough and not perfect. The therapist lets the new baby relationship down. This is to be expected and allows for the important repair function to occur. For example, while the therapist caught and reflected back many of the transformational changes occurring in the partners and their relationship, there were also times of missed important statements. Often the therapist was 'off the mark' when tired, at the end of the day, or towards the last moments of the therapy hour.

For example, the couple got up to leave the last session before a two-week break for the holidays. The therapist was planning a vacation and was feeling guilty about leaving the couple when they were just beginning to express their true and real selves and were making real progress. But in the rush of leaving, that feeling was ignored. At the door Barb said, 'I am amazed how much I feel about you leaving us. It is just like I used to feel – unwanted – in my family, and now suddenly I see that I am doing it with you. I mean, you have a right to have a vacation. It is only two weeks!' The therapist smiled and simply ignored this statement, whereas if she had been paying more attention she would have accepted the feelings of being unwanted as natural and perhaps also mention that the fact that Barb could both see this and say it was a step towards change.

Barb and Henry canceled two meetings after the holidays. Only when they finally showed up was the therapist able to replay that last scene and hold the pain that was being expressed. She was able to apologize for her lapse and mentioned that she had been feeling bad about leaving them when they were doing such a lot of work on themselves. She was forgiven and they moved on, actually making larger steps towards mature interactions than before.

An example of my own countertransference

A couple in their early sixties came for couple therapy after the wife had left home. I had seen her alone for several months and she had decided to return home, but only if her husband agreed to work on their relationship. Previously he had rejected her requests for couple therapy. But after she left, he had been seriously shocked and wounded by her actions. He was a public figure who commanded a great deal of respect. He perceived her going out, renting an apartment, and leaving him to cope as showing disrespect for him. He was humiliated by her action, afraid of a public uncovering of his personal life, and was seriously scared of losing her after what he had seen as a good marriage of 40 years. The couple's four grown-up children all took his side and were furious at her for making such a unilateral move. They were a family where major decisions were made together with all the family members. Her striking out on her own was no doubt both an insulting and a fearful move.

The case was complicated for me from the start. I had seen her for many sessions and already had an alliance with her. I had suggested they see another couple therapist because of that, but neither were willing and I agreed to give it a try. Perhaps that was the beginning of strong countertransferential feelings in which I felt prejudiced towards her. I had after all heard all her stories about his neglecting her over decades in favor of his work life. I knew a lot about her anger and nothing about his.

As mentioned earlier in the book, I was often flattered by being seen as a magician and in this case the compliment of such a high-status public figure wanting therapy with me was even more gratifying. I felt that I had a high stake in making sure that they stayed together. While she still had many grievances against him, she wanted to keep the family together.

I was aware of my role in my own family as oldest daughter close to my father. I did not consciously know that my job was to keep the family together. I only had the following facts – my parents were together for 7 years before deciding to have their first child. Before my mother got pregnant, both she and my father begged their own parents to let them get divorced. They were both told in no uncertain fashion that it would kill each of their mothers. So I was born. The other fact adding to my conclusion that I was the glue that kept them together was that my father left home when I went off to college. So my conclusion was that I had a powerful role in keeping my father from leaving and that my own coming into this world was a last ditch attempt by a couple who wished to separate.

Back to the couple in treatment, I felt a great deal of pressure to succeed in this case. It affected me in the tension I felt before each session. It affected my reactions when the husband had to cancel because of an important meeting at work. I reacted with anger and even disgust. I thought he was setting himself up to being left again and I would be blamed. I was aware that I was very worried about his being his old egocentric self and that she would have to leave permanently (which she did not want to do).

It turned out that the wife's feelings were very similar to mine all the way along. She felt pressure to succeed in the therapy so she wouldn't have to leave again. Her own children were clear that they sided with him and would cut-off from her if she left again. She was furious when he missed meetings, but was afraid to rock the boat and cause him to be angry. For me, our fear of his anger was much like my own fears of my father's anger. He had been so unhappy during his married life that he had taken his frustration out on all of us. He could be tyrannical and hit all of us impulsively when he felt bad. So for me anger was a problem feeling, one that could be dangerous.

Because of my exposure to Winnicott, I was able to access feelings of hatred towards my father. He had abused his powerful position in the family, could be a bully, and was never remorseful. My mother for her own reasons did not stand up to him. I came to see that she had been afraid of his anger all their married life.

It was possible here to see a pattern of women fearing the hate they experience towards a powerful man. I, my mother, and the wife in this couple had a lot to learn about standing up for ourselves to a powerful man. Hatred is key to accessing repressed rage, frustration, and aggression. Working on myself and my own hatred towards my father and to my mother, I was able to locate a connection with the man. Before that, I had taken the wife's side without questioning.

I asked to see the husband alone a few times. During these sessions I was able to create a new relationship with him. I learned about his early life and deep commitment to public service. I learned that he often tried to be there for his wife, but she was worried it would harm his career and he would blame her. She often rejected his attempts to give her more personal time.

These separate sessions were crucial in creating a therapeutic alliance with this formidable and famous man. I found that being able to work alone with someone like him made me feel strong and reliable. Facing my hatred was crucial in helping me access my fear of aggression and anger towards a powerful man. I was freed up to work without the baggage from my own past.

It turned out in couple work later that she admitted to her own role in encouraging him to think about his career more than about her. She felt guilty taking him away from his important public role because she also came from a background that highly valued public service. We finally started talking openly about dealing with anger and aggression. It turned out that both partners were quite afraid of anger and aggression. They had fantasies of anger getting out of hand and imagining that the press would find out and this would ruin the family.

Only after directly talking about hatred, rage, and anger, they finally revealed a family secret. The husband had violent temper tantrums in which he lashed out or cut-off for days. Neither of them seemed to know what to do about their mutual fear of aggression. Both of them colluded in hiding these events from their children and extended family. Sometimes he made up excuses as to why he could not attend a family event. He always had his career to fall back on, saying that people higher up needed him. But the real story only came out in therapy, which was that he was recovering from his own temper tantrums, which could take him days to calm down from.

We all learned something about coping with hatred and anger. We were able to do it by naming the problem and by my open discussion of my own fearful feelings about anger. I told them that I had experienced a childhood with abuse. I found them to be extremely generous (as they were in their public lives) to me and they helped me to also deal better with anger by their doing it first. I never shared my family story specifically with them, but let them know that they were dealing with a vulnerable human being who had her own issues around hate and anger.

They felt very good about therapy because it was the first time in their lives they had talked directly about powerful negative feelings. The pattern of denial was deeply entrenched in their lives. The wife had once gone on a trip with him and his entire office, hiking in the country. She did not feel well, but insisted on going on. It turned out she had had a heart attack and her heart was damaged by not getting treatment in time.

We ended the therapy when it was clear they could deal with issues without her having to get sick or leave home. For me it was a healing of my own fears of anger by coping well with a figure who reminded me so much of my own father and his rages.

8 The self of the therapist

In the last decade a wealth of literature on the therapist's use of self in therapy has been produced. Therapy methods have moved away from the idea that therapy is made up of standardized tools used in the same way by every therapist. Increasingly, the subjective experience of the therapist and the differences between therapists in personality, race, gender, and ethnicity have all been part of a push to see the therapist's self as part of the therapy procuress. The post-modern perspective has raised therapists' awareness of their own construction of therapy and the idea today is that the therapist's self is always in interaction in the therapy process. Also, with regard to couple therapy, the renewal of interest in the individual partner's own attachment and object-relations has led to renewed thinking about the therapist's self in couple therapy.

Tester gave us this definition of the therapist's use of self:

> Use of self is the active and purposeful use of the personal aspect of the (family) therapist to further the aims of therapy.
>
> (Tester, 1992, p. 53)

The use of the self in therapy can be traced back to Freud, who insisted upon a 'training analysis' for all aspiring psychoanalysts to rid their psyches of any wish-defense complexes or neurotic anxieties that might interfere with the analytic process.

Winnicott believed in a real encounter between the therapist and the client/patient. He was loath to give directions as to how to do therapy. He was more interested in how to be therapeutic. Winnicott shares a great deal with Martin Buber and his ideas about I–Thou relationships (Buber, 1970). Winnicott as a psychoanalyst went through several analyses of his own, over decades, with different analysts. He also was actively engaged in self-analysis. He saw many of his ideas as linked to his own childhood as a child of a depressed mother.

Winnicott's basic claim about good enough mothering/therapy was the ability of the mother/therapist to gradually demand more from the infant by a trial-and-error process. Through maternal preoccupation, the mother intuitively knows how much stimulation or reduction of stimulation her baby needs. The therapist is seen as being in a state of 'reverie' similar to the mother's preoccupation.

Bion's concept of maternal 'reverie' as the capacity to sense (and make sense of) what is going on inside the infant has been an important element in post-Kleinian thought: reverie is an act of faith in unconscious process. It is considered the equivalent of Stern's attunement, or Winnicott's maternal preoccupation. In therapy, the analyst's use of 'reverie' is an important tool in his/her response to the patient's material: it is this capacity for playing with a patient's images that Bion and Winnicott encouraged.

In the positional space created, there will be unconscious communication. The good enough mother/therapist will make some mistakes. Sometimes the unconscious creates links between therapist and patient or between couples and therapist or partners with each other. These 'ruptures' in lack of attunement need to be repaired. It is this process of mistakes and their repair that allows the child/client to develop at a pace that ultimately includes increasing independence with increasing trust on the mother/therapist. Without mistakes by the self of the mother and of the therapist, the child/patient/couple are denied the opportunity to experience the repair process. Winnicott placed a great deal of credit on this rupture/repair process for creating change. Thus paradoxically Winnicott is proposing that good enough in a relationship which then takes on the repair function is actually far better than perfect.

Use of the self of therapist in family and couple therapy

The literature on the use of the self in couple and family therapy indicates three distinct ways to make the self of the therapist prominent in treatment. One of these is helping therapists to know their own biases but to refrain from imposing them in therapy through self-awareness. Another mode of the use of self involves therapists tapping into their own life experiences as resources for increased compassion: it is the self of the therapist that constitutes the heart of the matter. This trend goes along with the idea of self-disclosure and there is an entire literature about when, what, how, and with whom to use self-disclosure.

Another way of looking at the self is to be aware how one's self is defined, constrained, or empowered by using different methods of treatment. Below is an example of a training method that attempts to heighten the trainees' understanding of the fluid nature of the self of the therapist, as well as how theoretical orientations bring out different kinds of selves. These and other training recommendations attempt to sensitize the budding therapist to the many ways in which the therapists' selves become part of the therapeutic process. Most of the professional literature attempts to increase therapist control over issues related to the self.

There are many methods available for increasing therapist self-awareness. Doing their own genogram is one excellent method. Individual therapy has an important role to play. A supportive supervision group in which safety has been established and honesty will not result in sanctions can help a lot in moving forward to more insight. Also training can be devised to amplify the issue of the self of the therapist. Different methods and theories bring forth and construct different aspects of the individual. In these training methods the idea is to help trainees see how different models bring out different aspects of their selves and how they have a choice with regard to what aspect of self they want to express. The didactic aspect includes a brief review of three models of therapy: structural, narrative, and collaborative. Grounding in these approaches was assumed, but further clarification and comparison was offered with a recap of theory of change, the skills and observable practice of each model. The following is a training tool recommended in 'Therapeutic Groundhog Day – exploring the impact of the theory/approach of the self of the therapist' (Boston, 2007).

> The students were divided into groups. Nine trainees were cast as the same three member families: two parents and an adolescent. The players were given character details, presenting problem, and time to 'flesh out' the referred family. The remaining trainees were divided into three teams, including therapists, coaches and observers. Each team picked two of the three models on offer and defined two skills within that way of working which they intended to practice. The therapist was also told that she could stop the role play periodically to seek consultation from the coach. Each family met with a team of two therapists, a coach and observers. Each therapist had a fifteen-minute turn at interviewing and trying out the preselected skill. Then there was brief feedback to the therapist before the coffee break, after which the same family members reconvened to repeat the first session with the therapist now having adopted another model and set of techniques. The 'groundhog' element comprised the opportunity to hold constant the same characters and events – differences being in approach and technique.
>
> Participants spoke from role position. The 'family' commented on what was more or less helpful, how it affected the relationship with the therapist and what impact the versions had on the hypothetical family. The therapists evaluated their ability to use each technique, how it fit for them, what they would do differently, and what they observed about themselves in each version. Coaches and observers also commented on the impact of different approaches on the interview and family, the gaps between intentions and implementation, and emphasized aspects of learning and skill. The final group discussion highlighted several significant aspects. They were concerned about moving from the expert to non-expert position. They became acutely aware of how they had been affected and had shaped themselves physically, emotionally and cognitively in relation to the models. The rapid juxtaposition of the different selves was a personal experience, confirming that theory influences self.
>
> (2007, p. 340)

Self and differences

Another issue in the literature about the self of the therapist highlights social differences and handling them well. The aspect of restraint is mentioned in the literature on gender, ethnicity, sexual orientation, race, and other social-demographic differences. By becoming aware of one's own taken-for-granted beliefs and assumptions, the therapist can be on the alert for how these assumptions might be limiting in therapy. Hare-Mustin and Marecek (1987) wrote about 'alpha and beta' biases with regard to gender biases.

Some work in feminist psychology has suggested that male–female differences are not as universal, dramatic, or enduring as has been previously asserted. Feminist psychodynamic theories, in contrast, assert that there are deep-seated and enduring differences between women and men in 'self-structure' and relational capacities. Proponents of these theories view gender differences as universal, highly dichotomized, and enduring. Using constructivism as a conceptual framework, gender theories can be considered as representations that either exaggerate or minimize male–female differences. The tendency to exaggerate differences is called 'alpha bias', and the tendency to minimize differences is called 'beta bias'. Alpha bias can be seen in psychodynamic theories, Parson's sex role theory, and in feminist psychodynamic theories. Beta bias can be seen in psychological research on men that is incorrectly generalized to women, in theories that view male and female roles as complementary, in some systems approaches to family therapy, and in recent social policies. All current representations of gender involve alpha and beta bias. The constructivist view holds that the true nature of gender is undividable. Theories are thus evaluated not by correctness but by utility, by examining how representations of gender have been used to provide the symbols and to support the scientific and sociopolitical aims of either the status quo or feminism.

Self-awareness about gender, sexual orientation, ethnicity, race, class, and other differences between people can be used to further therapy. For example, a Western-trained psychotherapist working with a Muslim couple in Istanbul has to keep her feminist ideas to herself and try to understand the more patriarchal stance of both partners in therapy.

The most common mistake is to make assumptions that ignore differences. Rather than ignore differences, we can use them in therapy. I have often used the fact that I was born in New York but am now working in Tel Aviv to give me permission to ask questions that might seem self-evident to a native. I can ask about how an issue (i.e. affairs, homosexuality, travel alone) is usually viewed in the culture I adopted. Opening up the issue of differences (between me and them, and then between the couple) is one way of making communication clearer and more open.

The danger of ignoring differences is greater for those therapists who occupy the dominant higher status in the culture. There is a kind of 'difference blindness' in those who make assumptions because of their entitled position. For example:

I was supervising a group of seven master's-level family and couple therapists. I saw this group once a week for an academic year. The group was all female. Out of the seven women, one was 'Sephardic', meaning coming from an ethnic background of Arab-speaking countries (Libya, Morocco, Algeria, etc.). The other six training therapists were of Ashkenazi ethnic background, coming from Western cultures. Israel is a melting pot of cultures with contradictions about differences. On the one hand it is not considered to be polite to point out a person's ethnic background. This is especially true when the person was born in Israel but of either Sephardic or Ashkenazi parents. Such a person is considered to be Israeli, despite the statistics showing gaps in educational level, income, status at work etc. for the two different ethnic groups. On the other hand, the status gap between the two ethnic groups is mirrored by different accents when talking Hebrew and darker colored skin.

As a supervisor of Ashkenazi-dominant cultural background, I never mentioned the differences between the one Sephardic student and the others. Only on the last day, which we spent evaluating the experience, did I suddenly (intuitively) ask the one Sephardic student if she ever felt different. I could see the other students recoil at my social ineptitude and blunder. But the student surprised us all by saying 'I never forget my difference. My accent is different, my skin color is different. I don't speak up freely; I am more a watcher so as not to be noticed. I stopped myself sometimes from offering an idea that later on someone else offered. I was angry at myself, but I never questioned that I need to be more careful.'

The other students and I were astonished that such a block in free expression had gone unnoticed for months. Had I not had a sudden intuitive need to break the social norms, we would never have known about her reticence and hesitation. Sometimes when I tell other students about this event, they cannot believe that such a thing really happened.

The differences between people can be used as a resource for understanding low self-esteem and acting out cultural stereotypes. The literature on the topic of the self of the couple therapist mentions that being aware of life experience can make the therapist more compassionate to issues related to all kinds of 'isms': sexism, racism, ageism, etc.

Life experiences enable one to work on deeper levels with greater identification of the feelings involved. A personal experience can blind a therapist as well as help the therapist understand better.

The self of the therapist in good enough therapy

For Winnicott, the idea of a true and false self means that the therapist has to be aware of their own false selves and have access to their true self. This is no small undertaking. Self-reflection on the part of the therapist is important in so many ways. In the previous discussion of countertransference it is clear that the couple therapist will have a hard time being neutral and not taking sides if the therapist's own issues are not dealt with.

For Winnicott (1965a), in the false self, other people's expectations can become of overriding importance, overlaying or contradicting the original sense of self, the one connected to the very roots of one's being. Winnicott thought that such an extreme kind of false self began to develop in very early infancy, as a defense against an environment that felt unsafe or overwhelming because of a lack of reasonably attuned care-giving. Winnicott used the term 'good enough' to refer to what he thought of as optimal parenting; he thought that babies need parents who are usually emotionally attuned and able to empathize with the baby, but not perfectly so. The danger is that 'through this False Self, the infant builds up a false set of relationships' which are incorporated instead of real ones. Such a child has a False Self that functions to prevent former trauma in any further relationships. Winnicott expects the reader to deal with his paradoxical thinking – the false self is compliancy to the environment and thus a negative thing. But the false self is also positive by protecting the real self.

The False Self in its pathological guise prevents and inhibits what Winnicott calls the 'spontaneous gesture' of the True Self. Compliance and imitation are the costly outcomes.

Winnicott was on one hand very open about the emotional baggage therapists bring to the work. He believed strongly in therapist self-awareness. On the other hand, he was clear that being self-aware was not a license to use therapy for doing one's own work. He advocated being very careful about what to share and what not to share. Self-reflection is a way of *not* bringing one's own issues into therapy by not acting them out unconsciously or at least of having control over what to use and what not to use.

The observing self of the couple

When the therapist in couple therapy works towards self-awareness, this carries over to the couple. Wile is one therapist who understands how important it is to stay with the negative feelings of each partner and to teach the couple to view their negativity from a different perspective (Wile, 2008). He writes about the couple's observing ego, the ability of the couple to view itself from an outsider perspective and see their negative interactions as their underlying need to connect and as a road to intimacy. He believes that fighting and withdrawing are inevitable in couple relationships, but partners can become increasingly skillful in reducing their frequency, duration, and damage, and even turn them into opportunities. He wrote:

> The quality of life in a relationship depends on the couple's ability to cope with their inevitable periods of fighting (quietly or loudly) and withdrawing (not talking about what mainly concerns them). Couples typically come to a therapy session in the midst of one of these two states. In either case, I move next to one of you and speak as if I were that person talking to the other. If you are fighting, I attempt to translate your angry and defensive comments into confiding ones. If you are withdrawing – that is, not talking about your feelings – I speculate about what these feelings might be and ask if my guess is correct. My goal is to turn fights or withdrawal into intimate conversations – to turn what is endangering the relationship into a means for deepening it.
> (Wile, 2008, p. 60)

In addition to whatever specific issues you are both struggling with (money, sex, children, in-laws), there is generally the added and often more significant problem of how you talk – or don't talk – about these issues: you fight or withdraw. Fighting is a deadlocked exchange in which each partner feels too unheard to listen, too misunderstood to be understanding, and too stung by what the other just said to do anything other than sting back. Withdrawing is a devitalized exchange in which partners don't talk about what most concerns them and may not talk much at all.

Intimacy, the alternative to fighting and withdrawing, occurs when partners confide to each other the main things on their minds – what's 'alive' for them at the moment, to use Marshall Rosenberg's term – in a way that works out, that is, that leaves each feeling closer rather than hurt, angry, defensive, or distant. Intimacy, this alternative to fighting and withdrawing, can be created by the way partners recover from fighting or withdrawing, that is, by means of a recovery conversation in which, unlike the fight or withdrawal, you confide feelings, make acknowledgments, reach out to the other, and look at things from the other's point of view.

In such a conversation, you create a meta-level, a bird's eye view, a perch, a helicopter look at the traffic, a vantage point above the fray, a platform. You operate as joint troubleshooters talking in a dispassionate, compassionate, and intimate way about your fighting, withdrawing, and lack of intimacy. You develop a shared picture of your relationship – how it is special as well as its trouble spots. Every couple has its own set of unsolvable problems that they grapple with throughout the relationship. Creating a platform – operating as joint troubleshooters – is the premier way to deal with such problems. Operating as troubleshooters, you commiserate over your unsolvable problems and put them in perspective. In couple therapy, I translate the partners' fights and withdrawals into conversations. I show them how to construct a platform from which to hold recovery conversations that enable them to turn problems into occasions for intimacy – to turn what is endangering the relationship into a means for deepening it.

We can look at different couple therapists from the perspective of the false or true self. If we work towards stopping negative interactions we run the risk of increasing the compliance to a false self that Winnicott saw as fundamental to not feeling real. He also makes it clear that the false self is a very early defensive measure that starts in early infancy when the infant's spontaneous gestures are constantly met by ignoring, stopping. or even retaliating in some way. Quickly the infant, whose entire existence is based on the connection with the mother, withdraws their own connection to themselves and begins a lifelong history of strengthening the false self in order to keep the connection.

The self of the therapist is not easily brought into therapy and therefore it is hard for the therapist to truly strengthen the real selves of the partners in a couple. The professional role is a kind of defensive maneuver that protects the interests of the couple by making sure that the therapist is in control of their own impulses and needs. We therapists try to make sure that we are getting our intimacy needs met elsewhere and try not to use therapy as a place where our intimacy is being fed.

I have often sensed at the end of a long day of doing therapy that my real-life relationships seem to be shallower than my relationships in the therapy room. I come out of the clinic and meet the daily life trials and tribulations related to who does the dishes and how much we spend. I have just spent hours getting beyond that stuff to deeper underlying issues. Now I have to 'go back' to non-intimate interactions. It becomes easy to be hooked and even addicted to the intimacy in the therapeutic relationship. At least with couples, we are clear where most of the intimacy is supposed to be. As we proceed and hopefully help couples, our role recedes in importance and prominence. But we can also be struck by the lack of intimacy in our own relationships as we emerge from successful couple sessions where intimacy between the partners is soaring.

No doubt our self-control, reality testing, and ability to keep professional boundaries are all important. But Winnicott also shows us that when the therapist is real and in touch with their own true self, the therapy will be more profound and involve deeper experiences with the patients. We have here another one of Winnicott's paradoxes. He is clear we need boundaries and control over our emotions while doing therapy, but he is also calling for being in touch with our deepest fantasies about our clients, which hopefully maps out for us what we are really feeling and why. Only then can we really be sure not to act out our own unconscious feelings.

It appears that how the therapist views the work he or she is doing contributes to the ability to hold negative emotions while knowing that the outcome will be good. As a supervisor and teacher for almost 40 years, I was often struck by the lack of self-esteem of trainees and students. Quite commonly there is more doubt and fear of failure than confidence and security about success. As one of the interviewees said, 'Every couple can destroy me.' Many therapists would agree with another interviewee's question 'What would a real therapist do in this situation?' Many therapists have shared a false-self consciousness with me – a persona they keep up for colleagues but that is seriously eroded inside. Some seem to feel like imposters who pretend to know much more than they feel they do.

Could it be that therapists are not helped to create a positive self-image that would hold all the self-reflection that is a part of training? Is it boasting or too self-confident for therapists to be in touch with their own strengths as unique beings? How can therapists keep a balance between openness to faults and vulnerability while maintaining a sense of being good enough in their professional lives?

What would Winnicott have said about therapist self-esteem? While I have not found specific writings on this, it would appear to me that he would focus on the therapist's ability to go on being. An infant is exposed to a myriad of experiences. The child experiences internally good feelings, bad ones, and then the return of good ones. How does a child develop an ability to integrate these distinct feelings into an integrated whole? Going on being is Winnicott's unique phrase for the mother's ability to hold the infant throughout all the ups and downs of internal life, helping the infant tie these experiences into a sense of connection that is the sense of 'I am'.

If the therapist did not have such holding to allow for a sense of being real, a connection between seemingly disparate parts, it would be harder to help couples who have the same problems.

Self-esteem and work with couples

As I previously mentioned, I expected myself to be a kind of magician, always helpful and able to create transformations of the couple's relationship. I tie this clearly into my own sense of futility with my mother, in which whatever I did was not enough. Also when I did achieve success, there was a loaded silence following my success. The message was 'You have to achieve to be good enough' and 'No success is enough to feel good enough about'. This is a heavy baggage to carry into the room with a fighting couple who themselves have feelings of not being good enough. They also might feel that they have created a relationship (baby) that isn't good enough. This makes them as partners (parents) not good enough to create a healthy marriage (baby).

The job of becoming a couple therapist involves splitting off of the true self with a false-self role as healer. That is, the more we accumulate knowledge (reading, workshops, and supervision), the more we expect that our professional selves will be secure. Thus the role of therapist can easily become a field for false-self development. I always noticed that when I came back from a workshop or conference about a certain method, I would use that method for about a week. Then I would go back to whatever it was that I did normally.

From its inception, therapy has longed to be recognized as a science. The more we can hypothesize, predict, and measure results, the better scientists we are. There is a definite pull towards developing a professional persona that can justify an intervention while the real self goes on doing whatever it is most comfortable to do. Only when in training do we feel the need to label the behavior or reaction we have in professional language. And the paradox might be that the more we can label our interventions, the less we rely on our true selves to create the bond for change.

One of the roads towards a true-self sense of security is in the relationship with the couples we treat. It is in this crucible of complex relationships that we can start to rely on our intuition. We have to rely on our intuition when we realize how many relationships are in the room in couple therapy. There is the relationship of partner 1 to partner 2; each of them to the therapist; the therapist's relationship to each partner and to the relationship as a whole; each partner's relationship with the couple relationship; and finally the relationship of all of them to the therapeutic relationship. How could we ever dream of being scientific within a context as complex as therapy relationships?

In his way of thinking, Winnicott shares a lot with existential writers and therapists. The question of science versus art is indeed a classic debate in the field of psychotherapy. In its beginnings, Freud clearly intended for psychoanalysis to become a science. Many of those who have entered the field since have sought the same goal. However, is psychotherapy best seen as an art or a science? In beginning, it is important to make a distinction between the field of psychology and the field of psychotherapy. While this distinction in many ways is arbitrary because they are both closely related to each other and highly influential upon each other, this distinction is still important. In more recent times, this distinction appears to be growing. This can be illustrated in the separation of PhD (Doctorate of Philosophy in Psychology) from the PsyD (Doctorate of Psychology).

Psychology has become more research-based (science), while psychotherapy is flexible enough to be an art, a science, or a mixture of the two.

An existential perspective would focus on the idea of an empirically informed art. In other words, existential thought would not devalue the scientific knowledge, but neither would it elevate it too highly. Science and research is one way of knowing. There are still many other ways of knowing that exist. This includes phenomenological, spiritual, intuition, and relational ways of knowing.

Existential thought would strongly criticize much of the field of psychology today for over-reliance on scientific knowledge. Winnicott, probably influenced by Freud, was looking for a scientific basis for his theories. Like Piaget, he went from studying the individual to making claims about the majority of people. But his strength was not in the prediction of differences, but in the strong evidence of his use of intuition in his work.

He wrote to mothers:

> Unthinking people will often try to teach you how to do the things which you can do better than you can be taught to do them. If you are sure of all this, you can start to add to your value as a mother by learning the things that can be taught, for the best of our civilization and culture offers much that is of value, if you can take it without loss of what comes to you naturally.
>
> (Winnicott, 1987, p. 5)

I would like to imagine how differently I might have worked with couples had my many teachers and supervisors sent this message to me. I was not taught to rely on intuition but on standardized protocols of treatment that could be replicated and thus held up to the scientific goal of predictability. But couple therapy is very different from a scientific endeavor. What would it have been like had I worked to listen better to my own intuition? Only then could I really decide which of the many subsystems and interactions I might want to respond to. I believe that the constant use of intuition combined with theories and scientific knowledge would develop a strong sense of self-esteem. This self-esteem would not just be a professional one, but a reflection of my entire being.

Here is one example where intuition was definitely useful in strengthening my own self-esteem. As my self-esteem became less shaken by events in therapy, I could hold more of the hate, rage, aggression, sadness, disappointment and withdrawal that couples bring to therapy.

Dorit and Eitan came to therapy when Eitan decided he wanted to end the marriage. Dorit was not against this but wanted to check with a professional since they had small children and were very responsible people. A couple in their mid-thirties, this couple did not at all seem on the brink of divorce. At first I was very unsure of what was going on. The couple behaved very nicely to each other, polite and respectful. They had built a good life for themselves with their own home, close relationships to family and friends, and satisfying work life. They rarely fought and when they did they talked about their problems openly. In effect they behaved as if they had undergone successful couple treatment! I was thrown off at first, as I wondered why they wanted a divorce and what I could offer them. They were as nice and respectful to me as they were to each other. Had I given them a questionnaire, they probably would rate high in marital satisfaction. So what was wrong?

It was only by accessing my inner feelings that I started to have a sense of the seriousness of their situation. Before every session, I dreaded their coming. I felt useless and vulnerable, even though neither of them seemed to have a complaint about the therapy. More important, I was constantly feeling tired in their sessions. I caught myself dozing off once, even though they were talking about events that were important to them. When I was able to stay awake, I felt something flat inside of me. I located this feeling in my belly and in my heart area. It was as if there was a contraction, a flattening out of everything. I realized that I could not feel anything when I was with them. I was relieved when they left the room.

I decided (having very little to lose, it seemed) to share my feelings with them. I worked on how to say things without sounding critical of them. I think my delivery was calm and not accusatory. It went something like this: 'You know, when you first came here it was not clear to me why you both seem so close to divorce. You have done a great deal to create a good home life in every way – and you have succeeded in that. So for the last few sessions I wondered how I could help you. Then I began to feel a certain flatness when we were all together. It was as if something alive was missing. I felt myself sort of drifting off. I had a hard time staying connected to you. Is this something you two have experienced?'

There was a silence in the room and a kind of heavy sadness. Dorit started to cry and when Eitan reached for a tissue for her, she moved her hands as if to say 'No'. It was the first negative thing I had seen between them and it felt good. The flatness was gone, something alive was happening. Over the next few sessions we talked about the flatness and when it started in them as well. It turned out that they had a traumatic birth experience in which their newborn third child died a few hours after birth. They had never discussed this event between them or with anyone else. They were told by the medical staff that the best thing would be to have another child soon. They tried, but found that they were not attracted to each other and neither wanted sex.

The next few sessions were the opposite of the early sessions. Instead of flatness, there was a process of grieving and anger at the environment that had not held their horrible experience, and also anger at each other for doing the 'stiff upper lip' routine with each other.

I wish I could report that the return of their feelings meant that they could stay together. What happened is that they revealed that the third child who had died had been for them a last attempt to resuscitate the dying marriage. Their grief had frozen them into a place of no feelings. When their feeling life started to return, it led to an increased wish to be free of each other. They apparently had lost feelings of love long before the sad third pregnancy and wanted to quickly move ahead towards the separation that they had originally wanted.

My intuition was based mostly on my observation of their physical and emotional responses, and my own responses. I think that this couple was satisfied with the therapy, although I was sad that their direction was to divorce. They were relieved to be able to separate. My own self-esteem was strengthened by my ability to acknowledge not knowing what was going on. Such a paradox would not be surprising to Winnicott, whose language and thinking was often paradoxical.

It is strengthening one's trust in intuitive knowledge that leads to stronger self-esteem and thus a greater ability to hold the very powerful feelings that exist in couple therapy. Self-esteem and holding are intricately connected because the one doing the holding is the therapist's self. Is this self good enough to hold the intense feelings between couples and between them and the therapist? No theory seems to me to do the trick in being there when the situation is hard. However, intuition allows us to then utilize the theories that were probably embedded in the intuition. In the case of Dorit and Eitan, I was later able to recognize the theoretical basis for much of what happened. I understand from theory and research what trauma does to people. I know how important timely grieving is for overcoming a serious loss. I know that as a couple they 'dropped' the relationship/baby by not dealing with the central pain in the relationship. Only when they felt I could hold all that could they begin to mourn and get back on track. In their case back on track was to continue in the direction of a desired divorce.

The other aspect of this case description is that it is, as couple therapy should aim to be, a process of repair. The rupture in Dorit and Eitan's relationship occurred before the third pregnancy. The pregnancy can be seen as their own attempts to repair some ruptures in their relationship. However, the catastrophic nature of the birth not only did not repair the relationship but added additional stress and even trauma to it. The relationship was not strong enough to overcome the grief in time to work on the relationship. By the time they came to therapy the best repair that could be offered would be help in moving on to a divorce. However, intuition does not spell all this out like a flow chart. The basic assumption about intuition is not that it is always right. It is just what it says it is. An intuition comes from some kind of unconscious process, which at the time we cannot label because intuition jumps out and grabs a hold on us, giving no explanation. Later on, whether the intuition was helpful or not, a theoretical understanding could add new and important information.

Ogden and Winnicott: the analytic third and intuition in couple therapy

Ogden, a psychoanalyst, has written extensively about Winnicott (Ogden, 1987, 1994, 1997). Here I will discuss the concept of the analytic third, which seems to me to be the same as the potential space or transitory space that Winnicott wrote about. It is in this space that the therapist and the patient (or couple) create a new potential space. Ogden called this the analytic third:

> It seems to me that I use the term analytic third to refer to a third subject, unconsciously co-created by analyst and analysand, which seems to take on a life of its own in the interpersonal field between analysts and patients. This third subject stands in dialectical tension with the separate, individual subjectivities of analyst and analysand in such a way that the individual subjectivities and the third create, negate, and preserve one another.
>
> It is in this space where intuition finds a voice.

Ogden continues:

> The analytic third is at first almost entirely an unconscious phenomenon.
>
> The unconscious, by definition, cannot be invaded on the wings of the brute force of will. The analyst and analysand must use indirect (associational) methods to 'catch the drift' of the unconscious co-creation. For the analyst, this means relying to a very large degree on 'the foul rag-and-bone shop' of his reverie experience (his mundane, everyday thoughts, feelings, ruminations, preoccupations, daydreams, bodily sensations, and so forth). The analyst's use of his reverie experience requires tolerance of the experience of not knowing, of finding himself (or, perhaps more accurately, losing himself) adrift and apparently directionless. The emotional residue of a reverie experience is usually, at first, unobtrusive and inarticulate, an experience that is more a sense of dysphonic emotional disequilibrium than a sense of having arrived at an understanding. And yet, in my own clinical work, the use of my reverie experience is the emotional compass upon which I most heavily rely (but cannot clearly read) in my efforts to orient myself to what is happening in the analytic relationship in general, and in the workings of the analytic third in particular.
>
> (Ogden, 1994, p. 17–18)

The analytic third may be of a powerfully creative and enriching sort. Such forms of the analytic third are enlivening in the sense that 'shapes' are generated in the analytic relationship (for instance, interesting, sometimes novel, forms of considering, dreaming, and fantasizing as well as richer and more fully human qualities of object-relatedness marked, for example, by humor, compassion, playfulness, flirtatiousness, camaraderie, charm, love, and anger which have 'all the sense of real'). Some forms of playing in the analytic setting involve an experience of the analytic third that might be thought of as an experience of the patient and analyst engaged in playing in the presence of the unconscious (jointly, but asymmetrically constructed) mother who facilitates the capacity of the child *to be* alone in her ('invisible', unobtrusive) presence (Winnicott, 1958). I place emphasis on the words 'to be' because it is the experience of coming into being as an individual with one's own distinct and unique qualities that is of central importance in the experience of this form of the analytic third. One can see and feel and hear and smell and touch something like oneself in the activity of playing. This experience of playful symbol- and metaphor-making allows one to create symbols that give shapes and emotional substance (sensate 'embodiments') to the self-as-object ('me'), which serve as mirrors in which the self-as-subject ('I') recognizes/creates itself. The creation of various forms of the analytic third that create and preserve conditions in which playing might safely occur evolves throughout the course of every analysis that is 'a going concern' (to borrow Winnicott's apt phrase).

In this type of work the therapist is a useful object for the couple's feelings, ideas, pain, and hope. But the therapist is also a subject reacting to the clients as well as to his/her own internal processes. Use of the self of the therapist is crucial in creating this potential space for change. It is a space where the selves of therapist, of each partner, and of the relationships are all taken into account and filtered through the dreams, feelings, fantasies that the therapist has about the couple. Using these through intuition allows a strengthening of the therapist–client bond; this bond creates a safe space. As therapy progresses well, there is a strengthening of the therapist's self-esteem.

When the therapist is able to become a subjective part of the therapy, there is less focus on figuring out the psychodynamics, projective identifications, introjection, and other formulations of the couple's dynamic as if they existed in a vacuum. That is, when the therapist is not included in the therapeutic model, it is as if the couple is bringing their 'problematic' child (the relationship) to the relationship expert to fix it. The expert has to first formulate what is the problem interaction of the relationship and locate impasses that reflect core issues. While the therapist has concrete tasks and is crucial to a safe space, it is crucial to conceptualize the therapist as part of the therapeutic system. Work on countertransference, the self of the therapist, and parts of the therapist that are involved in impasses are all necessary aspects of treating couples. Some therapeutic methods realize this and include the self of the therapist as part of the treatment. Other methods do not conceptualize understanding the therapist as a necessary element in the progress of therapy. Looking through Winnicott's lens, there is no therapy (baby) without the therapist (mother). Good enough couple therapy, no matter by which theoretical method or tools, needs to see the therapist and the couple as a system undergoing change all the time.

Therapist's own inner couple

What does self-reflection bring to couple therapy? I believe we all carry in us an internal object of couple relationships. Molly Ludham calls this 'the couple in the mind'. She writes:

> human beings commonly hold a life-long bond or attachment to an internal couple. This dynamic inner object may assume a variety of forms, symbolizing both togetherness and conflict, its presence helps to shape the individual's relationship to couples and the making of couples relationships in adult life … such an inner image would reflect both an outer and inner life.
>
> (Ludham, 2007, p. 100)

For the couple therapist, work on their own inner couple object is crucial to work in the therapy sessions with couples. In the example I gave above relating to my fear around a professional trip, I was able to change my relationship to my own internal couple. My internal couple is fraught with the conflicts between my parents, the rejection by my father of my mother, and my own reenactment of these rejections in my own actual marriage. Had I handled my pain in my usual way, I would have brought it to my husband, expecting him to magically make it better. In other words, my internal couple has the neediness for reparation and care, as well as the disappointment and even cruelty of rejection of these needs. I wonder if these patterns went on with my parents. I remember that during my childhood, before my parents' divorce, they often went off on long trips together. I remember a trip of two months when their four children (and me as the eldest) were quite young. What I picked up about them was that my father was always trying to get my mother away from her kids and her intense investment in the maternal role. I somehow picked up the idea that he wanted her to himself, but that she was always clear that the children came first. She rejected his attempts to get her away from her children, but in doing so also rejected her maternal role by giving in and taking long trips, leaving her children with strangers as nannies.

Work on my own internal couples object has allowed me to improve my own marriage and also see similar dynamics in the couples I treat. Many of the couples who come to therapy are struggling with similar issues of connection to each other, rejection of the other, and the need to gain security about being wanted and loved. It is far easier to locate these maps of internal and interactional acting out of invitations and rejections when I myself have come to terms with these dynamics.

Also, the very act of allowing oneself to be aware of the internal objects and their impact allows the therapist to differentiate themselves from the couples in treatment. While many couples do struggle with similar internal couples objects, others have different dynamics. It is easier to tease these out when one's own internal couple objects are clear.

The false self has mostly been viewed as a negative compliant part of the personality that hides the true self. Many writers, such as Miller (1981) and Masterson (1988), see searching for the real self as the crux of good therapy.

However, there is much that can be done by work on the false self and in re-conceptualizing the false self as an important potential space for change. The idea of a false self as necessary from infancy suggests the positive functions of this part of the personality.

The function of the false self is to hide and protect the true self, which is always potentially there. Winnicott considered that in every individual there is a split of a true self and a false self. He described a whole range of false-self organization. At the pathological extreme is when the false self presents itself as the real person, where the true self is completely hidden. Obviously, such individuals will have enormous difficulties in every type of relationship interaction because of an essential lack of the true self. At the healthy end of that spectrum or range in health, the false self is what we would present as our social self, our polite social self, our polite manner. That is an achievement. Obviously, the issues around which we comply in our social manner are not crucial, but that capacity also helps individuals fit in socially and respond appropriately. Within that range and moving towards the pathological, the extreme pathology end, is where the true self can be hidden by the false self, but it has in that split a secret life, a private life that the false self protects.

In other words, the false self can be a way, if it is in a flexible interplay with spontaneity and the true self, of negotiating very rich social relationships. This has important ramifications for couple therapy. The real self is actually very rarely totally unmasked. Masud Khan said 'I am false to my back teeth' (Hopkins,

2006). In a 15-year analysis with Winnicott, he only had three experiences of true self. All three were physical. That is, he found himself on his knees with his ear to Winnicott's heart and he listened to it. So there was a psychosomatic collusion at those moments that was not present at any other time. In another treatment at one point Winnicott says something to the effect 'Get the nurse of the false self out of the room' (Winnicott, 1972). That we talked as if we were two nurses talking about this child when he was talking about the patient.

Winnicott was concerned with socially adapted behaviors that were stifling the true self. He said that other people's expectations can become of overriding importance, overlaying or contradicting the original sense of self, the one connected to the very roots of one's being. Winnicott thought that such an extreme kind of false self is an illness that begins to develop in infancy. Negative false selves are a defense against an environment that felt unsafe or overwhelming because of a lack of reasonably attuned care-giving. The danger is that through this false self, the infant builds up a false set of relationships, and by means of introjections even attains a show of being real. The result can be a child whose potential aliveness and creativity has gone unnoticed ... concealing an empty, barren internal world behind a mask of independence. Yet at the same time the false self is the ultimate defense against the unthinkable 'exploitation of the True Self, which would result in its annihilation'.

By contrast, the True Self is rooted in, and '"does no more than collect together the details of the experience of aliveness" – this means the body's life-sustaining functions, "including the heart's action and breathing"'. Out of this the baby creates the experience of reality: a sense that 'Life is worth the trouble of living'. In the baby's nonverbal gesture which '... expresses a spontaneous instinct', the true-self potential can be communicated to, and affirmed by, the mother.

'The False Self in its pathological guise prevents and inhibits what Winnicott calls the "spontaneous gesture" of the True Self. Compliance and imitation are the costly results.' Some would indeed consider that 'the idea of compliance is central to Winnicott's theory of the false self' and add, paradoxically, that 'concern for an object is easily a compliant act'. When an infant starts to say 'no' in body language and movement, the mother can insist on having her way, or can try negotiating what she believes is necessary versus what the child appears to want. When the mother is not responsive to the baby's spontaneity, and instead a mother's expectations are too insistent, they can eventually result in compliant behavior and an impaired autonomy as the baby has to manage objects prematurely. The false self enacts a kind of dissociated regard or recognition of the object; the object is taken seriously, is shown concern, but not by a real person.

Nevertheless, Winnicott did not underestimate the need as well for a false self, seeing 'the False Self ... as a necessary defensive organization, a survival kit, a caretaker self, the means by which a threatened person has managed to survive'. Winnicott postulates that there is a continuum of false self development, distinguishing five levels of organization of the false self. He attempted to delineate the progression of false self from helpful to pathological:

1. At the pathological end of the continuum the false self acts as if it were the real person – the true self remaining concealed, only a virtual possibility. However, the false self always lacks 'something essential': socially, the person is perceived as false.
2. Less severely, the false self protects the true self, which remains not actualized – for Winnicott a clear example of a clinical condition organized for the positive goal of preservation of the individual in spite of abnormal environmental conditions.
3. Closer to health, the false self supports the individual's search for conditions that will allow the true self to recover its well-being – its own identity.
4. Even closer to health, we find the false self 'established on the basis of identifications'.
5. In a healthy person, the false self is composed of that which facilitates 'a polite social behavior, good manners and a certain reserve'. It is this essential courtesy that makes possible life in society: 'the false self acts to allow smooth passage through the world by inducing appropriate and socially acceptable ways of expressing love and hate'.

Winnicott was far more complex in his thinking about true and false selves. Neither was more or less than the other. But he had unique views on how the true and false self become compromised from early infancy. The infant arrives with a true self and the potential defenses of false self as need be. As the social world is navigated from the mother–infant relationship to other relationships, the dynamic balance between the true and false selves is crucial to feeling real as an adult. These ideas have important repercussions for couples in distress who are seeking therapy.

Use of the therapist's own relationship

Many of the couple therapists I interviewed mentioned the importance of their own intimate relationships in their work with couples. I firmly believe that in addition to bringing our childhood traumas into the therapy room, we bring our intimate relationship histories as well. One of the ways this can work (although certainly not the only way) is for the therapist to use positive experiences with overcoming difficulties in their own relationships. That is, we can use our relationships in the way Winnicott meant by 'use' of an object. That is, our marriages and intimate connections go through cycles of creation and destruction as well as recreation, and are eventually available to be used in our inner life. This does not mean that those of us therapists who have experienced divorce and the dissolution of a relationship do not have these internal objects for their use. All relationships have their moments of rupture and their moments of repair. Those who have had traumatic divorces might have more work to do in order to use their seemingly failed relationship in their couple work. But this is necessary anyway to go on believing in relationships and helping others repair their own relationships.

I have been married for 40 years and this makes using my own relationship at home almost inevitable. The question is not whether I am influenced by my own relationship but in what ways I am influenced. And more importantly, how can I make use of my relationship at home to help couples I work with?

At the age of 24, I married an Israeli musician. I brought to the marriage all the unresolved childhood issues discussed before, as well as cultural and class differences. Having been born and raised in the USA, in an upper middle-class family, outside of falling in love, I had very little in common with my kibbutz-born and -educated husband. In some ways, all marriages are intermarriages, as each member comes to the union from a different family. However, with these everyday differences united with cultural and class differences (and of course gender difference), I wonder what we found in common at all.

What we seemed to have was a kind of contract in which my husband gave me all the mothering I so gravely lacked. His was indeed a good enough mother to me for at least half of our marriage. He took over many of the functions of a mother (cooking, childcare) and supported me in my career achievements as well as my use of therapy along the way. I offered him something of the larger world. Having left Israel to study music abroad, my husband was eager to maintain his connection to the world outside of Israel. While we met in Israel, because of my doctoral studies in Berkeley, California we spent much of our first years of marriage going back and forth from Israel to the USA. I think I also offered him an interesting partner who was sophisticated and very different from his uneducated Polish parents. He had experienced some shame on the kibbutz as the son of these parents. While the kibbutz is supposedly an example of an egalitarian community, it had a clear social status pecking order, with his parents on the lower rungs. For him I fitted into his dreams of a life better than the one he left behind at the kibbutz.

What I find the most useful in my work with couples is my own experience of my marriage almost breaking up and its reconfiguration in a totally new way. Without going into too many of the personal details, after 15 years of marriage I was faced with a feeling that I had lost my love for my husband. The contract we had was clearly over. I wanted more access to my own children and was less caught up in my career, having reached all the goals I had formerly desired. I no longer felt the need for a good enough mother and in reflecting back on about five years of turmoil, I realize that in many ways we had succeeded in delivering me from absolute dependency to relative independence. The amazing thing about these kinds of crisis in marriage is that they occur without our control or planning of any kind. We are swept away in a powerful process of growth and differentiation that needs to happen for the marriage to either break up or renew itself.

There are many times I look back on those five years and remember a statement made in Israel by Florence Kaslow, a well-known therapist and researcher in the area of divorce. She came to Israel to give a workshop on divorce and began her presentation with the following comment: 'Hello, I am Dr. Florence Kaslow and I will talk to you about divorce. I know about it because I have been divorced five times [a gasp from the rather conservative professional audience in Israel of 20 years ago]. I have been married and divorced five times to the same husband.' I love this comment because it reflects my own life and it also offers a way of looking at couple crisis as a developmental stage crisis with growth potential.

My own marriage reconfigured and renewed itself through a great deal of confusion and crisis. I moved out, and eventually came back. I went through the terrors of living without my good enough mother (husband) and used many different transitional objects along the way. During the period of crisis I went out into the world with a sense of omnipotence, nurtured in my marriage. I discovered that not only was I not omnipotent, but that I was actually quite needy. After several years of conflict and a trial separation, I found myself back with my husband under some different conditions.

Accepting my own neediness was a crucial turning point for me. For most of my life I struggled to be independent while not having the kind of nurturing that makes this independence solid enough to build upon. At first it was a crushing blow to me to discover how much I needed my husband and how little I cared for the world out there without the family. I had to work through stages of growth on my own, which included cutting off from my husband. Eventually with good therapy we were able to create a new kind of marriage. What is interesting for me is that the new marriage had much in common with the first marriage. I still rely on my husband for good enough mothering. He still relies on me to bring the world into our lives. Yet there has been a profound change.

My new 'old' marriage

The change I see is that we are more separate, autonomous individuals who are also able to become far more intimate than we were in our 'first' marriage. In the past I had been the one who always wanted more closeness and he pulled away in a typical pursuer–distancer dance. In our second marriage, my husband takes equal responsibility for bringing up topics and dealing with issues. I no longer have to chase him because he is the initiator of interactions as much as I am. We still fight, but the depth of the aggression and the pain felt are less intense and more manageable. We are far more aware and thus accountable to each other for what is going on in the relationship.

This second marriage took its own time to develop. One aspect of the new marriage was our decision to work together. Although he was a musician, he had enough free time to learn about couple therapy and specifically about marriage enrichment. We took enrichment courses together. Whenever I had a sabbatical, he used the time to learn more about couples.

Later, we opened what we called 'The Marriage School', which combined several different models of couple enrichment. We led the groups together for several years, and this developed into working together with a couple in therapy. I find that when a couple feels most difficult to me, the work becomes easier when my husband helps out. During the period where I stopped working with couples, he began to see couples on his own. Increasingly, my husband searched for his own area of expertise within the joint area of couples work. He became a divorce mediator. His expertise was work with men and he developed his own identity within the togetherness of joining my world of couple therapy.

While few couples would want to work together in couple therapy, the idea of a joint project is very important when thinking of a long-term relationship. Couples married about 20 years or more have often instinctively had their own joint projects – having children and creating a family; building a house together; making joint finances work for them; and furthering joint hobbies (sports, collections, travel).

Having recreated my own marriage and having watched how other couples recreate their marriages, I find a positive and encouraging note has entered my individual work with couples.

Using relationships at home to help do couple therapy

It is hard to imagine doing couple therapy without having this inner knowledge of how much couples can potentially change. I have my own marriage as a story I can use to help me help others, generally without talking about it. Sometimes I do mention that I know how to remarry my own husband or I will just talk about having a goal of creating a new marriage from the ashes of their old one. In general, the knowledge of the flexibility of a couple's relationship helps me envision change even when the couple have given up. Sometimes I am overly zealous about what can occur. I have to give up when they are ready to give up and help people take a different route than the one I took. I have to deal with my own ambivalence about my route. Did I give up my independence too early on? Would I have been happier moving on, rather than going back to repair? These and other crucial questions come up when the couple in therapy are questioning whether to continue to work on their relationships or not.

Self-reflection about our own relationships is crucial in couple work. While most of us do not bring our actual partners into the therapy, they are there all the time in our fantasy lives. Some of our goals relate to lacks we feel at home. We can notice when we are on a mission to save a couple, when we are impotent to save our own marriage. Or, we can recognize when we are jealous of the achievements of a couple when they seem to be doing better than we are. We might be ambivalent about their choices of lifestyles (i.e. an open marriage) when we do not have such choices in our relationships. We might be outraged when a partner tells the other about an affair when we perceive their marriage did not deserve this, as our own does not deserve this. Perhaps we might be competitive with a couple in showing them how much we know (especially when at home we don't know enough). We might be discouraged about what can be achieved when at home we have a sense of failure. All these are countertransferences from our own couple lives and not necessarily from our early childhood experiences.

My own experiences have fostered an awareness of the unexpected and immense potential for change in a marriage. For me the opening up of my world of therapy to my husband has made me more transparent to him and him to me. Not everything we see is great, but it is real. I have a sense that when I faltered and had a burnout experience, my husband was there to pick up the load and help me go on, eventually coming back to therapy on my own.

Also it has fostered the option of leaving as a real possibility for me and others. That makes marriage appear to me to be a choice and I think I bring the sense of choice into the room after my own experiences. The essential question of whether to stay or leave remains a possibility in my life and in my thinking about my clients.

I do work hard not to impose my journey on others, while still having my own marriage as a story that might help my work with couples. I believe that the more we are aware of what we bring into the therapy room from our own lives, the less we might unconsciously act out our own stories through our couples.

9 Internal family systems therapy

The next step

While some interpret the self and false self as two different aspects of the same person, many others see the person as made up of many selves, sometimes called parts or voices. These ideas were developed after Winnicott and within the last two decades. But they appear to me to be ways of elaborating Winnicott and finding methods that fit with his views on people.

In a book called *Subpersonalities: The People Inside Us*, Rowan (1990) carefully follows the history of those thinkers who believe that we are all 'multiple personalities'. Here he follows many diverse trends in psychology and also transpersonal spiritual methods that all have the idea at their core that we have different selves. He has written about Richard Schwartz, who came to the idea of multiple parts of the self as well as one unified Self, and this is the model I will be discussing later on. At the core of this model was a family therapist who, in work with traumatized people, came to the conclusion that we can directly contact and work with these selves, not to get rid of them, but use them as resources. Schwartz wrote:

> I began discussing with Sally what her internal experience was just before she went on a binge and vomit spree. She described a confusing cacophony of voices that seemed to carry on conversations inside her head. When I pressed her to differentiate the voices she found, to her and my surprise, that with relative ease she could identify several voices that regularly participated in heated conversations with each other. One voice was highly critical of everything about her, especially her appearance. Another defended her against this criticism and blamed her parents for her problems. Another voice made her feel sad, hopeless and helpless, both because her report was so similar to the reports of other bulimics I had treated and because as I listen to her I became aware of somewhat similar voices within me.
>
> (Schwartz, 1987, p. 33)

I first met Richard Schwartz in the middle of 1980 at a family therapy conference. He was very enthusiastic about his discoveries of different personalities within each of us. I was then quite skeptical, especially as he insisted that these parts have their own histories, style of talking, and style of behaving. They interacted with each other just as family members might interact. For example, two groups might gang up against a third. He believed that some of the groups were managers and kept the overall personality functioning in daily life. There was another group that he called 'exiles', which were essentially inner children of all ages who carried trauma and pain. They were relegated to silence because it hurt so much to listen to them. However, they wanted to tell their stories. So there was a third group, which he called 'firefighters'. These protective parts binged, drank, did drugs, shopping, sexual acting out and everything that can be done to calm and quiet these very upset children parts. The firefighters were often destructive and their acting out called the managers back into action. The exiles were continuously relegated to some part of the psyche that is hidden and not dealt with.

I was extremely confused by his model, especially since he seemed to believe that these people inside of us have their own lives. I remember asking with disbelief, where did these parts live? Where did they do their shopping? Where did they sleep? He and I could not communicate at that point and it took another ten years for me to rediscover the truths available to us in his thinking.

I have since then found many other writings about multiple parts of the personality (Stone & Winkelman, 1985). In Rowan's book on subpersonalities he quotes and discusses Winnicott as well. Rowan writes about Winnicott that it is important to recognize that the events we are talking about (traumas) may be very unimportant to the adults and very important to the baby. Winnicott is precise about how this can happen (Winnicott, 1971c).

The feeling of the mother's existence lasts X minutes. If the mother is away longer than X minutes, then the imago fades and along with this the baby's capacity to use the symbol of the union ceases. The baby is distressed, but this distress is soon mended because the mother returns in X+Y minutes. In X+Y minutes the baby has not become altered. But in X=Y=Z, the baby has become traumatized. The mother's return does not mend the baby's altered state. Trauma implies that the baby has experienced a break in life's continuity so that primitive defenses become organized to defend against a repetition of 'unthinkable anxiety' or a return of the acute confusion state that belongs to disintegration to a nascent ego structure.

In his latest writings about internal parts, Schwartz has combined the group called the managers and the group called the firefighters to become a larger group of 'protectors'. These child exiles that are carrying burdens of traumas can be healed. The idea that Schwartz proposes is that because our personality relegates these pain-filled selves to the unconscious, we are always fighting them to keep them unconscious. When all kinds of acting out behaviors (drinking binging, etc.) do not work, the exiled selves have to be listened to in order to become unstuck and start to grow and develop. I will continue towards the end of this chapter to give examples of ways to use this method, which seems to reflect Winnicott's thinking. The false self had multiple selves. So there's a shifting shape in the idea of the false self that seems to be very, very protean, in terms of the way it shows up in various situations.

Since our own wounds and the problems people bring us tend to coincide in any interaction, we can start to rely on our intuition in making comments to the couple. As we increasingly rely on our intuition, we become like a good enough mother who is actively teaching her infant so as to bring that infant from a sense of omnipotence to relative independence. No two infants are alike. This idea means that we need to be careful when applying standard methods to couples without giving them the holding environment a good enough mother would do.

This is a simple but true description of good enough mothering in the therapeutic environment. The couple come often without a sense of self-reflection and certainly without a sense of the relationship being their own baby, an entity of itself. The therapist is in a state of presence called reverie or maternal preoccupation, in which we listen carefully to the partners but just as carefully to our own stirring up of emotions, fantasy, ideas, needs....

In this state of being fully present to ourselves as well as to them, we venture an intervention: a comment, a question, a request to try out a new communication. There certainly are enough methods around today for couple therapists. But the good enough therapist is intensely watchful for how any of their behavior is fitting or not to the partners and to the relationship. We are giving of ourselves in the way a mother offers an object to the infant. We expect the infant to hesitate, to take time and see if it fits. We allow that time, we pace ourselves, and learn to be silent and wait. If our statement or question seems not to fit (even one partner), there is an open recognition that rupture might have occurred and repair needs to be made. This is the process of teaching the couple (baby) that we are entrusted with. It makes the setting crucial, just as the warmth of the water for a bath has to be just right. We are on time, disconnect the phone, take time before a session to relax and look at notes, we schedule time in between sessions, we don't put all the hard cases on one day, we end on time with the sensitivity that an ending of a session has a powerful emotional reverberation.

Over the years I have developed the ability to watch the physical and emotional language in the room. I feel it in my own body and I have specific cues I have learned about my own inner children. I notice when my stomach is tight and that usually indicates fear or worry. I know that for me sadness is felt in my heart area as a heaviness. I notice when time flies by or when it seems leaden and slow. This often means I am not in touch with the people in the room and am experiencing loneliness. Every therapist could use the development of their own emotional-physical dictionary.

Any therapy method that helps the therapist develop this dictionary is useful. I have found that the most congruent method with Winnicott's thinking is the method called 'Internal family systems therapy'. Richard Schwartz, who developed this model, built it on the work of Murray Bowen and differentiation of the self. But in many ways the internal family systems (IFS) model is a practical way of thinking of object relating and a method for dealing with inner children in both the couple and in myself as a therapist.

Using IFS to help in good enough couple therapy

As I mentioned earlier, my first introduction to the parts that live inside us was less than successful. It took me ten years to somehow pick up the book I had bought at that first conference when I met Richard Schwartz. I don't know why after ten years I took the book with me to Eilat, a seaside resort where I was going to rest on the beach for a few days. I found myself reading the book and becoming very excited. I started to play with small rocks on the beach, giving them names of parts of my own personality. At the time I was working out some issue in my family life and so I mapped out my own parts and the parts I have contracted with my husband. I mapped out both his and my managers, both of our exiles (from stories I heard from his past as well as events I remember from my past) and finally my own and his firefighters.

Like Winnicott, Schwartz gives a very central role to a single Self (he uses the capital letter to designate the oneness of this aspect of consciousness). The Self is sort of like a soul in the sense that it has the power to remain potent and unwounded no matter what happened in childhood. The Self in the IFS model is the good enough mother who is able to help her children (all the parts) grow and develop and get along with each other. Recently IFS has been applied to couple therapy.

In IFS therapy, our aim is to help each client access the Self that will provide continual love and care to our inner family – a profound and transformative love. As a client once noted after witnessing his partner fall deeply in love with her inner wounded child, 'Finally I can really love and feel empathy for that little girl, knowing it isn't entirely mine to fix and heal.'

The IFS approach to couple therapy is a mode of treatment that aims to help couples develop a deeply satisfying relationship between many parts and two spacious Selves, letting our partner become an important – but not the only or primary – source of love.

As an IFS therapist, my intention is to invite partners to accept their humanness and their capacity to love deeply – first themselves and then each other. I extend an invitation for people to stretch into what's possible for their relationships, but I no longer try to convince them that they should.

For me, the grace of IFS has been to learn to be present with all that arrives in my office – to relax and trust the process as it unfolds. These days, I have learned to make the necessary interventions, more often than not, with much more clarity, genuine curiosity, and an open heart.

A case example

I have been experimenting with IFS work with couples and noticing the parallels between this work and good enough couple therapy. In both there is an attempt to reach the real self that is silent, accepting, secure, and empowering to the entire system. I like to notice which parts in each partner relate to parts in the other partner. I notice which parts come up for me during a session and increasingly I can talk to my couples about the parts that I experience in me.

This couple were in their early thirties, with two children (one age 3 and one 6 months). John was a lawyer and Jane stayed at home with the children. They came to therapy because of severe fighting. They were living in Jane's mother's house, all in one room, while their own home was being extended. They lived in a high-status neighborhood and John made a good income. Jane came for treatment this time (there was a long history of my working with them) because she felt that John did not respect her staying home with the children and was very critical of her. Obviously there were tensions and stress because of living the way they were, but they both felt that these were just triggers for deeper issues. Jane felt that John was driven to be increasingly successful financially and that this kind of ambition was alien to her, that it put her under pressure to work when she was happy staying home being a fulltime mother. In a session John told how he had a heart blockage and that he was changing his lifestyle, eating better and doing exercise. He did, however, feel that the marriage was going nowhere and he was very disturbed that Jane seemed 'not vital' and alive to him.

In a first joint session the atmosphere was extremely tense. There were many mutual recriminations and quite a bit of aggression. Jane told him that he 'disgusted her' and he attacked her for being boring and giving him nothing except 'making the food', which hurt her so much she left the room. After this session we did the parts work that is described below.

His/her story

Jane was in treatment with me over 10 years ago for depression and addiction to chocolate. At the time she was single, very career-oriented. A child of an abusive father and divorced parents, she had grown up on a farm next to the city, with a negative self-image due to her family's history and also her lower social status compared to the children of the schools she attended. Her dreams then were to succeed as a businesswoman. When her parents divorced, she cut off from her father and became extremely close to her mother. At the time she first came to me, her addiction to chocolate was very severe and involved having a 'fix' every hour. She was also depressed around feeling that she was going nowhere in life, was not successful and especially around feeling that she missed opportunities for success. For example, she had been offered a job abroad but because of anxieties as well as social problems she failed and had to come back.

Over the next two years I worked with her to wean her from the chocolate and to help her improve her self-esteem. She had many employment issues around fighting with authority and feeling unappreciated at work. She continued to feel that she was a failure as she went through two quite high-powered jobs, one in which she did well but the project ended and one in which she was eventually let go. She suffered from anxieties around job issues that continued to plague her, although with my support she continued to try. In addition she suffered from depression that came and went.

Seven years later she met John, a very successful once-divorced lawyer. They fell very much in love. During the next four years I saw them occasionally. They remained very much in love, but would occasionally come to treatment with the same recurrent symptom. John was a very verbal and intelligent man, but driven and ambitious. He came from a very successful and wealthy family, and had studied law at Oxford. He believed himself to be quite special and was easily hurt if Jane did not appreciate him in some way. He would have temper tantrums and could be quite aggressive to her. Jane was determined not to repeat the abuse she had suffered as a girl. Jane was an extremely beautiful and sexy woman, who prized her freedom, sexuality, and autonomy. She asked for a lot of sex and they had conflicts about his not wanting as much sex as she did. Jane continued to have conflicts around jobs, and occasionally would work with me about that. John sometimes had sessions with me about his driven, ambitious character as well as over his involvement and high-conflict relationship with his mother. His mother was a dominating and aggressive woman. John had an enmeshed kind of relationship with her and tended to be her best friend and worst enemy. She turned to him and demanded a lot of contact, but they also fought constantly and in those fights he was abusive to her. Jane was convinced that he was acting out his anger at his mother with her, and we had had sessions around this as well. Through therapy the marriage thrived and Jane managed to stay in her job as a PR specialist. John made a lot of progress with his mother and was increasingly kinder and less explosive at home as well. I was 'on call' for when they couldn't handle a fight on their own, and they would use therapy for several sessions and then stop.

The couple came back to therapy more intensively during Jane's first pregnancy and after the birth. Jane was very conflicted about whether to get pregnant. Her fear was that if she were to have a child, the balance of power between her and John would change and she might be dominated by him. Also, she was afraid she would lose her edge in her career. Her talks with me were around whether or not to get pregnant, and eventually she decided to do so. After the birth she had a serious post-partum depression which necessitated anti-depressants. I continued to support the couple in joint and individual sessions and after several months they no longer felt that they needed therapy. Jane found that as soon as her depression cleared up, she enjoyed being a mother very much and felt that she wanted to stay home. This situation continued throughout the next three years. During her next pregnancy, she came back in the hope of avoiding another depression and we decided (together with psychiatric advice) to start her on medication preventively.

Jane began (John had yet to arrive). She said she was worried about the 'rehabilitation of her feelings' because she didn't know if she loved John anymore. She felt she had lost respect. She also told how they couldn't talk much because they were living with her mother. John arrived and Jane said that nothing had changed. John said that they had had a good weekend because it was quiet and maybe they were ready to listen. He talked about watching Jane to monitor her moods and how her mood really affected him. If she wasn't happy or was down, he was immediately up or down, and he was tied up with her feelings. Jane said that when he was down she tried to cheer him up and when that didn't work she would get angry. Jane said that she used to be like him – watching all his moods and being affected by them, and that she used to cry at everything he said. But that she realized she had to be tough, because he used her expressing her feelings against her. She talked about becoming indifferent. I asked if I could interview her about this 'tough' part of her and she agreed. I asked John if he would write down all his ideas while he listened, that I would interview her for an hour and then him. They both agreed.

THERAPIST: So when does this tough side come up for you?

JANE: When John gets aggressive with me, I say to myself, 'He doesn't deserve to see me crying': I guess we could call it my ego or something.

THERAPIST: Where do you feel it the most, when this part comes up. We all have parts of us, many personalities. Like when you walked out the last session, that is a different part than the one who is listening now, right?

JANE: Yes, that is right. I feel this part in my stomach.

THERAPIST: Can you tell me about this part of you?

JANE: She is my age ... 38, but she has always been there so, I guess she is growing up with me. She is very secure and sure of herself. She is beautiful, she doesn't let me get emotional, and she thinks a lot. She never cries but she is logical.

THERAPIST: When does she tend to appear?

JANE: She always has been with me. When I have conflict with people, she doesn't let me show my feelings. Like with a boss, I would like to sit down on the floor and cry, but she helps me feel equal. She is a very dominant part of my life. She is there all the time lately.

THERAPIST: Would it be alright with you if we got to know her a bit more?

JANE: Ok.

THERAPIST: Would you try to see her inside a room, maybe in your stomach, but with you outside the room watching through a window. You aren't next to her, but have a distance between the two of you ... what do you see?

JANE: She is standing and looking at me. She is watching me.

THERAPIST: What else?

JANE: She used to come to me whenever it felt like some injustice was happening. Even when my father would hit me, she would be there. She did not let me talk in those days, because I would just get hit more (but he saw her in my eyes) and I used to get most of the abuse. Not like my mother or brother, who gave in to injustice; she did not let me do that. She made me feel I am ok, I am right, but this was a threat to my father and sometimes it made him hit me more. She didn't let him cut off my head or cut out my tongue (these are Hebrew expressions meaning that she didn't allow Jane to back down).

THERAPIST: Anything else?

JANE: I really love her, she takes care of me.

THERAPIST: So what is she afraid could happen to you if she didn't keep you 'tough' ... someone would 'Cut off your head. Cut out your tongue'?

JANE: She is afraid ... she doesn't trust John ...

THERAPIST: Is there another part that is afraid or is it the tough one?

JANE: No, you are right; there is another part of me.

THERAPIST: How does this part look?

JANE: She is very scared. She is around 20 and looks well kept up, more wild. She doesn't trust anyone, especially not John. She remembers how John made fun of my crying.

THERAPIST: So if we put her in a room, what is she doing there? Where do you feel her in your body? What do you feel to her?

JANE: I don't feel comfortable with her. She is very tight and tense ... looking around, seeing if anything bad is going to happen. I guess I feel her in my shoulders. She is worried all the time, watching out.

THERAPIST: Who is she worried about?

JANE: The crying girl?

THERAPIST: Is it ok if we get to know her?

JANE: Alright. She is about 14 or maybe 15, 16. She is very thin, has long hair and is very delicate and pretty. She has a very gentle heart, but she has been abused and humiliated and she is sitting all tied-up inside herself, she walks around too and is hurt.

THERAPIST: What do you feel when you see her?

JANE: I would like to hug her, help her. I feel her in my throat. (Looks like she is crying.) She is lost ... no one enjoys her.

THERAPIST: So let's see, so far, we have a part of you that is tough and is about 38, although she has been growing inside of your stomach for a long time. And then you have another part that is about 20 years old, and she is watching, and is worrying and tries to make sure that the crying part doesn't get hurt. And you have a young girl who is a teenager, who is very gentle but has been hurt and she is crying? How do they interact with each other?

JANE: I guess that the 20-year-old wild girl who is worrying watches to see if anyone is hurting the teenager and, if so, she calls in the tough one who doesn't feel the pain.

THERAPIST: When does that all happen?

JANE: When it seems like something unfair is going on. But I am getting kind of tired of all of this. It isn't natural and there is this fine-tuning that has to be done all the time, it is exhausting.

THERAPIST: So you feel tired of it all, but this fine tuning has to go on to make sure that the girl doesn't get hurt? By the way, was it the 'tough' part that got you out of the room last week when John said you don't give him anything but rice and schnitzel?

JANE: Yes, she removes the young girl, whenever something like that starts, they all just get her out of there.

THERAPIST: And why is that?

JANE: So that John won't think that she is weak, so that he won't lose respect for me. I use the 'tough' one to get the girl out of the way, but it gets tiring, having to fine tune all this all the time.

THERAPIST: So this enables the girl not to be hurt?

JANE: Well it doesn't really work; it isn't like there are impermeable boundaries. Some of the hurt gets in anyway.

THERAPIST: I am soon going to work with John, but while I do I would like us to think of what we can do to make sure that the young teen is protected. I know that we will be talking with some of his parts, maybe parts that aren't so nice, and I want to make sure that the girl is ok ... what do you suggest?

JANE: I don't know.

THERAPIST: Do you want to promise that if the girl starts to feel hurt, that you will go in the room and hold her?

JANE: No, that reminds me too much of what used to happen with my father. My mother would come in and comfort me. That makes it seem like John is like my father and that isn't true and I don't like that. He isn't my father and it isn't healthy for me too, to be too similar to my mother.

THERAPIST: Well, how about if we ask the 'tough one' to help out here ... that she will go in the room to help the teen?

JANE: That is fine.

THERAPIST: Can you see that?

JANE: Yes, I see the two of them together. It is fine. They are close.

[We all take a break. After the break John asks if he can ask Jane some questions. I say that maybe we should save those for the end, that we want to make sure that Jane's teenager is safe and that maybe we should take the time to talk with John. He agrees to wait, saying that he feels bad about the teenager and that it makes a protective part of him come out. He wants to know her more, the part that is in Jane's throat that is vulnerable and lonely. He says that he wants to be with that girl, but that there is something in him that gets indifferent and then he isn't there for Jane.]

THERAPIST: So maybe we can get to know that indifferent part of you?

JOHN: I would call him 'egoism'. He is always there, so I guess he is like me, 43. He just is interested in getting for himself.

THERAPIST: Can you see him?

JOHN: No, he is vague, amorphous, and maybe transparent, everywhere in my body, my heart, head and hands. He is greedy and likes to grab whatever is near him, whatever is within grasp, he is lazy though and kind of stupid, he doesn't plan ahead and does stupid things sometimes, but he is positive really. He is for survival ...

other people stop him from overdoing it and taking too much. I mean, he has boundaries, he stops since he knows that if he takes too much he will get nothing in the end.

THERAPIST: Wow – you seem to know him quite well. Is that him that says no and limits him?

JOHN: No, there is a 'social boss' that tells him to stop. Now that I think of it, they are both serving the 'big boss', who is the 'patriarch' – The father. He is in charge and he gets the egoism to go and grab things according to what society wants. This big boss, this patriarch, wants Jane to be happy, doesn't want her hurt and he gets the other to work for him. You see, the egoism is just a technical part, he doesn't think really. The social part thinks, but they all serve the father.

THERAPIST: Where is this big boss and how does he look?

JOHN: He is in my head. Everything starts from my head. And he looks like my father ... well, my father had the same thing, this 'patriarch' who was trying to get everyone's needs met. I have the same part, but even more than my father ... a better updated version.

THERAPIST: What about your needs?

JOHN: No, this big boss, he isn't interested in my needs. Same with my father, no one thought about his needs, he just had to make sure we all had a high standard of living. We are talking here about concrete needs you know, making money.

THERAPIST: So who is it that is saying that Jane should work?

JOHN: Oh, that isn't a very important part! – That is a rather fragile part, maybe frightened.

THERAPIST: What is that frightened part afraid of?

JOHN: Well, that all this system won't work, that there won't be enough money to bring about the stability we all need, the security. Maybe the whole thing will fall apart?

THERAPIST: Is that what he is afraid of?

JOHN: I don't know if I want to know him. Maybe it isn't going to be good for my health. I feel confused and a sense of insecurity now that we are talking about this. It is kind of unclear to me. Maybe it makes me want to run away, but where could I run too actually? I know how to neutralize this fear. The egoist gets very busy running around making money, and the social part also pushes for what needs to be done. They are serving the father, who is ... actually ... the family! Not something outside, but inside – the father is the family and serves the family. But I also know how to have a good time sometimes, I grab some fun.

THERAPIST: How does that work?

JOHN: When there is too much pressure from the big boss, and the egoist is running around and there is so much to do, these guys have a justification to have some fun.

THERAPIST: So the fearful part gets worried that maybe there won't be enough stability and money for the big boss, or the family? Can you tell me more about this fearful part? Would the egoist let me know more about this fragile part ... would that be ok? Maybe we could see this part and him or her in a room. Would you be willing to look in to see what is there?

JOHN: He is a 'dreir' (Yiddish for a 'sad soul') and I don't like him. He has had bad life experiences and a cautious worldview – he is kind of a miserable type, no life in him, a real pessimist and worrier ... well he is my mother actually! He is kind of paranoid, always afraid. He is weak and ruins the atmosphere ... poisons it actually and even gets panicked. He doesn't trust anyone. When he jumps out, Jane tries to get him back into his box. She explains that we have enough money. But she doesn't know him, he is rather grotesque. When he jumps out, he makes me really worry ... what would happen if I were sick and could not work or something and Jane was out of the workforce?

THERAPIST: You know, last week those words you used for him ... not very alive, killing all the fun ... you said that about Jane and now you are talking about this fearful part.

JOHN: ... yes, that is true. When he sees her like that, I hate it. Like I hate him ... like I hate the way my mother thinks. Then I guess the big boss sends the egoistic part to work, to get some more money, bring the money! But you know, this is getting to be too hard. I am falling apart, it is starting to feel like a noose, I mean emotionally I can't take this much longer. I used to be able to get the fear back in the box, but when I got sick, I couldn't control this anymore, the fear I mean.

THERAPIST: (turning to both of them) Would you like to continue to explore these parts in the next session? (They want to and ask for a session the same week to continue working.) It might be interesting for you two to pay attention in the next few days when different parts are triggered. Like, for example, when the fearful part comes up for you John, how does it make you behave towards Jane?

JANE: Well, if he would say 'I am afraid', I could help him. But instead he says 'What good are you to me? Making me rice?'

THERAPIST: Yes and it is interesting what part of you that triggers. The part that is concerned about justice and respect for the teen?

JANE: I know that I am very worried about being exploited ... or at least that the teenager will be exploited ... I don't want John to see her as weak ... it is true that when I get worried about that I can't really help him out.

THERAPIST: Let's stop now. Maybe you can take a break from all this for a few days, let all these parts, which do seem tired, rest a bit. Maybe after a few days it might be helpful to ask the questions you had.

JANE: But I don't want John to try to be the wise guy ... to figure all this out and be smart.

THERAPIST: Are you protecting the teenager now? Would it be helpful for you to hear that John doesn't want to 'win' but really wants to know?

JOHN: That is true ... I do really want to know ...

THERAPIST: So maybe we can agree that you won't analyze each other, but maybe just ask some questions ... that's all.

(They agree to that.)

The specific methods are derived here from IFS therapy. But in rereading this in light of writing this book, I see how much good enough couple therapy is available in this kind of work. The therapist is at first very directive and caretaking. There is a history of work with this couple at different stages in their life. The sense is of the therapy being part of their individual, and later couple, relationships.

But more important, we can see a gradual movement to accessing inner parts and especially trying to help the couple have a reflexive view of themselves and their parts. This is an attempt to bring out the real self, the aspect of the personality that is not a part, but that can be a good enough mother to all the parts. The self loves unconditionally and accepts all the parts as having something to contribute to the personality and to the couple. As the couple increase their use of this method, they access more parts but also their own true self. The self does not talk but holds the parts. The exiles are the babies that were not cared for adequately. The idea here is that through the therapist's true self, the self of each partner is activated and relied on by the individual. These are people who were hurt at some critical stages of childhood. But the idea here is that the self can do any healing that is necessary.

We do not need to go into spiritual explanations, although they might be true. We do not need to see the true self as an internal higher self or intervention by higher beings. We can look to the good enough mother, who has the power to re-parent any parts that need it. Holding, mirroring, increasing demands for independent work, repairing any ruptures in the work itself can all be seen as our own internal good enough mother.

Back to the good enough mother

So in ending this book we come back to Winnicott's good enough mother. I imagine that many of the therapies that work (for the individual or the couple) do so partly because there is a re-parenting process going on and an accessing of one's own Self. I venture to connect the true self with the good enough mother. Both have the power to build or to disappoint. Both empower others and both are always available to those who want to find them.

A poem by Winnicott, written late in life, shows the origins of his interest in good enough mothering:

> *The Tree*
> Thus I knew her
> Once, stretched out on her lap
> as now on a dead tree
> I learned to make her smile
> to stem her tears
> to undo her guilt
> to cure her inward death
> To enliven her was my living.
> (Rodman, 2003; printed here by permission of
> The Marsh Agency Ltd on behalf of The
> Winnicott Trust)

This was probably how Winnicott viewed himself and his depressed mother. Winnicott devoted his life to helping himself and others reach a sense of vitality and genuine joy as well as genuine hate. The last sentence shows how he took the situation of having a depressed mother into a lifelong mission to bring life back to the dead: To enliven her was my living.

A critique of Winnicott

In her critique of Rodman's biography of Winnicott, Martha Nussbaum makes the following comments:

> One can find much to criticize in Winnicott's ideas, as well as in his practical judgment. His account of the role of the father is grossly deficient, perhaps as a result of the fact that he never completely worked out his intuitive ideas about the malleability of gender and the relationship between rigid gender norms and the False Self. His ideas about the True Self sometimes verge on an excessive romanticism, as when he suggests that any communication with

> the outside world involves a deformation of a True Self, which is fundamentally incommunicado. At other times he more plausibly suggests that the True Self, if all goes well, will develop capacities for communication and reciprocity. But the mark of his childhood remained, and he repeatedly stressed (excessively, to my mind) the artificiality of the social, the radically asocial nature of all that is authentic. (Here he really is Brontë's heir.)
>
> I am also unconvinced by Winnicott's constant connection between self-assertion and 'hate', a word that he used too loosely. A person who has been repressed by demands for conformity might indeed hate those demands, and might feel the assertion of the self as a form of aggression; and such, clearly, was Winnicott's personal situation. But in the more benign case in which the capacity for concern and social interaction develops in partnership with love, self-assertion (and the sexuality that he linked to it) may take a wider range of forms. Winnicott implicitly acknowledges this, in his insightful remarks about art, culture, and play, but these notions remain inconsistently integrated into his writings.
>
> These are trivial matters, though, in comparison with the rich re-orientation that Winnicott gave to the theory and the practice of analysis. He was a poet among theoreticians, as he was a compassionate doctor among analysts. If one can derive many related insights from the reading of his favorite authors, such as Shakespeare, Wordsworth, and Henry James, he was able to formulate these insights into guidelines for the therapeutic treatment of unhappy people, giving psychoanalysis a hopeful face, one that emphasized people's capacities for love and society's capacity for 'holding' diversity, play, and freedom.
>
> (Nussbaum, 2003)

I would also add to her critique that at times his writing is so idiosyncratic and obscure that it is hard to comprehend. Yet there was a playfulness in his writings that also engenders playfulness in the reader. Nussbaum writes:

> A pediatrician first and always, with adults or with children, Winnicott was always willing to play, to respond to the moment, to surprise, to adopt unconventional methods if they seemed right. (All too often, he wrote, the patient brings his False Self into analysis and the analyst addresses himself to that, because it is easy to talk to a False Self.) Sometimes he sat on the floor; sometimes he offered a cup of tea; sometimes he held a hand. Sometimes sessions were daily and sometimes months apart. In the case of 'the Piggle,' a little girl named Gabrielle who was two and a half when she began to see Winnicott and five when she finished, we have Winnicott's own detailed notes of every session. The sessions were held on demand by the child, often months apart, and sometimes included participation by the parents (sophisticated and analytically aware) as well as letters and phone calls from them. This remarkable document shows us many things about Winnicott as therapist, but nothing more than his utter respect for the child's

world of objects. Almost his first remark, in notes of the first session, is: 'Already I had made friends with the teddy-bear who was sitting on the floor by the desk.' And throughout the analysis, we sense that Winnicott's poetic capacity, his willingness not to be 'only sane,' enables a degree of entry rare for any adult into the unhappy child's world, with its 'black mommy,' its 'Sush baby,' and the terrifying 'babacar'.

At the end of his analysis of Gabrielle, as the five-year-old prepares to leave him, he remarks, 'So the Winnicott you invented was all yours and he's now finished with, and no one else can ever have him.' The two sit together, reading an animal book. Then he tells her, 'I know when you are really shy, and that is when you want to tell me that you love me.' And he records: 'She was very positive in her gesture of assent.'

(Nussbaum, 2003)

10 Summary

The writing of this book has itself been a personal journey for me. When I began, I knew I wanted to understand Winnicott better and to apply his ideas to couple therapy. I hope that this fundamental goal has been reached. It would be very satisfying if others pick up this goal, since it seems to me that we are at a very early stage in understanding Winnicott's concepts as applied not just to infants but to the raising and parenting of couples.

During the writing of this book, I found myself compelled more than I expected to tell the story of my life as if Winnicott was listening and holding me. His writings have both a theme and a style that are congruent with each other: the theme has to do with authenticity and finding the true self; the writings are unique and even eccentric. Also, paradoxically (which was his way), the attempt to uncover the true self of my professional and personal life was in a dialectical interaction with Winnicott's ideas about protection of the true self. His idea of the right not to communicate, as one example, allows us to better communicate authentically because we don't have to get to everything. Once such boundaries are set up, we can offer more of ourselves because we feel safer. This is a kind of holding that even reading Winnicott can offer. We know we have false selves and Winnicott often proposed that these were protections of the true self. In peeling away some layers of the false self in me that led to my burnout, I was able to feel safe about sharing, knowing that I don't have to share everything.

As I dug deeply into the many different theories that influence me, I came upon similarities between different theories. A similarity across all theories I met on my journey is the creation and re-creation of new therapeutic languages. Each of the major theories I learned and the people I interacted with had their own unique language. Like in Monty Python's *The Life of Brian*, the crowd chants in unison 'We are all unique', 'We are all different': the different theories all claim to be unique. One of the ways these theories do this is by creating a unique language. When I studied with Michael White in Adelaide, Australia, I found myself mystified by the (to me) strange language of constructivism. One of the teachers said it takes about three years to feel comfortable with the language they were using. Beyond jargon, each theory accesses different senses and thoughts through different metaphors. The similarity is in the claim to be unique, which paradoxically is true. Each theory is unique and creates a unique language, yet they are the same in making claims about uniqueness. Sometimes it seems like a new problem is created when each theorist attempts to create a new language. As I delved into psychodynamic theories, for example, I was struck by how each one used its own words for the same thing. And yet each strand of theories has its own emphasis, almost like having an accent in one's language.

This book proposes awareness of the therapist is the main tool for working with couples. Regardless of the methods used, self-introspection adds the therapist's self as a major resource towards helping couples. One does not have to use psychoanalytic or object relations therapy to stay in touch with one's own self.

I do see a problem in this emphasis on the self of the therapist. As a therapist, I fully endorse this view. But as an educator I wonder what would happen if I placed self-awareness as the major tool in our training programs? Would all the students have to have their own therapy (as analysts have training analysis)? Would the program benefit from a strong emphasis on self-awareness or do students need to first get the basic tools and then work more on what these methods all mean to them personally? How much of their personal life is it expected they will share? In couple therapy the focus is on couple relationships and thus self-awareness has to include a piece on the therapist's own intimate relationships. What kind of effect on partners would a couple therapy training program with an emphasis on self-awareness have? How much responsibility about this does the program carry? If a trainee becomes more aware and then leaves his/her marriage, what responsibility does the program have for that? There is no doubt that we have to be careful what we wish for! While endorsing a strong emphasis on self-analysis, I am aware that it can be a double-edged sword.

The writing of this book has changed me. Just as Winnicott did not offer a cohesive therapeutic package, I have to acknowledge that the way I have been affected by Winnicott has not led to a new kind of therapy. Nussbaum says:

> Unlike Freud, Donald W. Winnicott is not a cultural icon, is not read in Great Books courses, revered and reviled. Unlike Jacques Lacan he is not an intellectual cult figure with a band of zealous disciples and an impenetrable jargon. There is no school of Winnicott; there are no courses in his methods. All this is as he wished it. Nobody was more skeptical of cuts and the righties they induced. All his life Winnicott was obsessed with the freedom of the individual self to exist defiantly, resisting parental and cultural demands, to be there without a word if silence was its choice. In his own writings he spoke in a voice that was determinately his own, surprisingly personal, idiosyncratic, playful and at the same time ordinary.
>
> (Nussbaum, 2003)

His work has enlivened my sense of what all methods of couple therapy can offer. His ideas make me think about how I go about being a couple therapist, no matter what method I use. The idea of rupture and repair, for example, can be applied to different kinds of therapeutic methods. I can now take a method, such as behavioral communications training, and contemplate what aspect of good enough mothering this type of work might offer to certain couples at certain times. It becomes increasingly clear that Winnicott's concepts can become a place for reflection of all types of therapeutic questions. Whatever our methods, we can benefit from asking questions that result from his work: Are we being present in the sessions as well as doing our methods? How are we using our selves in the therapy? Are we moving our couples towards authenticity or false selves? Are we being authentic or false? How do therapists working with individuals hold their clients in different ways? How do we notice if rupture in the therapeutic relationship has occurred and how can we repair it? How do we offer ideas for change to our couples? Do we force feed or adapt our methods for each individual? How do we create a potential space for change and what transitional objects are we offering to a couple in the process of change? If we started our family and couple therapy programs with an overview of Winnicott's ideas, would this affect the rest of the program and if so, how?

There are so many such questions we can ask along the way. I hope that this book has generated curiosity and questions. I hope that this work may be the start of a new dialogue on Winnicott and couple therapy. Winnicott leaves us a legacy of paradoxes. We can be renewed not by more techniques, which he does not offer, but by holding in tension the many paradoxes of human experience. Examples of universal human paradoxes include both self-assertion and recognition; independence and interdependence; autonomy and relatedness; and in the clinical situation, intrapsychic and intersubjective levels; discovery and co-creation; interpretation and expressive interaction; understanding and experiencing. The sense of dedication and playful seriousness that reading Winnicott engenders leaves me enriched. I hope that this book has a similar effect on the reader.

References

Abrams, J. (1996) *The language of Winnicott: a dictionary of Winnicott's use of words.* London: Karnac.

Ammons, A. R. (1986) Poetics. In *A.R. Ammons: the selected poems.* New York: Norton.

Atherton, J. S. (2013) Learning and teaching; assimilation and accommodation (http://www.learningandteaching.info/learning/assimacc.htm).

Barth, F. D. (2012) Making couples' therapy work. Off the Couch. *Psychology Today* 17 March (http://www.psychologytoday.com/blog/the-couch/201203/making-couples-therapy-work).

Bateson, G. (1971) A systems approach. *International Journal of Psychiatry* 9, 242–244.

Bollas, C. (1987) Normatic illness. In *Shadow of the object psychoanalysis of the unknown known.* London: Free Association Books.

Bookwala, J. (2005) The role of marital quality in physical health during the mature years. *Journal of Aging and Health* 17, 85–104.

Boston, P. (2007) Therapeutic groundhog day – exploring the impact of the theory/approach of the self of the therapist. *Journal of Family Therapy* 29, 338–341.

Bowen, M. (1978) *Family therapy in clinical practice.* Northvale, NJ: Jason Aronson.

Brown, J. & Wright, J. (2010) Inviting each partner out of the fusion: Bowen Family Systems Theory and couple therapy. *The CAPA Quarterly* 2, 17–20.

Buber, M. (1970) *I and Thou.* New York: Charles Scribner.

Caldwell, L. & Joyce, A. (Eds.) (2011) *Reading Winnicott.* New Library of Psychoanalysis. Oxford: Taylor & Francis.

Casement, P. (2014) *On learning from the patient.* London: Routledge.

Clulow, C. (Ed.) (2001) *Adult attachment and couple psychotherapy: The 'secure base' in practice and research.* London: Brunner-Routledge.

Coleman, W. (1995) Gesture and recognition: an alternative model to projective identification as a basis for couples relationships. In S. Ruszczynski & J. Fisher (Eds.) *Intrusiveness and intimacy in the couple.* London: Karnac.

Davis, M. & Wallbridge, D. (1981) *Boundary and space: an introduction to the work of D.W. Winnicott.* London: Karnac.

Fincham, F. D., Stanley, S., & Beach, S. R. H. (2007) Transformative processes in marriage: an analysis of emerging trends. *Journal of Marriage and the Family* 69, 275–292.

Freeman, J. & Combs, G. (1996) *Narrative therapy: social construction of preferred realities.* New York: W.W. Norton.

Gottman, J. & Silver, N. (2012) *What makes love last?* New York: Simon & Schuster.

Green, L. B. (2006) The value of hate in the countertransference. *Clinical Social Work Journal* 34, 187–199.

Gurman, A. (2008) *Clinical handbook of couple therapy* (4th edn). New York: Guilford Press.

Hamady, J. (2010) Performance anxiety; what really causes those nerves and how to overcome them. Finding Your Voice. *Psychology Today* 4 November (http://www.psychologytoday.com/blog/finding-your-voice/201011/performance-anxiety).

Hare-Mustin, R. T. & Marecek, J. (1987) Gender and the meaning of difference: alpha and beta bias. Paper presented at the 95th Annual Convention of the American Psychological Association, New York, 28 August–1 September.

Hendricks, H. (1988) *Getting the love you want*. New York: Henry Holt.

Herbine-Blank, T. (2010) *Intimacy from the inside out: advanced training for IFS couples therapists*. Boston, MA (http://toni.therapylinq.com).

Hirschberger, G., Srivastava, S., Marsh. P., Cowan, C. and Cowan, P. (2009) Attachment, marital satisfaction, and divorce during the first fifteen years of parenthood. *Personal Relationships* 16(3), 401–420.

Hopkins, L. (2006) *False self, the life of Masud Khan*. New York: Other Press.

Horney, K. (1950) *The collected works of Karen Horney* (2 vols.). New York: Norton.

Jacobus, M. (2005) *The poetics of psychoanalysis: in the wake of Klein*. Oxford: Oxford University Press.

Johnson, S. M. & Whiffen, V. (Eds.) (2003) *Attachment processes in couples and families*. New York: Guilford Press.

Kirschner, D. (2010) Is high marital satisfaction the fountain of youth? Finding true love. *Psychology Today* 14 July (http://www.psychologytoday.com/blog/finding-true-love/201007/marital-satisfaction-health-happiness).

Laing, R. D. (1960) *The divided self*. New York: Penguin.

Lambert, M. J. & Barley, D. E. (2001) Research summary on the therapeutic relationship and psychotherapy outcome. *Psychotherapy: Theory, Research, Practice, Training* 38(4), 357–361.

Lapides, F. (2010) The implicit realm in couple therapy: improving right hemisphere affect-regulating capabilities. *Clinical Social Work Journal* 39, 161–169.

Leone, C. (2008) Couple therapy from the perspective of self psychology and intersubjectivity theory. *Psychoanalytic Psychology* 25, 79–98.

Ludham, M. (2007) Our attachment to the couple in the mind. In M. Ludham & V. Nyberg (Eds.) *Couple attachments: theoretical and clinical studies*. London: Karnac.

Lundby, G. (2011) A stair of questions: a scaffolding of the maps of narrative practice (http://www.dulwichcentre.com.au/a-stair-of-questions-a-scaffolding-of-the-maps-of-narrative-practice.html).

Masterson, J. (1988) *The search for the true self: unmasking the personality disorders of our age*. New York: Free Press.

McCarthy, B. & Metz, M. (2008) The 'good enough sex model': a case illustration. *Sexual and Relationship Therapy* 23, 227–234.

Miller, A. (1981) *The drama of the gifted child: the search for the real self*. New York: Basic Books.

Nussbaum, M. C. (2003) Review of Rodman biography of Winnicott in New Republic 4632, 34–38.

Ogden, T. (1987) The transitional oedipal relationship in female development. *International Journal of Psychoanalysis* 68, 485–498.

Ogden, T. (1990) *The matrix of the mind: object relations and the psychoanalytic dialogue*. London: Karnac.

Ogden, T. (1994) The analytic third: working with intersubjective clinical facts. *International Journal of Psychoanalysis* 75, 3–20.

Ogden, T. (1997) *Reverie and interpretation: sensing something human*. Northvale, NJ: Aronson.

Ogden, T. (2001) Reading Winnicott. *Psychoanalytic Quarterly* 70(2), 299–323.

Patterson, G., Chamberlain, C. & Reid, J. (1982) A comparative evaluation of a parent-training program. *Behavior Therapy* 13(5), 638–650.

Phillips, A. (1988) *Winnicott*. Cambridge, MA: Harvard University Press.

Randolph, L. (1998) A Winnicotian approach to intimacy in the therapeutic alliance. *Journal of Analytic Social Work* 5(2), 19–33.

Rodman, R. (2003) *Winnicott: his life and work*. London: Perseus Books.

Rowan, J. (1990) *Subpersonalities: the people inside us*. London: Routledge.

Scharff, J. & Scharff, D. (2000) *Object relations couple therapy*. New York: Jason Aronson.

Schwartz, M. (1987) Our multiple selves: applying systems thinking to the inner family. *Networker* March/April 25–31.

Schwartz, M. (2009) Making use of Winnicott: a roundtable discussion. *PSYART: A Hyperlink Journal for the Psychological Study of the Arts* 15 December (http://www.psyartjournal.com/article/show/m_schwartz-making_use_of_winnicott_a_roundtable_dis).

Skowron, A. & Friedlander, M. (1998) Differentiation of self inventory: development and initial validation. *Journal of Counseling Psychology* 45, 235–246.

Stolorow, R., Brandchaft, B. & Atwood, G. E. (1987) *Psychoanalytic treatment: an intersubjective approach*. Hillsdale, NJ: Analytic Press.

Stone, H. & Winkelman, S. (1985) *Embracing ourselves*. Marina del Rey, CA: Devross.

Tester, S. (1992) The family therapist's use of self: a Delphi study (unpublished doctoral dissertation). Florida State University. Dissertation Abstracts International 53, 7-B.

Timm, T. & Blow, A. (1999) Self of the therapist work: a balancing between removing restraints and identifying resources. *Contemporary Family Therapy* 21(3), 331–345.

Tuber, S. (2008) *Attachment, play and authenticity: a Winnicott primer*. New York: Jason Aronson.

Wedge, M. (1996) *In the therapist's mirror: reality in the making*. New York: W.W. Norton.

Weisfield, G. E., Nowak, N. T., Lucas, T., Weisfield, C. C., Imamoğlu, E. O., Butovskaya, M., Jiliang, S. & Parkhill, M. R. (2011) Do women seek humorousness in men because it signals intelligence? *Humor: International Journal of Humor Research* 24, 435–462.

Wilberg, P. (no date) Modes of relatedness in psychotherapy: Laing, Winnicott and Relational Psychoanalysis (http://www.meaningofdepression.com/Wilberg's%20 articles.htm).

Wile, D. (2008) *After the honeymoon: how conflict can improve your relationship*. Oakland, CA: Collaborative Press.

Winnicott, D. (1931) *Clinical notes on disorders of childhood*. London: Heinemann.

Winnicott, D. (1945) [1978] Primitive emotional development. In M. Masud & R. Khan (Eds.) *D.W. Winnicott Through Paediatrics to Psychoanalysis*, pp. 145–156. London: The Hogarth Press and the Institute of Psychoanalysis.

Winnicott, D. (1949) Hate in the counter-transference. *International Journal of Psychoanalysis* 30, 69–74.
Winnicott, D. (1951) Transitional objects and transitional phenomena. In *Through paediatrics to psychoanalysis.* New York: Basic Books.
Winnicott, D. (1956) [1958] Primary maternal preoccupation. In *Collected papers, through paediatrics to psychoanalysis*, pp. 300–305. London: Tavistock.
Winnicott, D. (1957a) *The child and the family.* London: Tavistock.
Winnicott, D. (1957b) *The child and the outside world.* London: Tavistock.
Winnicott, D. (1958) The capacity to be alone. *International Journal of Psychoanalysis* 39, 416–420.
Winnicott, D. (1965a) Ego distortion in terms of true and false self. In *The maturational processes and the facilitating environment: studies in the theory of emotional development*, pp. 140–152. New York: International Universities Press.
Winnicott, D. (1965b) *Theory of emotional development.* London: Hogarth Press.
Winnicott, D. W. (1965c) The capacity to be alone. In *The maturational processes and the facilitating environment*, pp. 29–36. New York: International Universities (original work published 1958).
Winnicott, D. W. (1965d) Communicating and not communicating leading to a study of certain opposites. In *The maturational processes and the facilitating environment*, pp. 170–192. New York: International Universities Press.
Winnicott, D. (1965e) *The family and individual development.* London: Tavistock.
Winnicott, D. (1969) The use of an object. *International Journal of Psychoanalysis* 50, 711–716.
Winnicott, D. (1971a) *Playing and reality.* London: Tavistock.
Winnicott, D. (1971b) Mirror role of mother and family in child development. In *Winnicott's playing and reality.* London: Tavistock.
Winnicott, D. W. (1971c) Transitional objects and transitional phenomena. In *Playing and reality*, pp. 1–55. New York: Basic Books.
Winnicott, D. (1972) Holding and interpretation: fragment of an analysis. In P. L. Giovacchini (Ed.) *Tactics and techniques in psychoanalytic therapy.* London: Hogarth.
Winnicott, D. (1987) Babies and their mothers. London: The Winnicott Trust.
Wynne, L. & Singer, M. T. (1963) Thought disorder and family relations of schizophrenics. a research strategy. *Archives of General Psychiatry* 9(3), 191–198.
Young, R. (no date) Hate (http://human-nature.com/rmyoung/papers/pap126h.html).

Index